MW00975854

EMERITUS PROFESSOR JOHN PASSMORE is an internationally renowned philosopher and historian of ideas. Born in Sydney on 9 September 1914, he was educated at Manly Primary School, Sydney Boys' High School and the University of Sydney. He tutored and lectured in Philosophy at the University of Sydney (1935–49), and then became Professor of Philosophy at Otago University, Dunedin, New Zealand (1950–54).

In 1955 he became Reader in Philosophy at the Institute of Advanced Studies at the Australian National University, Canberra, later becoming Professor of Philosophy at the same university (1959–79). After his official retirement in 1979 and as Emeritus Professor, he has continued to be associated with the university as Visiting Fellow in the History of Ideas (1980–93) and History (1994–). For a few months each year (1984–91) he was Visiting Distinguished Professor and General Editor of the Russell Project at McMaster University (Ontario, Canada).

In the course of his long and internationally distinguished career he has also been a Visiting Professor at Brandeis University (New England, USA, 1960) and a Visiting Fellow at All Souls, Oxford (1970, 1978), Clare Hall, Cambridge (1973), and the London Institute of Education (1970). He has delivered named lectures in many universities, inside and outside Australia, including Japan. His many academic honours include honorary doctorates from Sydney, McMaster, Wollongong and the Australian National University, and fellowships of the Australian Academy of the Humanities (President 1974–77), the Australian Academy of the Social Sciences, the British Academy (Corresponding Fellow), the American Academy of Arts and Sciences (Foreign Fellow), and the Royal Danish Academy of Science and Letters (Foreign Fellow). He is also a Companion of the Order of Australia.

Professor Passmore is known internationally for his published works in philosophy, including *Ralph Cudworth* (1951), *Hume's Intentions* (1952), *A Hundred Years of Philosophy* (1957), *Philosophical Reasoning* (1961), *The Perfectibility of Man* (1970), *Man's Responsibility for Nature* (1974), *Science and its Critics* (1978), *The Philosophy of Teaching* (1980), *The Limits of Government* (1981), *Recent Philosophers* (1985) and *Serious Art* (1991).

Professor Passmore continues to work at an energetic pace, writing scholarly reviews and articles and addressing local and international conferences; he is also working on another book.

Memoirs of a Semi-detached Australian

From me to me

July 05

1= Chalmers

Memoirs of a Semi-detached Australian

John Passmore

MELBOURNE UNIVERSITY PRESS

Melbourne University Press
PO Box 278, Carlton South, Victoria 3053, Australia

First published 1997

Typeset in Malaysia by Syarikat Seng Teik Sdn. Bhd., in 10/13pt Sabon
Printed in Malaysia by SRM Production Services Sdn. Bhd.

National Library of Australia Cataloguing-in-Publication entry

Passmore, John, 1914–   .
    Memoirs of a semi-detached Australian.
    Includes index.
    ISBN 0 522 84766 8.

    1. Passmore, John, 1914–   . 2. Philosophers—Australia—
    Biography. I. Title.
199.94092

Contents

Illustrations

Acknowledgements

THE WORD 'memoir' suggests a reliance on the memory, a highly unreliable faculty. That largely has to be true of the memoir that follows, especially as, in the course of a somewhat peripatetic life, lived with no expectation of writing about it, I threw away papers. Wherever possible I have checked my memory by other sources, whether in the Mitchell Library, Sydney, the National Library, Canberra, or the libraries of the Australian National University, often having to call upon the help of librarians. There, too, I supplemented the material, dating back well beyond the range of memory, provided by my remote cousins, John Passmore and Ron Alt. For all but the first sixteen years of my life, my familial memories have been checked by my wife, born Doris Sumner. Unfortunately, her diary was begun only in 1948 and applies only to occasions at which she was present. Our memories are often far from coinciding; we have disagreed a great deal about many facts and events. She has often converted me, but sometimes I have insisted on writing the last word. In spite of this, she has read all that I have written with great care and improved the text considerably.

Although I technically retired in 1979, the Australian National University has continued to provide me with a home over the period in which I have been writing this book, along with other books and articles. My home has latterly been in the History Program of the Institute of Advanced Studies. Thanks are due to the director of that programme, Paul Bourke, the divisional administrator Beverly Gallina and particularly to Helen Macnab, Janice Aldridge and Anthea Bundock. They had the major, although not the sole, responsibility for putting this work on a computer disk. More than that, they have kept up my morale, very necessary since I have been writing a book so different from anything I have previously written, by telling me that they have enjoyed reading it.

My elder daughter, Helen Hoffmann, solved some library problems for me. My younger daughter, Diana Millar, spent her vacation practising her computer skills on my last chapter and suggested a stylistic change which I adopted for the entire memoir. Neither, however, takes any responsibility for what I have written. Neither does Dr Chris Cunneen from the *Australian Dictionary of Biography*, who was good enough to read the manuscript and drew attention to a few errors in detail. Finally, I owe a great deal to my editor Jenny Lee, who succeeded in reducing the length of this book, for economic reasons, without driving me into apoplexy, and made many suggestions of a more fruitful kind.

Conversions

In 1972 metric measurements were adopted in Australia:

1 inch	2.54 centimetres
1 foot	30.5 centimetres
1 yard	0.91 metre
1 mile	1.61 kilometres
1 acre	0.405 hectare
1 pound	0.45 kilogram

On 14 February 1966 Australian currency changed from pounds, shillings and pence (£, s, d) to dollars and cents at the rate of £1 = $2. Twelve pence made up one shilling; twenty shillings made up one pound; twenty-one shillings made up one guinea.

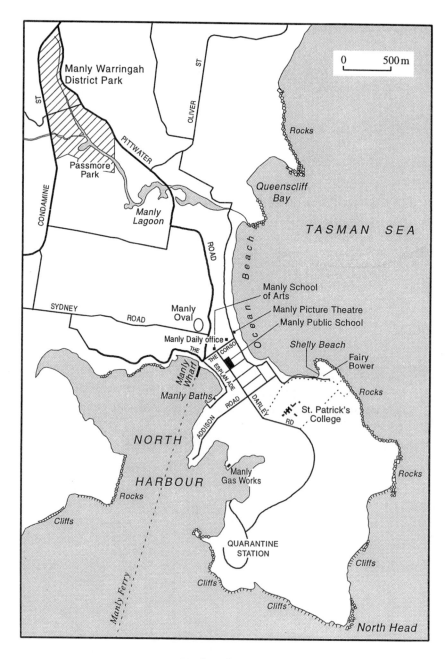

Manly in the 1930s

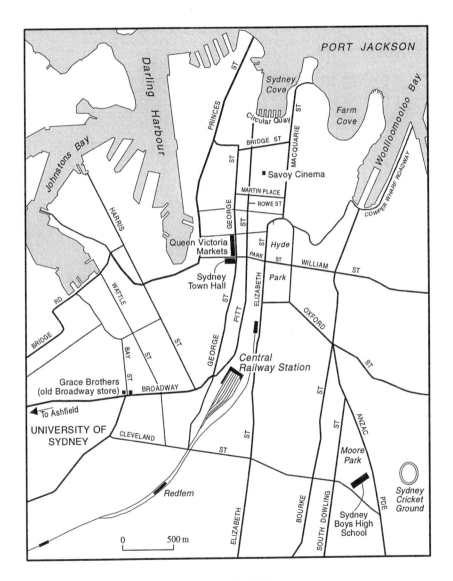

Sydney in the 1930s

1

My Ancestors Become Australian

S OME FAMILY TREES can boast of poets or prophets, bishops or actresses, scientists or scholars, or at the very least of millionaires or major criminals. Mine contains no such wonders. As a child I heard rumours of a family saint—Nan O'Nagel, was it?—an archbishop, a professor of English in Dublin, but these are lost in the mists of the Celtic imagination. Even so, no one ever went so far as to claim that we were descended from ancient Irish kings; that omission is significant in its modesty. If I begin with my family's history, that is to emphasise two things: my exceptional Australianism and my unexceptional ordinariness, at least so far as my background goes.

I had always supposed that my connection with Australia dated back only to 1826, when my great-grandfather John Passmore arrived in Sydney. It therefore astonished me to learn from the researches of my distant cousin Ronald Alt that I was a direct descendant of the Londoner James Thomas John (or Joseph?) Bean (or Baines?), who arrived in Sydney in April 1799 as a free settler on the supply ship *HMS Buffalo* with his Scottish wife, three daughters and two sons. It gives some indication of the state of the colony that on the ship's arrival the main complaint was that it brought no bedding, which was in desperately short supply. Captain Collins, from whose correspondence these observations are drawn, adds a further point about *HMS Buffalo*: its figure-head was not, as one would expect, a buffalo, but a kangaroo. This, he patronisingly writes, 'very much amused the natives, who could have had no idea of seeing the animals of their country carved in wood'. I have to confess to taking a childish delight in the fact that my first Australian ancestors were thus led across the seas by a kangaroo.

Why did James Bean take such an extraordinary decision, to migrate with his young family to a convict colony? In a superficial sense one can easily answer that question. Along with four other carpenters he came out to work on a hospital to be built in 'the Rocks', on the western side of Circular Quay, then Sydney's principal port. One might add that these were very difficult years in Great Britain, economically as well as politically. Even so, to take a family on an appalling six-month voyage to a convict colony with fewer than a hundred free settlers?

One can only guess. Perhaps, like many a later immigrant, he was given too little information or had too little imagination to envisage what could lie ahead. It may well be that his fancy swept away his prudence. The terms offered in the agreement he signed as John Bean must have seemed prodigiously generous to a London carpenter. They offered 'one hundred acres of land at Port Jackson, along with the right to be victualled and clothed from the public stores for the period of twelve months after being put in possession of our respective allotments and to be allowed the labour of two convicts (maintained by Government) for the same term'. He had no way of knowing how scarce clothing was, how poor the victuals. No doubt he envisaged his hundred acres in terms of such English countryside as he might have seen. Although he continued to practise his vocation, acting as a supervisor during the building of a later Sydney Hospital in 1810–14, he and his family worked hard at his farm, making it prosper in an environment that was anything but easy. Contemporary documents describe the farm as being at Toongabbie, but in modern terms it was at Castle Hill, now an outer suburb of Sydney.

The location of the farm was of some consequence. On 3 March 1803 a group of fifteen Irish convicts broke out of the Castle Hill Agricultural Settlement, supposing, as so many convicts did, that they could make their way to China. Some of them made their way instead to what the *Sydney Gazette* of 5 March called 'Mrs. Bean's house'—Bean was no doubt away working—where 'they gave a loose to sensuality, equally brutal and unmanly'. 'Resistance', the *Gazette* continues, 'was of no avail, for their rapacity was unbridled'. All the children were involved except the eldest daughter, who was already married. Their ages ranged from seventeen to eleven years.

It is from the youngest daughter, Ann Bean, that my descent runs. In 1808 Ann married an ex-convict 'freed after servitude'. That was Samuel James, arrested for theft at the age of thirteen and given in 1798 what was officially known as a 'light sentence' —seven years transportation. In fact, James served most of his sentence in the notorious prison hulks in England. It was 20 June 1802 before he arrived in Sydney, and just three years later he was released from his 'servitude' as a farm labourer. His good behaviour brought him eighty acres of land situated next to Bean's property. There James settled down, sired twelve children, and achieved respectability by becoming a constable. His petty English theft was indeed a 'Fortunate Fall'.

The James's ninth child, Sarah, followed in her mother's footsteps at the age of fifteen by marrying another ex-convict, the Yorkshireman Jeremiah Crossley, who had been arrested for stealing goods valued at the relatively large sum of £5. Nineteen years of age, a brickmaker by trade, literate, he had no previous convictions. He too was sentenced to seven years transportation, arriving in Sydney in June 1832 on the convict ship *John*. His 'Certificate of Freedom' came in 1838, after a period as an assigned labourer. With his wife, he was a pioneer farmer in various areas. Moving on, as so many early farmers did, when they had exhausted their land or improved it for sale, they ended their squatting days on a farm near Yass.

Yass, some 320 kilometres south-west of Sydney, was to be my archetypal country town. The town's prosperity largely rested on the fine quality of the wool grown in the surrounding countryside. Before the railway was built, Yass supported a considerable number of carriers and a startlingly large number of inns. It is not altogether surprising, then, that Jeremiah Crossley eventually abandoned farming to set himself up in business as a carrier. He died, according to his obituary, 'a respected and well-liked citizen'.

Had I set out to write this memoir a few years earlier, the reader would have been spared these details of my convict ancestry. Some years ago, when I was invited to join a get-together of 'Crossleys', my reply was that no one named Crossley formed part of my family tree. I was quite unaware that the great-grandmother known to me as 'Mrs Weatherby' had been born Martha Crossley, the eldest daughter of Sarah and Jeremiah, and had previously been Mrs Alt and Mrs Mote.

I remember my great-grandmother in her eighties—she did not die until 1937, at the age of ninety-four—as a formidably Victorian figure, her generous proportions clad from head to foot in black (bombazine?). If in a late-life photograph she bears a striking resemblance to the Dear Queen, in her earlier life she had been a pioneer woman of mythical dimensions.

Martha was six and a half when her first surviving brother was born, and her father had to call on her to do a man's job, as her time conceived it, on the farm. Interviewed by the Yass *Tribune Courier* of 19 October 1936 in honour of her ninety-fourth birthday, she referred with pride to her prowess in riding wild brumbies, and reported that in her father's judgement 'she could plough, reap and harrow as well as any man'. At the age of twenty-one, expecting her first child, she worked on the harvest until the birth was imminent and returned just four hours later—a story I might have regarded with greater suspicion had not my elder daughter displayed a comparable insouciance on the occasion of the birth of my only grandson. Martha went on to produce eleven children, as well as assuming responsibility for two stepsons from the first marriage of her German husband, Christoph Alt. 'Hard work', she once remarked, 'is a fine thing, provided that other people do it'. She spoke from experience.

It was not by accident that I was ignorant of my convict forebears until Ronald Alt rattled that particular skeleton. Only recently has it become socially permissible to admit to such ancestry, even when the convicts concerned, as in the case of my mother's family, developed into Protestant citizens, and sometimes Masons, whose respectability is somewhat intimidating. I suspect that my ancestors would be far more ashamed of me on account of my views than I am of them on account of their actions. One of my colleagues—the late lamented economic historian, Noel Butlin—commented on my news of Alt's discovery: 'You must be the only Fellow of the British

Academy with convict ancestry'. Perhaps so, but it is possible that some Fellows have ancestors who were greater rogues, if perhaps in less public ways, than my own.

If Ronald Alt's book, *Christoph Alt of Yass*, drew my attention to a British family link of which I was previously unaware, his main concern was with the German family that lent him his name. My British ancestors enter his story only because my grandmother was born Elizabeth Alt.

The Alt family came from Bannerod, a tiny village in relatively high country north of Frankfurt. There was little choice of occupation: difficult farming in the short summers, forestry, or service in the household of the wealthy if distinctly minor nobility in nearby Lauterbach. That is where Christoph Alt secured employment until 1849 when, at the age of twenty-one, he was conscripted into the Hessen Ducal Third Infantry Regiment. The main object of the army was to put down recurrent democratic unrest. Christoph was obviously proud of the commemorative medal and the testimonials that came his way when his service ended; they were carefully preserved.

In 1847 Christoph's brother Heinrich had emigrated to Australia, and five years later Christoph decided to join him, after Heinrich offered to pay his £12 fare. Christoph began his Australian life as a carrier. He travelled between Yass and Sydney by bullock cart, a journey of at least six weeks each way, along earth roads that were often impassably muddy and infested by bushrangers. As a way of avoiding their attentions, Christoph hid his money in a can of grease. The fact that he stood a sturdy six foot five inches tall was something of a help to him in any minor struggles that might ensue. When he married he gave up carrying, and in 1859 embarked on a successful career as a farmer and innkeeper.

Life in Christoph's first inn, the Carrier Arms, was not entirely peaceful. The inn was in bushland a short distance out of Yass, and was popular with the notorious bushranger Ben Hall and his gang, including the exceptionally violent young Johnny Dunn. To inform on them would have been fatal, but the police were naturally anxious to obtain whatever information they could. Christoph Alt, one might say, was caught between the devil and the deep blue police. One suspects that of the two he preferred the devils, who at least paid their way. On one occasion the police threatened to charge Christoph with receiving stolen money. 'How do you know', he replied, 'that the actual money I received was stolen?' A bush lawyer, if ever there was one.

Not until they had put aside sufficient money to buy the Yass Hotel, in the centre of the town, could Christoph and Martha feel reasonably secure. They were to make a great success of that hotel, which was once described as 'the best outside Sydney'. In his announcement in the *Yass Courier* that he had purchased the hotel he described himself as 'Christoph Alt, better known as John, the German'. Immigrants from countries other than the British Isles were still rare enough to make 'the German' a sufficiently discriminating nickname.

So much for my German origins. These were the days of the gold rushes, when thousands of immigrants sought to make sudden fortunes in Australia. But not the Alts. They sought independence in occupations where they could be their own masters, and did reasonably well without amassing riches. That is the pattern of my ancestors—on a Marxist analysis petty-bourgeois—both on the Alt and the Passmore sides.

The exception to this search for independence was that some of the Alts entered the railways, then a highly regarded form of public service. John Alt, my great-uncle, rose to be Stationmaster at Central Station, Sydney, which was magnificently housed in a sandstone building with a clock-tower. Meeting him there as a small child, I was tremendously impressed. The Stationmaster wore a splendid uniform, the like of which I had never seen outside a church. Part of his function was to see to the welfare of dignitaries, even of visiting British Royalty. His services won him the Imperial Service Medal. He had a wife, too, who claimed descent from Scottish nobility, even if she bore the name of Smith. So he represents 'aristocracy' in my family background.

The most interesting character among the Alts, from my point of view, is a great-aunt who never, I think, came my way, although her married name sometimes arose in family conversation. An elder sister of my grandmother, Sidonia Alt married Herbert Mellersh, an

English private banker's son who had abandoned university studies in chemistry in order to migrate, first to Fiji and then to Australia, where he gravitated to Yass. There he set up in business as a stock and station agent with my grandfather Frederick Moule, and married Moule's sister-in-law, Sidonia Alt. Mellersh soon tired of stock and stations and, no doubt hoping to draw upon his knowledge of chemistry, set up a factory for the extraction of eucalyptus oil. But that too did not hold his interest for long, and he decided to abandon Yass for the Big City, Sydney.

Mellersh was not a blood relation; that comes out in the fact that he developed into a modern-style entrepreneur, devoted to horses and unsuccessful companies, to say nothing of alcohol. Sidonia had her problems, as her husband died just eight years after her marriage. But her mother-in-law, feeling perhaps that Sidonia deserved some reward for putting up with Mellersh, left her the vast income of £1500 a year. To secure her inheritance, Sidonia had to travel to England. There she encountered the serious wealth and the delights of Edwardian London, which converted her into a semi-detached Australian. If she ended her days in a Sydney mansion, this was only because she did not want to live in England through yet another world war. Much of her life was spent in England or in the British colony in Egypt. She had first encountered Egypt during the 1914–18 war, doing volunteer service as a nurse in an Australian Army Corps—an experience that included being torpedoed in the Mediterranean.

I really should not have written about her at such length, but I am fascinated by everything said about her in Ronald Alt's account. She could by no means have been my model, and I have had no experience of the wealthy milieu in which she lived, but she makes me feel less of an oddity. I am not, after all, the sole multi-coloured sheep in my family.

My grandfather, Frederick Moule, I never knew; he died young, less than a year after my mother's birth on 1 September 1890. His death was one of the most important events in my life. Before explaining why, it will be as well to say a little about him. He was the only one of my grandparents to be born outside Australia, in that quintessentially Southern English town, Cheltenham. His father, a master craftsman in cabinet work and upholstery, migrated to Christchurch, a New Zealand city designed under the Wakefield plan to be a sort of transplanted Cheltenham, reproducing the rigid class structure of Southern English society.

That is how it came to pass that my grandfather was educated in Christchurch; I still have a medal for history and two rowing cups he won there. But along with his brother, followed later by his father, he migrated to Australia and more particularly to that magnetic town, Yass. There, at the age of twenty-five, he set up in business as an 'auctioneer and commission agent'. On his death, just five years later, the *Yass Evening Tribune* published an obituary that was a little more specific than the customary, always favourable, tribute. He was 'energetic and honourable'; 'the district can ill afford to lose men as capable as F. G. Moule was generally acknowledged to be in commercial matters'.

The reason why his death is so important is not that I lost contact with such virtues, but rather that my grandmother remarried, this time to an Irish Catholic, John Sheekey. I was not brought up, then, in the austere Protestant tradition of the Alts or the Moules.

That this marriage took place is more than a little surprising. 'Mixed marriages' were regularly anathematised from the Roman Catholic pulpit. For such marriages to be considered valid by the church, any children born to them had to be baptised and educated as Roman Catholics. Whether this automatically included stepchildren I do not know, but anyhow my mother was rebaptised. She always felt indignant about this, believing that she should have been left free to make her own decision when she reached maturity. Her indignation, I suspect, was an important factor in my life.

When my mother came to marry, however, there was no question of another mixed marriage. Like the Sheekeys, to whom indeed they were very vaguely related, the Passmores were Irish Catholics. It is time to say something about my remoter ancestors on that side, although that lineage is much less surprising than my mother's. Much less, too, is known about it; I can speak with some confidence only about my great-grandparents.

John (inevitably) Passmore arrived in Australia on 4 November 1826 as a humble non-commissioned officer, described as a paymaster, in a humble branch of the army, the Royal Staff Corps, on one of the most appalling convict ships, the *Chapman*. About his parents nothing is known, as the relevant documents have been destroyed. He enlisted as a private on one shilling and threepence a day, enticed into doing so by a recruiting officer in 'the central district', some twelve days' march from the corps' headquarters in Hythe, Kent.

The Staff Corps' commissioned officers were mainly civil engineers and surveyors, and its privates and non-commissioned officers were all tradesmen. It had been founded in 1799 by the Duke of York for his Netherlands campaign. The British Army at that time was hopelessly Balkanised and, although he was officially Commander-in-Chief, the Duke of York could not persuade the Royal Corps of Engineers, then under the control of the Master of Ordnance, to give him the kind of support he needed. The new corps was put under the control of the Quartermaster-General, who was directly responsible to the Commander-in-Chief. Commissions in the corps could not be bought, presumably so that the engineering qualifications of the officers would not be in doubt. In a way the members of the corps were trouble-shooters, sent in small companies wherever they were needed. In Passmore's case, this was to supervise the convicts who were building roads and bridges along what was to become the Hume Highway, the route out of Sydney to, among other places, Goulburn and Yass.

Another, older, member of the corps was John Ward, whose daughter, Elizabeth, John Passmore was later to marry. Ward had been a member of the corps when it was on a very different mission —to St Helena, there to repair the house of the exiled Napoleon and adjacent buildings, while no doubt also acting as guards. (In France I keep quiet about this.)

I had always associated the Passmores with Devon; it is only there, especially in the neighbourhood of Ilfracombe and Coombe Martin, that the name is instantly recognised, with no questions about how to spell it. But at the same time I knew that there was somewhere an Irish background. Indeed, I used to pride myself on my Irishness until I came to be persuaded that many of the things I most disliked in the Australia of the 1930s were of Irish origin, although not peculiar to Ireland: the bigotry, the prudery, the sectarianism, the false bonhomie, the alcoholism, the 'tall poppy' syndrome, the mateship-style corruption. Nevertheless, my Irishness could not be shaken off. The family legends, as I earlier said, were Irish. To read Joyce's *Portrait of the Artist as a Young Man* was to find expressions, turns of phrase, that I had otherwise only encountered in domestic circles. 'Don't be so antimacassar' for 'don't be so proper' was such a one. The Irish vices are not my vices, and are by no means universal among the Irish. But I hope that I have some, if not enough, of the Irish virtues that are so conspicuous in the Irish friends we have made over time and in the Irish branch of my own family.

Whatever his remoter origins, John Passmore was born in Dublin on 16 December 1804. People with the same surname in various parts of the world have often written to ask whether we are related to them, but the answer is always in the negative. Indeed, although the name is not a common one—it is said to be a corruption of Passe-mer, the man from across the sea, so, presumably, 'the Norman'—there were, curiously enough, several John Passmores in the colony in its earlier days. I have many times been confused with the well-known painter and art teacher, the only John Passmore to be found in most Australian encyclopedias. When he died, indeed, my photograph appeared in the *Sydney Morning Herald* alongside his obituary. At one stage we both wrote about art at much the same time, with the result that I was accused of inconsistency. He told a mutual acquaintance that he was a remote cousin; some have said that he is descended from my great-grandfather's son, Henry, by his second wife. But I suspect that this is legend.

There is, however, a good deal of evidence, even apart from the authority of the *Sydney Morning Herald*, to demonstrate that the painter and myself are one and the same person. Did he not have one of his very rare exhibitions in Sydney in 1951, precisely when I was visiting from my then home in New Zealand? And later in New York when I was briefly there? How else to explain my authorship of a book called *Serious Art*? If he is said to have lived in London in 'Gloucester Park' that could well be an error for the 'Gloucester Crescent' where I lived. Was not one of his paintings of Fairy Bower beach, so close to my own Manly home? He went to England on the *Oronsay*—but was not that the name of our house at a time when it was customary to name houses after ships one had travelled on? Is this autobiography 'ghost-written', in the most literal sense? An Australian dictionary of events tells me that John Passmore, philosopher, was born in 1901; the painter was born in 1904, which is near enough. I remain unconvinced. But I have always been a rather sceptical person.

There is a story that my great-grandfather and other members of the Staff Corps protested about the treatment of the convicts on the *Chapman*. This is the sort of story I like to believe, but I have only very indirect evidence. The corps was not used to the kind of task that was required of it on the ship and in New South Wales. Indeed, in June 1829, when Governor Darling announced that the corps was to be disbanded, one explanation he gave was that its members were not severe enough in their treatment of the convicts they were supervising—although the *Australian* of 2 January 1829 alleged different motives, contending that the governor's move was designed to provide his cronies with work as builders and engineers.

Apart from this general consideration, there is some reason for believing that John Passmore was particularly unpopular with the powers that were. The letter to members of the corps announcing that their services were no longer required could serve as a model for modern masters of the art of 'letting go'. Their disbandment, they were assured, was a blessing in disguise: they were now relieved from their obligation to the army, were therefore free to make their fortunes in the colony, if they so desired. (They did have the alternative of joining the forces in Mauritius.) There would be no question of their getting pensions, but they could receive land in the colony, along with rations for twelve months until their land could be made productive. The rent would be a peppercorn a month.

Members of the corps had the choice between a smaller block of land in a township, where they could practise a trade, or a larger area in the country, which they would be expected to farm. If at the end of seven years they had made improvements on the farm equal in value to the farm itself, they would be granted the freehold of the land. Convicts could be assigned to them to help them work the land. John Ward was sensible and took up land near Parramatta, already a flourishing township, although he later abandoned it for an inn in Parramatta itself.

John Passmore, in contrast, was foolish and chose to take the hundred acres. This was near Goulburn, on the Southern Highlands, at a point on the Wollondilly River very close to what is now the Murray Flats railway station. It is about 217 kilometres from Sydney and about 100 kilometres north of Canberra and north-east of Yass. Canberra, Goulburn and Yass can be mapped as a triangle on the somewhat bleak plateau, rising to about 700 metres, where most of the nineteenth-century and some of the twentieth-century history of my family was worked out.

One of the local magistrates protested when he heard that it was proposed to allot this Goulburn land to soldiers. It was, he said, quite unsuitable for close settlement. Indeed, the successful farms on the nearby Goulburn Plains were 6000 acres in size, on better ground. But the Surveyor-General had drawn his straight lines on the map and, like many of his kind, Major Mitchell was not easily persuaded that geography and his straight lines were not wholly in accord, even if he did sensibly insist that the farms should have a water frontage where possible. Then, too, Goulburn was a military barracks and housed the notorious Towrang convict stockade. The government may have wanted ex-soldiers to settle there as a form of insurance. So, after a brief period checking cargoes as they entered the port of Sydney, which gained him a mention in the first number of the *Sydney Herald*, John Passmore became a farmer. He was, however, allotted only one of the two convicts he needed to work the rocky, heavily wooded, difficult country.

When his seven years were up he wanted to borrow against his land, but it took three years of pleading letters—I have a dismal one in my possession—before he could persuade the authorities to grant him the freehold. Obviously his farming had not been particularly successful; he managed to get himself appointed poundkeeper to supplement his income at the farm that he called, significantly enough, 'Passmore's Retreat'. But he did well enough to feel in a position to marry. The date was 1835, the place St Mary's Cathedral, Sydney, and the bride Elizabeth Ward, whom he had known as a child on the *Chapman*. As soon as he had possession of the land, John Passmore too became an innkeeper, establishing his Harrow Inn not far from Goulburn and near the old road to Sydney. Nothing remains of it now except the pathetic remnants of a bulb garden. He continued to work as a poundkeeper, and is thus described on his death certificate.

What I have written above is, I believe, largely correct. Although I have supplemented it from other sources, most of the information it contains derives from my conscientious cousin—grandson of my great-grandfather—yet another John Passmore, who died, alas, before his work was completed. It contrasts sharply with the distinctly Irish myth that was created around my great-grandfather. I shall quote the myth in my mother's words, as formulated in a letter to my wife:

> Pop's grandfather came to Australia in charge of a shipful of convicts; he gave such good service to the government of the day, he was rewarded with land 'as far as the eye can see' at Goulburn. The Passmore family, in early days, owned nearly all Goulburn. The old great-grandfather went out on a spree to celebrate an event and someone got his signature to papers re the land at Goulburn, and this prevented the Passmore family from being millionaires.

Is it any wonder that I have always resisted attempts to blur the distinction between fact and fiction, with such examples in my own family? Much of my writing is an argument with my mother. It was only towards the end of her life that my mother produced this version of a family legend. As a boy I had only been told that my great-grandfather gave away the deeds of his land to a stranger in his pub. Fact or fiction? I do not know, but the story does not surprise me. Our family has never been good at buying or hanging on to property.

Some of the information about my great-grandfather on which I have relied is contained in an article by cousin John on the Royal Staff Corps, published in September 1974 in *Descent*, the journal of the Society of Australian Genealogists. In the same number there is an article on the family of Patrick White. There could be no greater contrast in family histories, although the first White and the first Passmore arrived in the colony but a few months apart. The first White had the advantage of coming to Australia as a flock-master; none of my ancestors was a farmer by training and none of them ended his life a farmer. They preferred the more gregarious occupations—carrying, hotel-keeping, shopkeeping or the exercise of a trade.

So my Goulburn grandfather John Passmore was a saddler. I know nothing else about him, nothing at all about his wife Elizabeth—once more that name—Walsh. My father, born in 1880, was the youngest of their seven children and his parents died while he was still barely in his teens. From what I can make out, he was terribly disturbed by their death. Perhaps this is why I never heard him mention them, although he did call upon his mother as he approached death, rather to my mother's distress.

Whatever the explanation, none of my direct ancestors, unlike the Whites, made use of an early arrival in the 'Land of Opportunity' to acquire wealth or power or fame. That is true, so far as I know, of the family as a whole. The disclaimer is necessary, because the Passmores were anything but a tightly knit clan; about many of them I knew and know very little. There was, for example, the Uncle George who would occasionally descend upon us with a box of chocolates. What did he do? When did he die? No idea.

Thanks to my cousin's researches, however, I now know that my great-grandfather married twice. His first wife, Elizabeth Ward, from whom my descent runs, died after giving birth to only four children; my grandfather was the eldest child and only son. In contrast his second wife, Mary Lenehan, gave birth to nine children. One of these made himself known to a beloved aunt of mine, Aunt Emmeline (Aunt Emmy) with 'I'm your Uncle Henry', to meet the retort 'I don't have an Uncle Henry'. I knew nothing of the researcher John Passmore until he got in touch with me as a cousin. (I have used the word 'cousin' very broadly, never having mastered such expressions as 'twice removed', which some of my English friends use with such confidence.) One has only to look at the thousand or so names on the family trees in the Alt volume to see how many relatives I have on that side—even if most of those mentioned are only related to me in the remotest possible fashion.

But on the evidence at my disposal, it will be obvious why I began by saying that my family has been ordinarily ordinary but extraordinarily Australian. Of the many people I have mentioned, only Sidonia Mellersh could possibly be regarded as a semi-detached Australian. If we had needed a family motto, General Macmahon's 'j'y suis, j'y reste' would have been fine. I, too, have remained in Australia, but with relatively long absences, greater hesitancy. Ordinarily ordinary, extraordinarily Australian? Yes and no.

2

My Informal Education
1914–1930

O N 9 SEPTEMBER 1914 I first drew public attention to myself by a primal wail with a narrowly practical import. My mother's labour had taken three days; I had been set aside as dead and would no doubt soon have been so had I not peremptorily proclaimed: 'I wail, therefore I am'. A more traditionally philosophical child might have been quietly content with Descartes' 'I think, therefore I am' and would have died unnoticed. But I have always been outward-looking.

Unfortunately, I cannot be wholly confident that the dramatic tale I have just unfolded would bear closer investigation. It comes not from the presiding doctor, Dr Holmes à Court, whose name I was often to hear in my childhood as the epic struggle to bring me into existence was once again related, but only from my mother, never one to let brute facts stand in the way of a good story. Such traits, the reader should perhaps be reminded, are not heritable.

This much, however, is indisputable. My mother heeded the injunction to have no more children, and at a relatively early age she was prevented from doing so by what she always called her 'big operation'. Most of my ancestors' families were large to very large; I was that notorious misfit, an only child, with the typical symptoms of that condition but also its economic advantages, particularly in a low-income household.

It might have been expected that my birthplace would have been the Southern Highlands, as both my parents' had been, my mother being born in Yass, my father in nearby Murrumburrah. So it very nearly was. My father's occupation fluctuated in a somewhat odd way. His marriage certificate describes him as a book-keeper, my birth certificate as a painter—in the tradesman, not the artistic, sense of the word. I knew him only as a pay clerk. Apparently he reverted to office work after a period as a house-painter.

More precisely, for a time after his marriage, perhaps pressed by my mother, he was a small building contractor. But he encountered one of the periodic depressions to which Australia is subject, refused to go bankrupt, and so had to try to repay his creditors by painting houses. For that purpose he went to Canberra to help build Royal Military College, Duntroon, the training school for officers that had been set up in the still almost uninhabited new national capital.

There was nowhere to live except in a tent settlement erected for Duntroon workers in what is now the suburb of Kingston. By Australian standards it can be quite cold in a Canberra winter, and tent-dwelling in this climate was too much for my mother's health. She was told to move to a warmer climate, and chose Manly. So nearly did I come to being born in the place where I expect to end my life. If Canberra—as it was officially named in 1913, when my parents were still there—had been able to supply houses and my family had not left, my life, even my attitudes to life, would have been very different. For Manly, and the kind of life we lived in Manly, shaped me in a great many ways.

Although officially the Municipality of Manly is a suburb of Sydney, we never thought of it as such; it was 'the Village' and we were 'Villagers', sharing a fierce local patriotism. But this is not to suggest that Manly was remote, isolated, quiet, peaceful. It was the leading New South Wales holiday resort. A recent visitor, Jan Morris, has described Manly as a 'populist paradise'. In my boyhood it was even more so. The social columns of the *Yass Tribune* abounded in reports that Mr X. had just departed for Manly, or that Mrs Y. had just returned. It is not surprising that my parents chose it as their place of residence.

Manly's image of itself as a village and its place as the leading seaside resort are explained by its geography, which is not easy to describe to the unfortunate multitudes who have never been there. Although I have travelled a great deal, I know of no close analogue to Manly. It had a curious role; cartoonists used 'the little boy from Manly', dressed in a sailor suit, to represent Australia, seen as young and unsophisticated in a world of Great Powers. I could identify with that 'little boy'.

Manly's admittedly undistinguished centre is a narrow stretch of land about 300 metres across. We hill-dwellers called it 'the Flat' and were fond of saying that under no circumstances would we live in its humidity, but it was the centre of Manly's animation. The ferry boats from Sydney disgorged their passengers on the harbour side of Manly after a thirty-five minute trip across from Circular Quay. On their way the ferries passed the heads that form the entrance to Sydney Harbour—sometimes a very rough crossing, sometimes no more than a perceptible swell. During my boyhood the only alternative to this ferry-trip was a trip of more than two hours, involving a tram, a punt, another tram and finally a ferry that sailed through more placid waters. This was our only recourse if the seas were exceptionally severe or if the harbour was fog-bound. That sense of isolation united us as 'the village'. Even our supplies were brought to us by cargo-boat. 'Seven miles from Sydney, a thousand miles from care' was, and still is, Manly's motto.

The harbour side contains relatively narrow, relatively peaceful beaches. But although such beaches had their devotees—particularly after a shark-net was erected—it was not their placid charm that attracted visitors in such numbers to Manly. Crossing the rather attractive pine-lined Esplanade, tourists would make their way up the shop-lined Corso to the Ocean Beach. Here the Pacific swell breaks in great waves on a broad sandy beach more than a kilometre long, again backed by a pine-lined promenade, stretching from South Steyne through North Steyne to Queenscliff. (It will by now be apparent how cosmopolitan Manly was in its choice of names.) That beach is the heart and soul of Manly; that is where the life-savers display their muscular daring, that is where surf-riders display their skills (in my boyhood on heavy boards, very difficult to manage), that is where the prettiest girls in Australia used to congregate, along with suburban and country families and children brought from the Far West of New South Wales to seek health and see the sea for the first time. There, too, were camel rides and slot machines, turned by hand, with such delights as 'What the Butler Saw'.

On the eastern side of this central Flat rises a peninsula. On the harbour side, its cliffs are interspersed with beachy coves as far as the formidable North Head. Then it swings back with unbroken cliffs, their rocky bases largely inaccessible, to the incongruously named Fairy Bower. In my largely carless childhood Fairy Bower's bush-clad hill was the great resort of lovers. Now it is a park with a network of paths. At its base lies Shelly Beach, where we used to gather small shells to weigh down the crocheted covers that protected milk-jugs from flies in those pre-refrigeration days. These names are as we used them; in recent maps what I have called Fairy Bower is named Shelly Beach Park and the name 'Fairy Bower' is assigned to an inconsequential strip of sand beside the pedestrian 'parade' that leads back to South Steyne. The authorities are determined to leave nothing of my childhood alone.

The long peninsula was largely inaccessible to me as a child, occupied as it was for the most part by a quarantine station and a Roman Catholic seminary, St Patrick's College. It used to make me furious to encounter the seminary's impenetrable walls in my wanderings over the headland. There were still, though, rocks and wildflowers to make more interesting the solitary rambles I so greatly enjoyed.

My memories of boyhood, until I was twelve years old, were of living on the 'Eastern Hill', the first ridge of the peninsula, although I was actually born on the Western Hill. My mother was not easily satisfied with the accommodation she could find when she first arrived in Manly; house agents came to know her, she liked to say, as 'Mrs Shiftmore'. The house she settled on to rent was named 'Wentworth'; unusually in Sydney then for private houses, it was two storeys high. The top storey fronted on to the ridge road, Addison Road. Looking at it from that level, one would have supposed it to be a normal weatherboard bungalow. It stood on a corner, however, and on the Wood Street side the footpath fell quite sharply downhill. The doors from the lower storey opened directly out on to that path. My mother saw what an agent would call 'its potentialities'. My father, versatile as ever, removed the central staircase—although not before I, always clumsy, had succeeded in falling down its two flights, an experience that left me permanently uneasy on staircases. Three flats were then created on each floor, each with its own kitchen but sharing bathrooms and lavatories. These are the circumstances in which I lived my childhood.

Since the house was wooden, I had to be taught to be as quiet as possible and could not learn to play the violin, as I should like to have done. That apart, I certainly do not seek sympathy for my living conditions, especially at those times when we lived in the best flat at the front of the house. (Potential tenants always seemed to prefer the flat we lived in, since my mother had a genius for making flats look habitable.) What Mr Whitlam demanded for every child —'a desk with a lamp and his own room'—was something I never had. In our best flat, however, I could sleep out on an open veranda and, waking early, could have the first look at our daily paper, which was the relatively populist *Daily Telegraph* rather than the austere *Sydney Morning Herald*. Thus began an unfortunate addiction to newspapers from which I have never been able to shake myself clear. I can scarcely exaggerate the role newspapers have played in my informal education from early childhood to the present day.

Manly was not, in my childhood, primarily a hotel resort. Many of the tourists were day visitors only. The longer-term visitors from the country spent their two or three weeks in expensive flats or in rooms in furnished houses. My mother did not cater for such visitors. Her tenants mostly stayed for lengthy periods, often while they were considering the purchase of a house. We only once, in my recollection, had a short let. That was to two New Zealand girls—my first acquaintance with New Zealanders. The American fleet was visiting Sydney at the time and the girls brought home two American sailors—this was also my first acquaintance with Americans—who tried, unsuccessfully, to explain to me the mysteries of American football. But these were also the only tenants we ever had who left without paying the rent, and my mother did not repeat the experiment.

Life in these flats was not at all like life in a modern apartment, where the flat-dwellers are resolved as far as possible to ignore the fact that they have fellow tenants. Sharing bathrooms and 'lavatories' in itself diminishes psychic distance. Somewhat to my surprise, I cannot remember its giving rise to any animosities. Beyond that, we acted as a kind of social centre to the flats. There were cards almost every night—cribbage, five hundred, euchre or old-fashioned 'auction' bridge, in which I participated. There was even an occasional spiritualistic seance, with table-rapping and ouija boards. I remember being delighted to discover how to produce such phenomena as automatic writing or table-rapping without anyone discovering that I was consciously directing it.

My mother 'didn't take children'. So my life was lived in a kind of extended family consisting of tenants who functioned as honorary uncles and aunts, but with no honorary brothers and sisters. I had plenty of conversation, and if all else failed there was always the white cockatoo in the house across the road, even if he was rather repetitious. Many of our tenants remained my mother's friends and took a distant interest in my welfare long after they had found houses for themselves. They were mostly middle-aged and of English or Scottish origin, but one pair consisted of an Australian with a French wife he had met and married while in France with the Australian army. (I am writing, it should be remembered, of the 1920s. My first clear memories are of the Armistice Day celebrations and the white-mask-wearing influenza epidemic of 1919–20.) I was very fond of the Frenchwoman and spent a lot of time in their flat. Although I was too shy to try out my school French with her as she wanted me to do—one of my many stupid failures to take advantage of an opportunity through shyness—I nevertheless think this early acquaintance helped in my dealings with the French on my visits to France.

Did this contact with so many people who were not born in Australia, something by no means common in the 1920s, already tend to detach me from Australia? Not in the slightest. I used to lie in bed dreaming of an Australia that had a great defensive wall around it to keep out the foreigners, the source of all evil. Labor defence policy in the 1930s, with its concept of a 'Fortress Australia', suggests that I was not alone in my childish dreams. A very argumentative child, I violently defended the Australian ideal of a house on a quarter of acre against one of our English tenants, an advocate of terrace living, which was known to me only from photographs or from a glimpse of the run-down Sydney terraces of the day. What could be more Australian than that defence?

I grew up, then, in an adult world, though not wholly so. There were friends, one of them the only son of a South African pair who were to my eyes very well-off, since the father earned £8 a week and the son could afford such luxuries as Hornby train sets and advanced-level Meccano sets, out of which, for some reason, I delighted in making cranes, although too rapidly and therefore inefficiently. The instinct of workmanship, which I greatly admire, has never been my strong point—except perhaps in respect to writing.

There were other friends from this period, more Australian, and I have dim recollections of boyhood gangs, as of soft-ball cricket played in our back yard with a sewer-pipe as a wicket. Nevertheless, it was certainly a childhood surrounded by adults. Of course, there were then always quite a few adults in every child's life. The grocer came to the door each week, and so did the Chinese greengrocer—all the fruit and vegetable shops in Manly were then run by very elderly Chinese—who sometimes gave me a lift on his horse-drawn cart up the rather steep hill to our house. Then there was the baker, the iceman, the milkman, for whom we had to leave out our 'billy-cans', the insurance man who called every fortnight so that we could pay our instalment on a life-insurance policy. More rarely there would be itinerant tradesmen, perhaps shouting in the street their 'clothes-props, clothes-props' or 'rabbitto'. And, importantly, the twice-a-day postman.

Then, too, I was called upon to do quite a lot of shopping for my mother, at a time when shopping was a personal transaction with rarely changing individuals. I also did a little shopping for our tenants, although my mother strictly forbade me to take any money for my services. Perhaps this is why, in adult life, I have always felt uncomfortable about being paid. I enjoyed sitting on a high stool talking to the grocer and was certainly not averse to accepting the little gifts he would offer, in the form of what we always called 'lollies'.

There is one other person who has to be included in this category of adults—the family doctor. Our family doctor, Roy Minnett, was for a small boy a very special person in that he had actually played Test cricket for Australia against England. But it was not for his cricketing skills that my mother hero-worshipped him—about sport she could scarcely have cared less—it was as 'the doctor'.

This was not because the doctor could do so much but, in a sense, because he could do so little. When I contracted pneumonia at the age of six, there were no antibiotics; nothing could be done except to nurse me until the climax was reached at which the disease would either kill me or gradually diminish in potency. But just for that reason, the doctor had to be prepared to offer hope or solace. Home visits were commonplace. The doctor knew from personal experience the conditions under which his—there were few, if any, women doctors—patients lived and could then adjust his recommendations to them, deciding whether or what to charge and whether a patient should go to hospital or could properly be cared for at home. It was not surprising that a child could think of his doctor as a member of his extended family, or at least as a close family friend.

I spoke earlier about '*our* tenants' not '*my mother's* tenants', regarding them with a sense of proprietorship. Our telephone was affixed high on the wall, and I remember standing on a stool to answer inquiries when we had a flat vacant. At the age of eight or so, I would probably have dropped an advertisement for the flat in the *Manly Daily* office; at a somewhat later age, I might even have written it, in the peculiar telegraphese used in such advertisements. Sometimes, if my mother was out, it fell to me to show tenants around a flat, descanting upon its virtues. It is not surprising that I was verbally precocious, becoming the sort of boy of whom people who know nothing about politics say: 'Mark my words, that boy will become Prime Minister some day'. As a Prime Minister, I would have been my own Leader of the Opposition.

One thing I did not do was to help my mother with the heavy cleaning work in the common hallway, bathroom, lavatories. On my twenty-first birthday, one of our former tenants remarked that she had mentally rebuked me for sitting reading rather than helping my mother with such tasks. Certainly once I had taught myself to read at the age of three, reading became an obsession.

Most of my reading in early life consisted of schoolboy stories, especially from the pen of 'Frank Richards' (George Hamilton), best known as the inventor of Billy Bunter, in such weeklies as *Magnet* and *Gem*. There were mysteries in these works that I could not solve—what on earth was 'Remove', what were 'prefects'?—but that did not diminish my enjoyment. Then there were the Sexton Blake thrillers and such annuals as the English *Chums* and the Australian *Pals*—my favourite Christmas presents, willingly given in the vain hope that they would keep me quiet for a time. My taste did not run to the English *Boys Own Annual*, with what I should now see as its rampant imperialism. I remember from that annual only my bewilderment at 'Elephants in the coffee, sir!' (In the *coffee?*)

These schoolboy stories helped me to read fluently, and I soon went on of my own accord to an extraordinary medley of reading, quite different from what we read under instruction at school, which for the most part bored me to tears. There were no books in our house, except for a few tattered volumes of indeterminate provenance and one or two manuals on signwriting, suggesting that my father had once contemplated that as a career. Nor could I have borrowed books from any of my equally bookless friends. Fortunately, the 'School of Arts', as the Manly Municipal Library was then called, sat next to the school, and the children's section was cheap to join. I spent hours there. (Writing an autobiography sometimes makes you think. I would have said that as a child I had no vast ambitions. Then why did I so greatly enjoy reading and re-reading *From Log Cabin to White House?*)

In her autobiography *The Missing Heir*, the novelist Kylie Tennant describes the librarian at Manly as detesting her. With a novelistic gift for description, Tennant describes the librarian as sitting 'majestically on a kind of dais', as 'having three chins' and as having 'doled out fiction as if it were a gift from the gods'. The 'kind of dais' is right, and she was certainly fat, but the 'three chins' is not the kind of detail I should have noticed. It is the 'detested' that pulls me up and the phrase 'doled out', which suggests a reluctance I never felt at all. Was it not this same librarian who suggested to Tennant's mother that the 11-year-old Kylie should attend a course on Greek culture? Scarcely the action of a librarian who detested her. If she handed over fiction as if it were a 'gift from the gods', no novelist should object to that. I shall continue to think of her as one of those librarians who were vital to the education of children from bookless homes.

I would spend much of my time in the library putting books back into the alphabetical order so often disrupted by the onslaught of children. As a result I was no longer charged a subscription fee and, well below the official age, was allowed to take books from the adult part of the library. My reading soon moved up through Edgar Wallace to Wodehouse and Wells and Dickens, whose *Pickwick Papers* was the first novel I ever bought. There was a reading room, too, with periodicals such as the *Tatler* and the *Illustrated London News*. After doing some shopping in the Corso for my mother, I would repair there on a Saturday morning. How strange these journals made England seem, mixed up with Wodehouse and Dickens!

In later years, when much of my reading was demanded of me by my formal education, the facility I had acquired as a child was obviously of use; the problem was to teach myself to read more slowly once I embarked upon philosophy and literary scholarship. What my informally acquired reading speed helped me to do was to read around, outside my professional spheres. And that led me, later, to find new themes, to look for new cross-connections. Perhaps in consequence I have ranged too widely; perhaps I should have confined myself within some narrow professional boundary. If that is so, then the Manly 'School of Arts' must take the blame.

Had my parents expected any kind of academic life for me, they might have rebuked me for my populist reading. But they had no such expectations. Given my family background and my very erratic progress at school, this is scarcely surprising. There was, however, one member of my extended pseudo-family who apparently saw me rather differently and opened up to me a wider world. That was Henry Hawkins of Bromwich, England—my 'Uncle Harry'. Exactly how he entered our circle I do not know, but there he was, as a family friend who sometimes lived with us. He was a musician, a clarinet player when I first knew him, although in later life his lip broke down and he transferred his affection some octaves lower to the double bass. In England he had been a member of the orchestra in the Carl Rosa opera company, which played a conspicuous part in the musical life of the English provinces.

In England, as far as I can make out, he went bail for a friend who then skipped the country, so that 'Uncle Harry', not having the money at his disposal, was obliged to do likewise. That did not prevent him from becoming the conductor of the Police Band in Sydney, which he made into a fine military band. At that time it was quite customary in the cinemas—'at the flicks'—to have some form of musical entertainment on the stage as an interlude. In one of Sydney's larger cinemas, I proudly saw him in his full glory as a conductor.

We talked a great deal, often on walks together, sometimes about operas he had played for, sometimes about the puppet plays he had seen in Indonesia, once, I remember, about Chaucer. He must have noticed that I had spent my step-grandfather's annual birthday present of a five-shilling postal note, the largest sum I ever had at my disposal, on a *Pear's Cyclopedia*, which I then devoured, particularly in the long hours I spent in bed as a sickly child. Certainly it would not have occurred to anyone else I knew to present me on my tenth birthday with a large dictionary and on my eleventh with a volume the title of which may have enticed him, since I was then always known as 'Jack', *Jack's Self-Educator*. Two of the essays particularly took my fancy: one on logic, which fascinated me, and one on English literature by that great iconoclast A. S. Neill.

Uncle Harry ended his days in a melancholy fashion. After quarrelling with the government, he resigned as conductor at the worst possible time and then encountered a period marked not only by the Depression but by the advent of 'talkies', so that cinemas no longer needed orchestras. He was reduced to making eye-lotion and selling it from door to door. But I feel a greater sense of gratitude to him than to any childhood teacher; he opened up so many worlds to me.

It might be wondered how I could make anything of his descriptions of opera, since I had certainly not seen an opera performed. But as a seaside resort Manly followed the British tradition of offering entertainments other than films. There was, in particular, the Manly Municipal Band, which played in a bandstand on the Ocean Beach to the background noise of the Pacific rollers. The young, as no one now needs to be told, delight in noise. My favourites were the overtures to *Tannhäuser* and to *William Tell*, largely in the latter case for the storm scene. Then there was the never-to-be-forgotten occasion when the Manly band co-operated with bands from visiting warships and several cannons to perform the 1812 overture, on one of those unsurpassable balmy Manly nights, with the rhythm of the surf pounding away in a manner Tchaikovsky could certainly not have anticipated.

The other source of entertainment was 'The Serenaders', a visiting troupe who set up a tent for the summer season in the centre of 'The Flat', with weekly changes of programme. Here the distinction between 'high' and 'low' cultures was ignored, even if the low was lower than the high was high. The lower jokes of the low comedians, led by Sid Beck, later to make a name for himself on the stage of the Sydney Tivoli, largely passed over my head, but there was rough humour enough to amuse an innocent child. At the opposite extreme there were reasonable singers in the company, one of whom, Sidney Burchall, was later to be a favourite baritone on the Sydney musical comedy scene. I delighted in the opera extracts the Serenaders performed, whether it was the prison scene from *Faust* or the march from *Tannhäuser* or bits from *Carmen* or *Pagliacci* or *Cavalleria Rusticana*. By normal critical standards these extracts must have been appalling, with their tatty scenery and their second-rate singers, but they whetted my appetite for more and allowed me to listen to Uncle Harry with a degree of understanding. Attempts to dance extracts from *Les Sylphides* were a different matter, and put me off ballet for many years.

My informal education related not only to pleasure but to work. Our house was not too far from the gas company where my father worked, ostensibly as a paymaster but in fact with a considerably wider range of responsibilities—over Christmas, for example, it was his duty to check the output and ensure that no household suddenly found that the Christmas dinner would have to go uncooked. I sometimes walked with him, up hill and down dale, to the Gas Works, situated at the cape of a bay where ships could unload their coal. Becoming friendly with the chemist there was a way of getting some grasp of gas chemistry; I acquired, as time went on, some sense of the way in which science and engineering could overlap. That experience freed me from any illusion that to be a scientist was automatically to have an interesting job. Important though the regular analyses of the gas were, the chemist's job was extremely repetitious, less varied than my father's.

Contact with the workers was no less important, in a very different way. They were a tough lot; although they never troubled me, they left me with no tendency either to romanticise, or to generalise about, 'the workers', in the manner of some of the middle-class socialists of my later acquaintance who had never sniffed the richly scented air of a gas works.

More important than any of this was one tiny incident that occurred when my father and I, along with his immediate superiors, were being driven home on a truck together. To explain my life-long response to that incident, I must say a little more about my relationship with my father. In some respects, I must have been a disappointment to him. He had been a more than ordinarily good tennis and golf player as a young man; there are medals to prove it. He still played a respectable game of tennis in the local competition, and was a good golfer. I was considerably worse than mediocre in both games—except on one never-to-be-repeated occasion, when I, for once relaxing, out-drove him from every tee. My school results were not such as to compensate for this. When my academic career got under way, he incredulously asked my wife-to-be, 'Is he really that good?' My wife puts this event considerably later—the disadvantages of undocumented autobiography—but I have stood by my recollection, since the earlier date is, I think, artistically more satisfactory.

Nevertheless, we got on well, despite his somewhat distant manner. I only once remember having a serious row with him when, of all things, I defended the French Revolution—surprisingly enough, since most of my information derived from historical novels, which were generally pro-Royalist. It did not interfere with my relationship that he would sometimes come home from work to find my mother telling him that I was to be strapped for my misdemeanours that day—usually, perhaps always, either for wandering away or for impudence. I accepted the strappings as an inevitable fact of life, bearing no grudge. The idea that fathers at that time were tyrants, ruling the household with a rod of iron, was certainly not true in my father's or my grandfather's house. My disputes were with my mother; she was the decision-maker.

I knew, too, how hard my father worked, as he often brought his office books home, where he filled their columns with his beautiful handwriting and impeccable arithmetic. And that is to say nothing of the additional duties that came his way. All this for £2 a week, which explains why my mother converted herself into a landlady. When ill-health forced his retirement, two men had to be appointed to replace him.

This was the man whose immediate superiors, that day on the truck, jeered at him, humiliated him in front of his son. He was in no position to respond. That episode had a permanent effect on me. As I said, I never romanticised the workers and there were other reasons why I never became a communist. But unlike my father I could never bring myself to vote for the conservative parties and, exasperating though the unions sometimes were, corrupted by wealth and power, I saw in them the sole protection workers had against this kind of maltreatment. My father, of course, did not belong to a union.

There was one other occasion, also involving my father, which contributed to my political education. My father had a somewhat unusual hobby: he liked to lay out golf courses—in an unpaid capacity, naturally. In a vacant area of land, where other people might see an opportunity to make money, he saw a place to lay out a golf course. So far as I know, his first such attempt was on a headland north of Manly, at Long Reef, Collaroy. Never one to boast, he had said nothing to me on the rare occasions when we caught the tram to Collaroy for a picnic. But decades later a secretary of the golf course went through the golf club's old records and a letter came out of the blue thanking him for what he had done. Of course, my father could not afford to join the club he thus made possible. Later, compelled for health reasons to take a lengthy holiday, he went to Little Hartley, on the western side of the Blue Mountains about a hundred kilometres from Sydney, and did the same thing there.

The project in which I was involved was much nearer home. This was at North Manly, some three kilometres from Manly, then linked with it by a tram. It lies in a valley, cut off from the ocean on one side by a considerable hill and looking across to another low range of hills. In its original condition the valley was largely occupied by a swampy lagoon, which was fed by the waters from the rocky sandstone hills. The hills were quite unoccupied at that time except by low scrub and the wildflowers characteristic of the sandstone country around Sydney, flowers so strange to European eyes that I once saw some of them exhibited in a surrealist exhibition in Paris. There, too, were Aboriginal carvings, cut on a wide expanse of flat rocks. This was the first, and for a long time the only, contact I had with Aboriginal culture. The paintings added a sense of mysterious human antiquity to what was otherwise a fairly standard example of Sydney bushland.

The better land in the valley had been taken over by Chinese who had created splendid vegetable gardens there, but at the foot of the hill where the carvings were inscribed there was a length of reasonably flat, unoccupied land, in which no one seemed to take any particular interest. My father saw it as an opportunity to construct a nine-hole golf links, and unofficially took it over for that purpose. Its owner must have been complaisant; about this I know nothing. It became known as 'Passmore's Golf Course'. There were no fees, but the fifty or so people who joined in paid threepence each. This was to pay boys for collecting wood to make fires where billies could be boiled for picnic lunches and to cut the grass with a cutter my father supplied. Was this the cheapest golf-course in the world? There he tried to teach me to play golf, along with many friends, acquaintances and acquaintances of acquaintances— all at no cost to them. When it came to converting people to golf he had the zeal of a fundamentalist preacher, with none of the mercenariness such preachers commonly display.

One day in 1923 he had a vision. That great lagoon-swamp— could it not be converted into playing fields? We moved to North Manly when I was twelve years old, to own an unsewered brick cottage overlooking the swamp, a distinctly less salubrious location for all its view into the hills. In Addison Road there were some quite wealthy houses. One I particularly admired: a double-storey brick house with a great sweep of lawn, a tennis court, English-style garden and croquet lawn. Little did I imagine that I would some day own a similar house! Which is just as well, because I have never done so. There was nothing of that sort to be admired in North Manly.

I was told that the move from Addison Road was for my sake, now that I was at high school. But if I had no room of my own in Manly, the same was to be true in North Manly; I shared a bedroom with a young uncle, two years older than me. And my mother could now play the radio at a high volume, as she became slightly deaf.

The real reason for our move, I suspect, was in order to be nearer to where my father's heart lay, even if he then had a relatively long journey to work. There was no question of our owning a car. (I knew only one boy in Manly whose father owned a car—a minute Austin in which I rode once or twice.) On the rare occasions when we needed transport from our previous house, we called upon the 'creamy ponies' who picturesquely plied from Manly Wharf.

Yet oddly enough, my favourite hobby was a variant of English train-spotting, about which I then knew nothing. Although cars were few in number, there was a great variety, including steam-cars, 'Stanley Steamers', one of which regularly got up steam by driving along Addison Road, and a single 'electric brougham'—very like a horse-driven brougham, but with a battery-driven engine replacing the horse—which conveyed its owner from his home to the Ocean Beach. What we would do—for I was often joined by another boy in this enterprise—was to write down on each page of a note-book the name of a car and underneath it the registration number of each car of that sort. This must have been a fairly widespread hobby; the poet James McAuley tells us that he, too, enjoyed it, although he had the additional advantage of living near a railway line so that he could also 'train-spot'.

Manly had been a good place for this exercise; Pittwater Road, North Manly was even better, as it was then the only way to the northern beaches. I became very good at recognising cars, although I knew nothing about how they were driven. When I was taught to drive, very many years later, it had to be explained that the accelerator was used to get the car moving, not only to make it move faster as its name suggested. As for the thing called 'the choke', surely it was obvious that this was used to cut off the petrol and stop the car if the brakes failed.

If North Manly lacked the amenities of Manly, it had the advantage of being in a genuine sense a village, except that it did not display the hostility to strangers for which villagers are notorious. There was a ready constituency there for my father's vision. Very rapidly, he became secretary of the local Progress Association, meeting in the Baptist Church hall, an official position from which he could address the two councils that would have to take the financial responsibility for building the park or securing State funds for it. He was not entirely without experience as an organiser. He liked to tell a story about a concert he had organised at Yass, when he asked one of the most wealthy of the local graziers to attend. The grazier agreed, but a week later came up to my father with a request: 'If I sing a song, would I have to pay to go in?'—a story that, if nothing else, illustrates what town dwellers in places like Yass thought of the graziers who land-locked the towns and had their supplies railed in from Sydney.

My father's experience, however, did not run to the keeping of minutes or the writing of official letters. I participated zealously in the campaign and, in spite of my juvenile years, helped out in such respects. That gave me practical experience in types of writing, enlarging my registers, but also helped me to see what was involved in such negotiations. My father triumphed, if not finally until 1934. The result is what is called 'The Manly Warringah District Park'; only a small segment bears the name 'Passmore Park', which should really be applied to all of it. With its public golf course, its soccer fields, its cricket pitches, it gives pleasure to large numbers of people. Does not anything I have achieved look pale and ephemeral by comparison?

One other element in my informal education arose in a somewhat odd way. My parents and some friends were involved in a tram accident—a mild affair, but rare enough to be reported in detail in a Sydney newspaper. The interesting thing was how many errors there were in the report, in names, ages, addresses. This was certainly not out of malice, and I make too many such mistakes myself to be able to think of that occasion with any feeling of superiority. It was just that it made me realise that I was not to trust newspapers on points of detail. This by no means led me to give up reading them; simply, I read them more cautiously.

That reaction has been fully justified on a number of later occasions, as late as 1991 when an article on myself and my work in the *Times Higher Education Supplement*, although quite flattering in its general tone, is hopelessly wrong in detail, even about the name of my birthplace. Only once, indeed, have I been reported in a totally accurate fashion. It was the common practice when an ocean liner entered Sydney from overseas to send reporters to interview selected passengers. I was interviewed by a small group of reporters, one of whom, for some odd reason, was a sports reporter of an evening tabloid, the *Daily Mirror*. I was talking about university life in England, a subject on which he would not have claimed to have any expertise, but he took good notes and produced a completely accurate record. As journalistically experienced friends have pointed out to me, if a sports reporter gets details wrong about cricket scores or betting odds, howls of protest will rise to the heavens.

There is one other kind of informal education that has been very important in my life: that is learning by looking at the world around me, including people, events, buildings, nature, works of art. I am a spectator or, if you like, a voyeur. That is linked with my fondness for walking, which is the best way of looking intimately. From when I was twelve years old, we took many holidays in the Blue Mountains to avoid Sydney's summer humidity. The Blue Mountains are not like the mountains in Virginia or Upper New York State or North Wales, although their maximum height—not a peak but just a slight rise in the road—is much the same at about 1200 metres. They are more like a set of Grand Canyons. Think of the skeleton of a fish. Then mentally raise it in the centre so that the backbone forms a curve, and imagine the side bones to be the edge of cliffs dropping precipitously into deep valleys, with waterfalls tumbling from the heights to the bottoms of the valleys. The railway and the only through road ran along the backbone where the tourist towns lay.

You could walk, or ride by bus or car—in my case by bus when I was a child—to where these cliff edges projected into the wide, uninhabited valleys below. But walking was the only way to penetrate to the bottom of the various falls or to the heart of the valley. That did not mean that you had to scale sheer cliffs six hundred metres high. You could travel down paths and steps, following a gully, and take paths hacked into the cliffs to the next such gully. In the Blue Mountains I spent most of my holidays for over twenty years. And there I developed further my love of flowers, of the great trees, sometimes having the character of a rainforest, and the birds. Never more so than on a very long walk into the heart of the eucalypt forest in the Grose Valley, where the trees' mighty trunks rose from great expanses of maidenhair fern. (No Freudian interpretations, please!) It was these experiences, not books, that lay behind my later interest in environmentalism.

Yet with love of the wilderness came a fear of its loneliness. Before breakfast was a good time for long, solitary walks. Walking along the cliff-edges, I would sometimes experience adolescent suicidal impulses. There were no other human beings about, and the wilderness seemed in a curious way to want to pull me into it. The mysticism that many environmentalists display when they talk about wildernesses is indeed a form of death-wish.

Many years later, in 1957, I returned to the Blue Mountains, and more precisely to Blackheath. Sitting on a bench overlooking the Grose Valley was one of Australia's greatest and worst-treated intellectuals, the archaeologist Gordon Childe. He was then sixty-five years old; I had only recently met him. We had a pleasant talk. Next day his body was found at the bottom of the cliff.

There were many ways in which the Blue Mountains taught one to regard its wildernesses not only with love but with respectful fear. As a university student I used to spend a week or so each year in the lower Blue Mountains town of Woodford, waiting for my examination results while being mothered by an elderly Welsh woman who was so alarmed by my thinness that she would thrust wormwood on me to awaken my appetite and prepare vast meals for me in the old-style kitchen that also served as a bedroom for her husband and herself. Doris and I were once walking, perhaps two miles from Woodford, when in a rocky gully we came upon a fire, still quite small but impossible to stamp or beat out. We hurried back to warn the local bushfire officers, who assured us that the fire was so small and distant as to be quite unalarming. Back in Sydney we were to read in our newspapers two days later that, now a great fire, it had swept up to the mountain ridge, destroying many houses and causing several deaths.

Environmentalists are annoyed when I point out that not everyone shares their feelings about wildernesses; my own mixed feelings of love and fear help me to see this, even if I finally come down in favour of the wilderness. I once wrote that some people welcome the sight of a tin or a bottle in a wilderness as a kind of reassurance. It irritates me when critics ascribe this attitude to me. They seem to be unable to comprehend how one can describe with any degree of sympathetic understanding a view one does not hold.

In emphasising learning by walking and looking, I do not want to elevate this way of learning above book-learning. The botany I learnt from my wife-to-be helped me to see on our walks much that I had previously not observed, even if that previous experience enlivened the botany she taught me and made it concrete. Neither do I want to suggest that learning by looking is peculiar to the experience of nature. If I have emphasised learning about nature through walking and looking, that is because it was so important in my early life, and with permanent effects.

From my childhood on, however, I also liked to wander the streets, then so much more full of a diversity of activities than the streets of today's car-dominated suburbs, and in consequence much safer. Neighbourhood watch was taken for granted, for both good and ill. But it was not until I began to travel in Europe that city walking came to fascinate me. I have by now walked many more kilometres in European cities, big and small, than I ever did in the Blue Mountains. If my mountain walks were not without consequence for my *Man's Responsibility for Nature*, my city walks were responsible for much else that I have written, not only in *Serious Art* but whenever I touch on human affairs. G. E. Moore once remarked that all his work was provoked by what other philosophers had written; in my case that is only partly so.

One other species of informal education has run through my whole life and carried spectatorship to its extreme point: film-going. When I contracted the measles, which culminated in pneumonia, my main, and very vocal, complaint was that going to bed meant missing the last instalment of a Saturday afternoon serial I had been avidly following for weeks past. I should also have missed the sixpence that I used to spend on as many 'lollies' as I could get, quality disregarded. (My wife knew nothing of such luxuries as one shilling a week to spend; we were relatively well-off. Or was it sixpence in all with threepence for lollies? How hard it is to recall such fundamental details!) So I can safely claim to have been a film-goer for at least seventy-five years. In these early years, apart from the 'cliff-hanging' serials, the instalments of which very frequently ended with someone in that particular predicament, the matinees mainly served up a diet of Westerns, with Tom Mix as my favourite, and comedies, in which I selected Buster Keaton with difficulty out of a field otherwise consisting of Lloyd, Chaplin, Langdon.

Sometimes I went to the pictures in the evening with my parents, my mother trying to hold me firmly in my seat as I jumped up and down with excitement. With them I saw a film that gave me nightmares for a long time afterwards, *The Four Horsemen of the Apocalypse*. Another such was Lon Chaney's *The Hunchback of Notre Dame*, which left me terrified, although I was at least eight years old, as we walked home along the rather dark Ocean Beach front. There were also the Gish sisters' sentimental dramas—who could fail to be moved by *Orphans of the Storm*?—and, in early adolescence, the blonde charms of Laura La Plante in *The Cat and the Canary* entranced me.

Education? Surely. For much that I knew, or thought I knew, about human beings and their worlds derived from films. Often misinforming me, no doubt, but so much is true of every form of education, formal or informal. And I recall few aspects of my childhood with greater pleasure than 'Saturday arvo at the flicks'.

3

At School in Manly
1919–1928

T HE INFORMAL EDUCATION I have just described took place outside the school environment. But a great deal of schooling is also informal education. Children learn by watching the behaviour of teachers and fellow students, whether in the class-room or in the playground, by experiencing the diverse ways in which teachers and students react to particular forms of action and belief. That experience can have a considerable effect on a child's own behaviour and beliefs. It certainly did in my case. And it also made a very considerable difference that my parents chose to send me to a school that, given the character of our family, was not the obvious choice.

Once again, geography was important. Had we continued to live on the Western Hill where I was born rather than on the Eastern Hill to which my mother soon afterwards moved, my schooling would have been very different. Given that we were a Roman Catholic family, the natural thing would have been to send me to a Roman Catholic school. After all, if there was one thing more often anathematised than mixed marriages in the sermons of the Sunday Mass my parents regularly attended, it was those Roman Catholic parents who sent their children to the 'public' schools. I am very grateful that my parents did not succumb to this ecclesiastical pressure. I know enough about the Christian Brothers who would otherwise have become my teachers to know that their regime would have been fatal to me.

Why did my parents make that choice? The official reason was that, only four years old, I could not safely cross the heavily trafficked Corso, which lay between the Eastern Hill and the

Roman Catholic school. The public school, in contrast, was a relatively short, if steep, walk from our house. There was no question of my being driven to school and such luxuries as school buses were unheard of. In 1918 the age of the horse had gone, the age of the car was only in its earlier stages. There were no longer horse-riders in our street, no longer sulkies or carriages. The manure that I gathered with spade and bucket from the road outside our house to fertilise our garden came from cart-horses, or from the horse-cabs that acted as our taxis.

Could I not have been taken to school by the elder child of a friend? Asking myself that question, I have just realised that most of our friends were childless and none of them, so far as I can remember, was a Catholic. Ours was a relatively wealthy area and at that time wealth was very largely a Protestant prerogative. But I wonder how far these geographical and sociological considerations, plausible excuse though they provided, were the real reason for my going to a public school. Or was my mother taking revenge for that involuntary rebaptism?

'I went to a public school.' To English readers that might conjure up visions of architectural grandeur. But once they know that 'public school' simply means 'state school' a very different vision may be conjured up, of a mean brick building, cramped and asphalted. Anyone now inspecting the site of my old school would certainly conclude that it must have been of that kind, consisting as it now does of an asphalt parking area backed by mean modernist buildings. But archaeologists know that a site should be carefully inspected for fragments. And there, beneath a shrub, lies—or lay when I last looked—a fragment of a marble entabulature, inscribed with a date, the sort of thing one might find with less surprise among the ruins of a Roman forum in some such relatively modest setting as the hill above Trieste.

The comparison is not wholly absurd, for the school was built to a classical design, in one of the New South Wales government's architecturally ambitious moments. No architectural masterpiece to be sure but, constructed in 1882 of Sydney sandstone, a memorial to the seriousness with which New South Wales had embarked on its programme of free, public, secular education. Alongside the school was the headmaster's residence, a simple bungalow with a garden, weeded at intervals by forced labour from the classroom. There was also a large playground, its dirt surface relatively safe for games. The school did not have a tuckshop but the Corso was near by and it was easy to buy a hot Easterbrook's meat pie, dripping gravy everywhere, or something a little more refined from Gowanlock's 'ham and beef shop', as we then called delicatessens. That German name would certainly not have done when I first went to school in 1918, when 'German Sausage' had been translated into 'Devon Sausage'.

As time went on most of the school amenities vanished, particularly as the demand for secondary schools increased and Manly Public School was converted into Manly Intermediate Boys' High School. The playground was tarred, the headmaster's house was demolished, the present nondescript buildings were erected on most of what remained. But it gave me one of those shocks to which the elderly flesh is particularly heir to see the old building so completely razed. Not only the body but the soul has gone. There is no longer a Manly Intermediate Boys' High School.

Perhaps my nostalgia for the school's body would be less if I had recently examined it in its original form. For its soul, particularly as exhibited in its playground, I feel no nostalgia whatsoever. As a Catholic in a public school, I was automatically something of an outsider. That did not matter too much, apart from such baffling phenomena as that 'h' was pronounced 'aitch' at school and 'haitch' at home, as it would have been in a normal Irish-Catholic school. When the clergy came to the school for religious instruction on Wednesday mornings, we Catholics, very few in number, were shuffled off into another classroom along with Jews, agnostics and an occasional member of one of the wilder sects, much as we would have been grouped together as outsiders in eighteenth-century England. From what we heard of the noise coming from the other classrooms on such occasions and what we saw of the strained look on the face of the clergy as they left, I do not think we lost much illumination by not taking part in such religious instruction. The regular classes were wholly secular. But at least I had valuable experience of what it meant to be a member of a small minority, as I was to be for most of my life, as distinct from the ghetto experience of going to a Catholic school.

The real problems arose in the playground and in the swimming baths and playing fields on 'sports afternoons'. Manly was a very physical place. It delighted in the story that 'Manly' was so named by the first white visitor to its beaches, Governor Phillip, in memory of the 'manliness' of the Aborigines he encountered there. 'Their confidence and manly behaviour', he wrote to Lord Sydney, 'made me give the name "Manly Cove" to this place'. And in Manly's eyes 'manly' meant 'muscular'.

I was the despised weedy child of schoolboy fiction, particularly after my attack of double pneumonia. A recurrence a little later made me for a time an invalid, pushed around in a pram, and even after I had recovered control over my legs it left me extremely thin. I remained exceptionally thin, which was indeed a family tendency, until after my marriage, and continued to be rather thin until after my first trip to England, in 1948.

At one stage my mother, having failed in her attempts to improve my health by homeopathic medicine, decided that masturbation must be the cause of my ills and got from 'Uncle Harry' a book called *Man the Masterpiece*. This was at a time when sex education books had two objectives, first, to put the reader off sex and, secondly, to do this while offering the minimum of information. I was not in fact masturbating, let alone engaging in any other form of sexual behaviour, but I was distinctly curious. I soon returned the book as useless and resigned myself to acquiring sexual information from the drawings on the back of lavatory doors. My next piece of pseudo-sex education came a decade later when the Fathers and Sons movement showed pictures at school of the development of the embryo. But as a friend remarked, 'what I want to know is how the baby gets in and how it gets out'. In her autobiography *A Window in the Dark* Dymphna Cusack tells us that one of her senior colleagues at Sydney Girls' High School learnt with astonishment, at this late stage in her life, that babies were not born through the navel. So it is a good job that sex education was not left to the teachers! My later views on sex education, as developed in the final chapter of *The Philosophy of Teaching*, reflect these experiences.

To go back, however, to my relations with my fellow school-boys. Sometimes it might have seemed that I was deliberately trying to be outrageous, to fix myself in the role of The Outsider. To take one example, we were once commanded to write a 'composition' about whether we preferred summer or winter. I was alone in expressing a preference for winter. A preference for winter in a seaside resort! But as always when I say something that the rest of my little world regards as being outrageous—as happens, of course, very rarely—I have excellent reasons for my judgement.

The fact is that I am a Northerner. Anywhere in Northern Europe I am taken to be a local and addressed in the native tongue. My Jewish friend and colleague, Eugene Kamenka, once confessed that he at first found me hard to take, since I was the only person he had met who lived up to Hitler's description of an Aryan. In consequence, my skin burns easily and severely. I loved to lie on the sand and to gambol in the surf. But as to the first of these I soon found—perhaps not soon enough—that I could not lie on the sand, even soaked in coconut oil, without suffering severe burns. Surfing remained just possible when I could wear a shirt under my costume. But as I grew older and costumes were replaced by trunks, a shirt looked ridiculous and my thinness already offered more than enough reason for ridicule. I gave up the surf. There was no parental pressure to do otherwise. I do not remember my father ever being on the beach. If I have such a very early memory of my mother, her fair complexion preserved by a massive hat, no doubt protected by hat-pins from vagrant winds, it was as sitting on the beach, not as swimming.

Could I not at least have gone swimming in Manly Baths, famous as the home of 'Boy' Charlton, whose Olympic wins created a degree of patriotic sporting fervour scarcely matched until Australia won the America's Cup? The ramshackle wooden baths, which were later swept away by a great storm, were the home of some of my least favourite memories, school swimming competitions. I could not learn to swim any more than I could learn to dance; my physical co-ordination was too poor. Eventually, at Sydney Teachers' College, I was forced to pass some elementary swimming tests but I suspect that I was passed only out of favouritism. It will be apparent, then, why I was not an ardent summer-lover, whereas I greatly enjoyed long walks along the winter beaches, nearly empty in the days before wet-suits, along with winter climbs around the rocks and over the headlands. But that was far from normalising me.

These remarks may suggest that I was a Romantic-style solitary, innately hostile to all plebeian pursuits. That was not so; I enjoyed the animated crowds of the summer months, the 'Venetian Carnivals' when the streets of Manly were lined with chocolate wheels, side-shows, the usual mechanical contraptions for swinging human beings up into the air—in later life I was the only member of my family prepared to accompany my grandchild on such a contraption. In such a carnival, for the only time in my life, I won something—a tin of the then-famous Minties. Above all, I loved the culmination of the carnival, when decorated boats competed for attention on the dark waters of a Sydney Harbour night. It was on such an occasion that I arrived at the third stage of growing up, which began in shorts, went on to knickerbockers and ended at the age of thirteen in long pants, the then fashionable 'Oxford bags'.

As well, my poor sporting abilities did not stop me from being an ardent spectator, especially at Rugby Union, then the only form of football played in Manly, but also at cricket and, perhaps more surprisingly, at motor-cycle racing. All of these took place on Manly Oval. Pythagoras is said to have remarked that three classes of people go to the Olympic Games: those who take part, those who go there to sell food and those who go to look on. Of these, he added, the last are the best.

I wish I could believe him; for I have been the spectator of spectators. This has sometimes made me quite knowledgeable; my spectatorship does not consist in looking with glazed eyes. My comments on Rugby Union once led a new boy to say 'You must have played a great deal of football', much to the amusement of those who knew me better. But it is the participants, not the spectators, who attract my admiration, as did that wonderful winger Nimmo, when I was watching Rugby Union, or Gregory, when I was watching cricket. In later life my spectatorship has been directed elsewhere, towards science, politics and works of art, with-

out my being a scientist, a political activist or an artist. My passionate boyhood interest in sport largely faded out by the time I was
twenty. But it did for a time make me less of an outsider. That I
could not now name the members of the Australian Test team
clearly indicates what a semi-detached Australian I have become.

My mother's actions did not always help me to be less of an
outsider. She knew nothing about boys. Her only brother was born
after she had married and gone to live in Manly; she was brought up
in a household of girls. So she could see nothing wrong with sending
me off to school on an unusually hot day without a jacket, at a
time when jackets were universally worn. I was unmercifully teased.
Nowadays I continue to wear a jacket, however hot the weather. I
can give good reasons for this; I need my pocket diary, my keys, my
wallet, my sun-glasses. Nevertheless I sometimes wonder if I am still
affected by that day at school.

My thinness and muscular weakness made me a safe boy to
bully. Bullying increased when the dirt playing-field was tarred over
and we were forbidden to run on it. I could participate in the games
we used to play on the dirt and they gave boys something to do. As
so often, technological changes had unexpected social consequences.
But that is not the whole story. A boy can sometimes escape being
bullied either by being servile to the bullies, then playing the role of
a parasite, or by making himself so inconspicuous that he escapes
notice. I was not good at either of these things. I would respond to
taunting, and for all my total lack of pugilistic skill was involved
in quite a few schoolboy fights—although, with the curious logic
of schoolboys, those with whom I thus fought later became firm
friends, as the bullies did not.

To make matters worse, when taunted I would often lose my
temper or even dissolve into tears, with the natural consequence
that I came to be described as a 'sissie' and was nicknamed accordingly. This, I resolved, must stop. I devoted all the forces at my
disposal—and also for the only time in my life called on divine
help—to changing myself. I succeeded; even when the occasion
clearly called for it, I have never wept, and I have very rarely lost my
temper. That is one effect, although not a deliberate objective, of my
teachers, of my schooling. Has it been a good thing?

My not crying has sometimes led people to think of me as being callous—as a policeman thought I was when he announced a family death to me. Some would say that the cancer I developed in later life had this emotional restraint as its cause, or at least that it led me into the bouts of depression, common among academics, to which I was subject in my middle years. These, however, are speculations. In respect to losing my temper, my restraint has sometimes been useful, sometimes not. I have sometimes been in situations where it was generally agreed that my capacity to 'keep my cool' under singularly exasperating circumstances had saved the day. In the playground, the advantages were obvious; there was much less point in taunting me if doing so provoked no weeping, no outbursts of temper. For good or ill, emotional control was one of the most important outcomes of my schooling.

Bullying continued, although mitigated as a result of these character changes. The changes in behaviour did nothing for my physical strength, nothing for my lack of physical co-ordination. In consequence, I am completely free of that longing for a lost, paradisiacal childhood so common among Romantics, for all that a child's life in a place like Manly could easily have had that effect. 'Trailing clouds of glory' my school-fellows were certainly not. As for 'except ye be as little children, ye shall not enter the kingdom of heaven', that dictum seemed to me to identify the kingdom of heaven with Hell. Beyond that, I was never surprised, however disgusted I might be, when I heard reports of horrendous human acts; I could readily understand, for example, why it was so easy to find guards for the concentration camps. The school bullies were not monsters but perfectly normal human beings who in later life performed no particularly appalling deeds; it was their very normalcy that was so frightening as a preparation for life.

My going to a state school did not entirely cut me off from the Roman Catholic world. I went regularly and not unwillingly to Mass. I enjoyed the sensual side of the Mass, which was then more marked than now, to judge from services I have stumbled across in Rome. True enough Australian Catholicism was Irish Catholicism, as many later Italian migrants were to discover to their dismay. Not for me the enchanting female figures, legs and breasts bared, to be seen in many a church in Rome. (Someone should write a thesis on 'The Leg as a Sex Object in Baroque Art'.) The music, however, was more theatrical than it was later permitted to be; one could still hear Rossini sung not too badly by the choir. The days of congregational singing had not yet arrived. In a period when everyday dress was at its drabbest, the spectacular clothing worn by the clergy was a splendid relief, the more so on the occasional visits of a Bishop or Archbishop or Cardinal. So I was made ready for my later passion for the theatre by a somewhat curious mixture of High Mass and the Serenaders.

Oddly enough, what nevertheless disturbed me were not any qualms about transubstantiation or the like but the extracts from the Bible selected for reading to a congregation that was unlikely to have any further access to that book. It was certainly not among the few books in our household. The unease these extracts created in me was increased by the formal education I received each Sunday, in preparation for confirmation, at about the age of eight years. As so often happens on such occasions, the public-school boy shone in the confirmation class—so much so, indeed, that a priest was moved to ask me whether I had ever felt that I had a vocation. The reply 'I am not good enough' was perfectly genuine; to stand up in a pulpit and preach morality to other people is something I could never bring myself to do. My favourite biblical quotation has been 'He that is without sin among you, let him first cast a stone', although I have not always lived up to it, especially when the sin is intellectual. I am told that this passage is a later interpolation, but the fact that it succeeded in finding a place in the New Testament suggests that some Christians, at least, were troubled by the recurrent self-righteousness there to be found.

This formal religious education unsettled me. Just as English lessons often leave children with a hatred of literature, so my confirmation lessons helped to weaken my religious faith. What I loved was the casuistry, such complicated questions as 'if a man sincerely intends to make a good confession but is run over on the way to the church, does this count as his having made a good confession even although no priest has granted him absolution'? But I was upset by the moral implications of what we were being taught and also by the actual conduct of the class. (Meeting Catholic boys robbed me of any illusion they would be morally better than Protestant boys.) A tiny incident again. We were asked where was the body and where was the blood of Christ in the Communion service. The Catholic school children, unorthodoxly but not unnaturally, said that the body was in the bread, the blood in the wine; I knew that on the official teaching they were both in the bread and both in the wine. The teaching nun announced that, since this was Sunday, she would not at once cane the unwitting Protestants but would leave doing so to Monday. As someone in whom anticipatory fears have always been powerful, I found this appalling. Why should the boys have to suffer more because it was Sunday? And would not this have meant that I should have escaped punishment, had I got the answer wrong, since on Monday I should be safe in my public school? Children generally have a strong feeling for fairness but in me it was particularly acute.

In the same spirit I looked at much of what I was hearing in class or heard in sermons. The story of Adam and Eve particularly disturbed me. Why should other human beings have to suffer because Adam and Eve had succumbed to temptation? A nun told me, somewhat to my surprise, that I need not take that story literally. But the essence of the story had to remain, with its doctrine of collective punishment. That the sins of the fathers would be visited on the children, 'unto the third or fourth generation' seemed to me immoral, as did those hints of the doctrine of predestination that, while played down in the Roman Catholic Church, were clear enough in the biblical extracts. And why should there be more joy in heaven over the repentant sinner than over the ninety-nine who did not sin? And if there was no salvation outside the church, why did God wait for nearly 2000 years before giving the Aborigines access to Christianity?

It might seem impossibly precocious for a child of eight to be thinking in these terms. But I did. The moral ideas that underlay such questions were crude, but when I came to write *The Perfectibility of Man*, and read widely for this purpose, I soon discovered that they had occurred to many others in the history of the Christian church, the last of them leading Augustine to conclude that the

Antipodes did not, could not, exist. Admittedly, if one removes the theological element, the views I was criticising are realistic enough as a description of what happens in human affairs, in which people do suffer from what their ancestors did, in which favouritism is everywhere to be found, in which the reformed criminal is likely to attract more attention than the honest man, in which what happens to anybody is largely a question of luck—certainly in my case—or of 'grace' in the form of good parents and good teachers rather than of personal effort. Nevertheless, I was always condemning favouritism and collective punishment in the classroom; how could I believe that a world was morally governed if these were written into it by divine decree? Critics of Christianity often say that it is intellectually unacceptable but at the moral level unexceptionable, but it was the moral implications of Christianity that first shook my faith in it, well before I had any doubts of a more metaphysical kind. And my confirmation lessons confirmed my doubts, not my beliefs.

I had one other, longer, period of Catholic education, of a much more enjoyable kind. This was in Yass, where I was sent to recuperate from my pneumonia with my grandparents and a bevy of uncles, aunts and cousins, both on my mother's and my father's side. I loved being in Yass. It was oddly comforting to walk down the main street past Weatherby the shoemaker, Mote the greengrocer, Delaney the grocer, Williamson's garage—with its amazing collection of old cars, which I loved to climb over—Sheekey the cordial manufacturer, Sheekey the insurance agent, all relatively close family members, whether directly or by marriage. When I went to see a film, the accompanying music was played on a piano by yet another Sheekey, my aunt Jean. The Williamson cousin who showed me his wartime bullet-hole, which passed through his chest to the middle of his back, hand-pumping water up to our tank, my Aunt Emmeline's cream-cake afternoon teas, my grandmother's fowls— these are all persistent memories. My step-grandfather, the insurance agent, was amused by my verbal precocity; he allowed me to sit in his office, on one dramatic occasion when Yass was ringed by fires, or he would take me to the billiard room. I was, in short, 'spoiled', although my grandmother always ensured that there were limits to this spoiling. My step-grandfather, I should add, was far from being a Bohemian. He fits my stereotype of an Edwardian gentleman, in bulk and in dressing, with every day a flower, often a carnation, in the button-hole of his meticulously kept dark suit. The gold watch, with its gold chain, was also there, crossing a vest swollen by his corpulence.

I have wandered back to informal education rather than to schooling. Perhaps this is because the months I spent in the Yass convent school have in my memory the character of an informal education. It helped a great deal that I was not bullied there; as a city boy, I was respected for my 'sophistication'. Sport was of no consequence, which suited me fine. But my memories of the class-room were of plays being acted, stories told and an atmosphere of relative informality. (One certainly must not generalise from these experiences. Proximity drove my wife, a Protestant, to a convent school at about the same time. She remembers it as a regime based on knuckle-banging by rulers, a distinct shock to a child from a home where physical punishment was strictly eschewed.) The delights of that few months, however, were short-lived, the outcome bitter.

Public education at that time was rigorously governed by a Department of Education that was generally abominated by practising teachers, and consisted entirely of those 'basics' to which teachers are now being urged to return. We were taught skills— reading, writing, numerical calculation, drawing, singing, mapping. And we acquired information about other times, other places, and the Australian system of government. Unfortunately, what we read in school I mostly found tedious, my writing was a scrawl, my singing a caterwaul, my drawings—always of such enticing objects as boxes or bananas—bore little relation to their objects, and my maps, had anyone taken them to be what they were supposed to be, would have changed the course of world history.

The 'civics' course created a boredom that made the task of Sisyphus look interestingly varied, and it was not the most fascinating of tasks to turn tons, hundredweights, quarters into pounds. Children brought up on the metric system do not know what they are missing. The part of my primary school classes that I remember with most pleasure was 'nature study', because I would sometimes be sent out of school to gather tadpoles or mosquito larvae—

'wrigglers'—from the freshwater pools that were scattered around the rocks. There was woodwork, too. Like every small boy of the time I triumphantly took home a very rickety match-box holder.

When I returned to Manly, and to fifth grade, I found that I was hopelessly behind and had to cope with a teacher, Mr Hodge, with whom I was wholly at odds. He was not an absolutely unimaginative man; on Friday afternoons, that bane of every teacher's life, he would tell us another episode of a cliff-hanging serial he had composed, although as a published author he was known only for his pamphlet list of sequentially arranged railway stations, which we had to master. I thought him unjust, with his fondness for collective punishment, his refusal to brook any questioning. He thought I was impudent, and I finished the year ingloriously near the bottom of the class. Since he had some acquaintance with my father, it is not surprising that my father was always somewhat sceptical about my abilities. The figure of this teacher looms over my book *The Philosophy of Teaching*. If I hear about 'back to basics' I think of Hodge.

It was the teacher, however, who was at fault, not the basics as such. The following year, my last in primary school, was a very different story. Modern educationalists would no doubt be horrified to learn that, even if we were near the top of the class as I rapidly came to be, we were caned if we got a simple sum wrong. But this was caning without malice and with no preferential treatment. We did not enjoy it, but took it to be part of the order of things. Here was no tyrant, but an officer of the law. He taught the basics well because he had the capacity to make them interesting. So, for example, we learnt how to place the major cities of the world by a game that involved a large map of the world stretched across the blackboard. A boy was chosen to go out to the front of the class with a pointing stick; we were then to ask him where various places were. So long as he could point to them he remained out front; if he were defeated, the challenging boy took his place. Simple, but very effective. Not only my memory of the game but what I learnt by means of it has remained with me, very usefully, throughout my life.

In the contrast between these two years, there was a permanent cause for reflection: that although there are basic information and basic skills that every child ought to have, the personality of the teacher is the thing of crucial importance in teaching, assuming only that the teacher is well informed. This may seem to be an observation so trivial as not to be worth making. But it is surprising to find, in so many schemes of educational change, teachers being regarded as a mere conduit for official decisions, much as privates are commonly regarded in an army. In fact, without their whole-hearted co-operation, any such change is doomed to failure.

I have used the word 'change' rather than 'reform'. That word has had a curious history; it once meant to take something back to its original form but it has come to mean to remove defects. Many so-called 'reforms' are in fact simply attempts to satisfy particular interests—like the so-called Dawkins reforms in Australian universities in the 1990s, and comparable reforms in Great Britain. That is why I wrote 'changes'.

So far as 'basics' are concerned, my problem as a schoolboy is that I had different ideas from my teachers about what counted as 'basic'. Writing a composition, I wanted to use the best possible words, to make my precise meaning apparent. As many typists have learnt to their cost in subsequent years, such wordings seldom come to me immediately. So I would cross out a word in order to write what seemed to me a better word and in that process—in pen-and-ink days and given my natural clumsiness—might well create a blot.

Ink was a monster I had to conquer. In my earlier schooling there had been problems with slates. The slate-pencil always seemed to squeak more loudly than was permissible as I laboriously pushed it across the slate—for if reading came easily to me, writing most assuredly did not. At the next stage my pencils were given to breaking at a higher than average rate, but at least pencil-sharpening was an agreeable break in the day's routine. Steel-nibbed pens—fountain pens were strictly forbidden, as 'spoiling our writing' by not distinguishing in width between up and down strokes—and the small white ink-wells inset into the sloping wooden desks constituted a much more serious obstacle to a peaceful life, with so much of the ink making its mysterious way on to the tips of my fingers, on to my shirt-sleeves or on to the paper in front of me as blots and blurs rather than as legible words. I vividly remember those awful occasions when, as 'ink monitor', I had to pour ink from stone bottles into the minute mouths of the ink-wells.

My teachers, and particularly my fifth-class tyrant, thought of themselves as training children to become clerks at a time when my father's neatness was the ideal. That the new word was better than the old word was a matter of indifference to such teachers; that the page should contain no blots or ugly crossings-out was basic. Many of those who introduced the subsequent changes in primary schools shared my attitudes; they were not attacking the basics but rather taking a different view about what counted as basic. If I should now criticise many of these changes, this is because the older practices were not wholly mistaken, only partly mistaken, in what they took to be basic. But that what is now needed is simply a 'reform' in the original sense, a going back, I should certainly not agree. Remembering my endless hours of boredom, my battles with my teachers, and my attempts to spend as little time as possible at school, I cannot uncritically support conventional 'back to basics' movements. What is basic is by no means uncontroversial, any more than it is uncontroversial what constitutes that 'national interest' to which some political 'reformers' uncritically appeal. But the difference between two successive teachers, each working with a centrally controlled syllabus, with one of whom I was a total failure, the other a considerable success, brings out how far it is the teacher who matters, never more so than in the early years of schooling. The morale of teachers, the morale of students—these are considerations not easily factored in by economic rationalists, yet their effect on 'efficiency', another highly controversial concept, can be crucial.

Doing so well under my sixth-class teacher, Mr Fisher, I became, in spite of my dislike for this parable, the prodigal son, since the prize awarded to the most improved pupil was more valuable than the prize for the boy who came first. But what next? Once again geography was important. Manly had just been converted into an Intermediate High School, which we could attend for the first three years of our secondary school. There was a good deal of pressure on us to stay on; we were to be the first pupils under the new regime, and local patriotism was in question. In fact the

cleverer boys left. But I was only just eleven years old and would
have had to travel to Sydney High School by two trams and a ferry.
It was going to take me an hour and a half to get to school, with a
return journey rather longer, thanks to the vagaries of the ferry
time-table. So I stayed where I was.

In some respects this had a permanent effect of a rather calamitous kind. With the sudden expansion of secondary education,
teachers were hard to find. In a boy's high school there had to be
teachers of Latin, French, Elementary Science (physics and chemistry) along with the History, English, Mathematics and Geography
that the Continuation School had provided. Not for the first or
last time, educational innovations were introduced without any
consideration of where the teachers were to come from, it being a
common assumption that anyone can teach and that a teacher can
teach anything.

The effect of the sudden changes was that for considerable
periods of time, amounting in one case to months, we went entirely
without teachers, and in other cases we were taught by teachers
whose control over their subjects was unsteady, to say the least.
When I did finally go on to Sydney High School the teachers there
took the view that my control over fundamentals left much to be
desired. That was certainly true in mathematics and in Latin—I
have no recollection of who my mathematics teachers were in
Manly—but not in science or in French, where the women teachers
in Manly enabled me to read French with reasonable fluency.

Yet the boys who went on directly to Sydney High, although
the cleverest in primary school, did not do well there, exhausted
I suspect by their daily voyage, and they certainly missed some
picturesque characters. Not everyone can claim to have been
taught French and geography by a Polish count, Count Lionel de
Noskowski, who simultaneously acted as the critic of classical
music recordings for the *Sydney Morning Herald*; not every English
teacher would have allowed me, as Mr Jeffery did, to read out of
Jack's Self-Educator, which I had lugged along to school, passages
from A. S. Neill, scarcely the most orthodox of critics; not everyone
had a Latin teacher, L. C. Carrington, who stood for election as a
conservative Member of Parliament and who never ventured into
class without a very large Liddell and Scott Latin dictionary in case

Caesar should present difficulties; not everyone was taught history by a man, Jock Weeden, who later became Head of the Commonwealth Office of Education.

It is curious how scattered one's memories of school are. I remember getting 99 per cent in geography from the Polish Count, losing a mark for misspelling Nijni-Novgorod. To think that I would have got 100 per cent if we had been taught about that town under its Soviet name of Gorky! But that would have been unimaginable under Noskowski. I feel sure that no other schoolboys in Australia learnt as much about Russian and Polish geography as we did. Then there was the occasion when a chemistry demonstration went wrong and we had to rush to the windows to avoid being asphyxiated by chlorine; the time that Jock Weeden announced that he would not teach the Irish section of the British History course because it was 'too controversial' or when, in his capacity as sports master, he asked me what form of physical activity I preferred to engage in and I replied, to unanimous laughter, 'walking'.

Of greater influence was what happened when the English master, teaching in a secondary school for the first time, prepared a lesson on Longfellow's 'The Arrow and the Song' for the benefit of the much-dreaded school inspector. We were not to make it plain that we had discussed the poem in an earlier lesson and were carefully coached in the allegorical interpretations we were apparently to be perceiving at first sight. But the inspector shot an arrow into our class which came to earth in our brains. 'How', he asked, 'did we know that it *was* an allegory and not just a poem about a man who shot an arrow into the air?' Total consternation. I was often, in later life, to play the role of that inspector.

We were more than ready to assist Mr Jeffery in his failed attempt to deceive the inspector because he had won our sympathies. There were other occasions on which he needed our assistance. He greatly disliked our headmaster and would fulminate against him in class. But occasionally he would find the headmaster about to open the class door, having very likely heard the first words of his denunciation. Then he would switch in mid-sentence. Thus 'It's really a problem why he' [gives his teachers so little support] . . . 'changes from verse to prose at this point'. With solemn faces we awaited the headmaster's entry. Jeffery must have supposed me to be a reliable boy; he was paid his salary in cash, and would entrust it to me to put it into his bank account. That meant walking on a narrow footpath outside a particularly raucous pub. Trustworthy I may have been; scared I certainly was.

But I have a special indebtedness to Jeffery, because if we asked him a factual question, he would reply, 'Look it up'. (We had a dictionary and an encyclopaedia in the classroom.) I was already a devotee of reference books but this attitude reinforced my habits; scarcely a day goes by when I do not open some such book. I made an early resolution not to clog my memory with details which were easily discoverable if I needed them. This can sometimes make me seem very stupid. I have written several encyclopaedia articles on David Hume, but if I want to know his dates of birth and death I have to look up my articles. I am convinced that this is a perfectly sensible policy unless one has an exceptional memory, for numerical detail in particular, where mine is pathologically poor.

Why bother the reader with this flotsam and jetsam washed up on the quicksands of memory? Because it illustrates how different what one remembers of schooldays can be from what the teacher sets out to make one remember. At Manly I learnt a lot of that kind, too, particularly from the two women French teachers, but anyone whose passion for literature could be aroused by Vachell's very English schoolboy story *The Hill* or for French by the Perrault fairytales—our set books for the public examination that marked the end of Intermediate High School—would have had an extraordinarily low combustion point.

I remember only one case in which something I learnt at school aroused my passionate enthusiasm in these years. That enthusiasm-engendering course was parsing and analysis. We were taught them by our headmaster, 'Farmer' Brown, who was a genuine enthusiast. I decided later that he must have been a close reader of Jörgensen's book on the development of the English language. So while other boys and girls were being taught that 'the' was the definite article and 'a' the indefinite article, we were looking at the use of 'the' in the phrase 'the more the merrier' or of 'a' in 'Johnny's gone a-hunting'. I was delighted by the complexity of the English tongue and have remained so.

It was also my first acquaintance with close analysis—mathematics had been taught to me only as a set of techniques. In grammar lessons we went far beyond examination requirements, and for the first time I grasped what intellectual excitement was like. This was while pupils in other schools were reduced to utter boredom by parsing and analysis, taught as mechanical techniques rather than as an attempt to solve intellectual puzzles—and by teachers who were bored by what they were teaching. Of all the educational calamities a pupil can encounter, the most calamitous, if the most readily explicable, is the bored teacher. To make matters worse, such teachers too often welcome changes, just because they *are* changes.

What about the boys I went to school with? One reason why parents send their children to private schools is that they believe the children will meet 'the right sort' of children—those with influential parents who will be useful to them in later life. That would certainly not have been a good reason for sending children to Manly school. We were all the products of relatively poor—or at the very least, uninfluential—parents. I have never had occasion to call upon school-fellows for assistance and have no idea what became of most of them in later life. Recently, however, I met one of them who had had a distinguished military career, culminating in his becoming Chief of the General Staff. Whether there were other dark horses in the class I do not know.

Of my particular friends, one became a biologist, another a doctor. The doctor, George Whyte, was the only son of a widow, and could not afford to go on to a full high school for a further two years. Leaving school at the Intermediate level, as most then did, he joined the staff of a Sydney evening newspaper, the *Sun*. There he taught himself until he could successfully sit the examinations for entry into the university's medical school. Not only that, he went on to complete the first four years of medicine while retaining his position as night duty officer at the *Sun*, which required him to ring around the police and ambulance stations at regular intervals.

How he managed to do this, study, and get any sleep at all, I do not know. His newspaper made a one-night hero of him when he finally had to leave to undertake his clinical years, and gave him some financial help. He remained through all of this a singularly nice and simple person, choosing to be a doctor when that was by no means a path to financial success and involved living almost as disrupted a life as he had lived on the *Sun*. How George Whyte fared in later years I do not know.

For the rest, the boys were a mixed lot, ranging from a gentle giant, a country boy, seven years older than I was, through boys whose life was the surf, to the kind of boys who might have been found in any such school at the time, destined to life in an office or as small businessmen. Only three of us went on to Sydney High School and I have reason to be grateful to them. They decided that I was not effeminate, only physically weak and athletically inept. So I did not enter Sydney High School with a nickname that condemned me at the outset. Indeed, I came to be known, in a school that generally used surnames, by the vaguely affectionate nickname 'Jacko'.

An autobiography is an excellent place for airing one's prejudices. What, after all, could be more revealing? So let me take this occasion to say that I fully approve of the old custom of using surnames, reserving first names for those with whom one is on close terms. That was still the custom when I first dined at an Oxford High Table; although introductions were thin on the ground, one could soon pick up who was there, as their surnames were used. That was still true in 1955, on my second such visit there. Of all Oxford men, the one I was closest to was the philosopher Gilbert Ryle. We knew one another for twenty years before we used first names—until then we were simply 'Ryle' and 'Passmore'.

In later years at High Table one would find oneself surrounded by unknown faces addressing one another by first names, so that one did not find out, all night long, who they were. The function of surnames, after all, was to distinguish between the many persons with the same first name, and although first names have in recent years become more exotic, that usefulness remains. For my part, I still find that I tend to remember only a person's surname, which is often a source of embarrassment. Can I find supporters for a Society for the Resurrection of Using Surnames? Coupled, perhaps, with a Society for the Abolition of Acronyms, the most potent of our age's many contributions to communicative unintelligibility. As a home of lost causes, my house can certainly outdistance Oxford.

4

Sydney Boys' High School
1929–1930

THAT MY SCHOOLING should continue beyond the intermediate level was by no means to be taken for granted, although my results in the public examination were reasonably good by the standards of our school. The examination had been held in Sydney, and the harbour crossing was very rough. While only one of our number was violently seasick, the rest of us felt rather queasy. Not many people, I imagine, have sat for a public examination feeling seasick. In terms of 'A's and 'B's, my results were the best in the class, but George Whyte had surpassed me in total marks. This was to be a characteristic pattern in my examination results, to come second rather than first.

I was already fourteen years old, the normal school leaving age. In spite of my relative success, my father suggested that the best thing to do was to leave school and join the Shell Company, with which he had contacts through the Gas Company. I was determined, however, to become a secondary school teacher, and that involved going on for two more years to the Leaving Certificate—the normal entrance examination—and then to university. It must have seemed to my father an intimidating prospect to have a student in the home for so many years. True enough, there were other teachers in the family. My step-aunt Kath Sheekey was a splendid teacher, able to cope with classes of tough country boys, but after the Intermediate examinations she had gone straight to Blackfriars, which was then the Sydney Teachers' Training College.

My uncle, Arthur Passmore, had become a pupil teacher at the age of twelve, according to the nineteenth-century custom. He was rarely visible while I was a child, since he spent much of his life on

Norfolk Island, an island in the Pacific about 1900 kilometres from Sydney, but administered as part of New South Wales. There my uncle had a safety-line back to Australia, but he was not subject to the bureaucratic intervention of the Education Department, that bane of all innovatory teachers. When I did see him later in his near-country or outer-suburban postings, I found him not unfriendly but somewhat distant, austere. Indeed, there was a touch of that in my father. Do other people see me in the same way? Only gradually was the range of his achievements fully apparent to me.

I knew that he had invented a device known as the 'Passmore number tray', which was designed to teach children numerical relations by slotting together pieces of cardboard of various lengths. In principle it was identical with the now familiar cuisenaire rods, invented some quarter of a century later, but with the very important difference that cuisenaire used metal rods, whereas my uncle used much more fragile cardboard. (My father had similar technological difficulties with an invention to which he devoted a great deal of time, a device that enabled golfers to cultivate their golf swing in a minimum of space. It could have made a fortune in contemporary Japan.) I knew, too, that my uncle had been awarded a Carnegie Fellowship. I was to be similarly honoured in 1955, but it was more remarkable in his case, given his lack of academic qualifications. He was the only Passmore to venture abroad since the family had first arrived in Australia.

The story ran that he had got into some difficulties with the Department of Education because he was the first to teach schoolchildren to paint in the impressionist manner. Yet I was also told that while he was headmaster at Beecroft, then on the outer edge of Sydney, he was much in demand by that same department for dealing with exceptionally recalcitrant pupils.

His obituary in the *Yass Tribune* of 9 January 1936 does not help me to confirm either of these stories. But it does tell me that he was artistically gifted, that he was in great demand as a lecturer at teachers' associations, that he was well known as a music teacher, getting the local children on Norfolk Island to perform a Gilbert and Sullivan opera—just about the height of musical sophistication in those days—and that when he taught in the country he formed physical education squads. And I have sometimes been described as versatile! He is the only member of my family who might, I think, have properly found a place in the *Australian Dictionary of Biography*. But I suspect that few, if any, schoolteachers occupy a place there, if that is their sole claim to fame.

It was not, however, my uncle's example that led me to think in terms of secondary school teaching and thus going on to Sydney Boys' High School. Teaching lay open, as other occupations with some intellectual interest did not, to the sons and daughters of relatively low-income parents. It was thought of, too, as being particularly safe, secure. My future wife followed much the same pattern through Neutral Bay Intermediate High School to North Sydney Girls' High School. She had contemplated becoming a secretary, one of the few alternative occupations open to women, but that would have entailed fees at a secretarial school. When I entered high school I had no other occupation but teaching in mind. Law and medicine were ruled out as being for the rich. Buying cheap and selling dear never appealed to me, although I suspect that my mother's ideal would have been for me to own a shop just around the corner. Of commerce beyond that level I knew absolutely nothing.

Sydney High, situated some three kilometres south-east of Circular Quay, was then a very pleasant building, sprawling in a vaguely Mediterranean manner—now mutilated, as usual in Sydney, by subsequent architectural additions—in the middle of a reasonably large playing field. Its grounds had once formed part of the old Zoo, and still contained bear and monkey pits—not inappropriately. At the bottom was a fence and on the opposite side lay the Sydney Girls' High School. Fraternisation with the girls was distinctly discouraged. (There is a legend that it was in the course of such prohibited talking across the fence that I first met the girl who was to be my wife, but in fact she was miles away in North Sydney Girls' High.) For games, Moore Park lay near at hand. Opposite was the Sydney Cricket Ground, with which we could informally communicate when Test matches held the city in thrall.

To that school I travelled each day from North Manly, as later to the university, leaving home by tram at 7.20 each morning to catch a ferry across the harbour, followed by another tram-trip to arrive at school before 8.45. Leaving school at 3.15, I had little time to spare before the departure of the 4.15 ferry. Yet I would often make my way to the Sydney Municipal Library. This was housed in the then decrepit Queen Victoria Markets, notable mainly for the smells of dust and stale wine that clung around its mouldering walls. I was not one to be disturbed by such obstacles, any more than by the shuddering antiquity of the lift that conveyed us to the higher floors, which contained the library. There were books there, on a scale not inferior, say, to one of the better London branch libraries.

I was now a devout bibliomaniac. My funds, mostly presents on special occasions, did not permit much in the way of purchases, but on the other side Everyman's library at one shilling and the World's Classics at a slightly higher price offered considerable bargains, to say nothing of the then prolific second-hand shops. Wanting a lot for my money, I favoured anthologies, particularly volumes of short stories that led me across the centuries. But neither school nor bookshops would have provided me with the *Madame Bovary* or the Maupassant stories with which the municipal library supplied me. These I read in French, no doubt partly in an unavailing search for the sexual information that was otherwise nowhere to be found. But anyhow I read them with interest and some profit to my French, as part of an extraordinarily omnivorous reading, facilitated by my speed. It was nothing to read two light novels in one evening along with doing my homework.

Thus, too, I was introduced to the city of Sydney, which I had previously only glimpsed from the tram up to Central Station on the way to Yass or, in later years, to the Blue Mountains. There was not much time to explore; if I missed the 4.15 boat, my tram pass to North Manly ceased to be valid. Still, when I could wheedle money out of my mother, I began to go on weekends to the Sydney theatre. Pavlova, whose visit was everywhere advertised, might be out of the question, but there was a notable revelation when—from a back seat in the gallery—I was able to see *The Mikado*. Here was colour, music, wit all in one.

'Poor boy', I hear someone say, 'three hours a day travelling!' Well, yes, I deserve a modicum of pity but there were compensations. Except when crossing the Sydney Heads on a rough day, one could work much more effectively on a ferry than on a train or a tram. I usually arrived at school better equipped to translate from our set texts than most boys, with work prepared on the way. I could even write; a girl once told me I was known as 'the boy who is always writing on the boat'. That remark illustrated another point; on our ferry we formed a small informal society, with much the same members every day and with the seats so arranged that one could survey a considerable area. Those who caught the boats leaving before 8 a.m. were described as 'the strivers', from 8 a.m. to 9 a.m. 'the drivers', after 9 a.m. 'the thrivers'. As a schoolboy I was a striver, but only marginally so.

In my role as a spectator, this social situation fascinated me. I was surrounded by people whose faces and public gestures became day by day more familiar but whose names and occupations were quite unknown; I liked to guess their occupations, then try to get close to them in the departure queue to overhear fragments of conversation that might verify or disprove my guesses.

Exactly why I have told this story, I do not know. It would be nice to be able to add: this was the origin of my success as a playwright or as a member of the Secret Service. But neither vocation came my way. It does suggest that I have been constantly curious about human beings, which is true. This is curiosity at a speculative distance; I have never been one for gossip, and have sometimes been surrounded by scandals of which I had been totally unaware. But it does not exclude talking to a great range of people when the opportunity offers. Some people dislike public transport because it brings them close to the sort of people they do not ordinarily meet. I like it for exactly that reason, except when it is taken over by drunken louts.

But I have often found that young people who had the outward signs of loutishness were by no means dull to talk to, once the ice was broken. I do not look like the sort of academic who might put them off, or indeed like any kind of academic. When strangers have tried to guess my occupation, farmer and seaman have been the most popular guesses. On a train to Cambridge, I once had a most instructive, if somewhat one-sided, conversation on how to use concrete floors as an aid to the more efficient servicing of cows by bulls. You live and learn!

Looking out of the ferry could be as interesting as looking within, although the vision was not then of human beings, except when we occasionally rescued the crew of a collapsed yacht or, more often, watched them try to right their boat. Or we might wave to passengers on a passing ship. (I should at that time have called that, too, a boat. On my first voyage abroad, I thus described our liner in the presence of an officer, to get the response: '*That*, sir', pointing to a life-boat, 'is a boat. *This* is a ship.')

There were pilot boats on their sometimes perilous journey out through the Heads, tugs, dredges, coal-boats, some of them making their way to the Manly Gas Works, so that I looked at them in a semi-proprietorial way; yachts of every size, sometimes engaged in their mysterious races, sometimes blown over by sudden winds, sometimes triumphantly displaying their spinnakers; there were tramps and liners on their weekly departures to England or California.

It was an animated and visually gratifying scene, even if more than a little terrifying when a great liner loomed through the fog. This was especially so after the notorious incident when the liner *Tahiti* bore down on the *Greycliffe*, a ferry containing schoolgirls, with more than forty deaths. It was far from being a boring trip—somewhat too exciting, in fact, when we crossed the Heads in the smallest and oldest of the ferries, the last boat to get through that day, with great waves breaking over us.

It could be too exciting even for spectators. One of our tenants was watching from our bathroom window when the old *Kuringai* was battling the waves, momentarily disappearing from sight. 'She's gone', the tenant called out. But it was she herself who was gone, tumbling backwards into the bath in her excitement. In later years, the ferries discovered a somewhat different navigational route that let them ride some of the waves, instead of plunging directly through them. Much less exciting! The ferries were also enclosed, whereas as schoolboys we chose the upper deck, which was open to winds and waves.

So much for transport. Now for a little more about Sydney High School. It was in fact the oldest public high school in Sydney, originally located in the heart of the city, not far from its great rival, the private Sydney Grammar School. Over time, there came to be a group of such selective high schools, each of them drawing upon a wide geographical area. They very roughly corresponded to English grammar schools. But one difference, very important to me, was that they did not encourage, or indeed permit, specialisation. There was a limited timetable choice—for me irritating, as we had to choose between German, history and physics. I chose history, but still had two more years of chemistry, along with the compulsory French, two mathematics, the also compulsory Latin and English. We were preparing for the Leaving Certificate, success in which meant matriculation to the university, except that for Arts and Medicine one had to pass in Latin. I do not regret having studied any of these courses, I only wish that I had been able also to take German, physics and particularly Greek, which had not been taught in Manly. These were omissions I could only partly repair in later life. I was particularly grateful for the very well taught chemistry, which I could also later use as an entry point to biology. Classes were carefully graded—selection within selection—the top class in any subject being reserved for those who wished to take the subject at the honours level, which involved additional work for additional papers.

In its general outline—forgetting the idiocies in detail—this was, I think, a good system. When I went to England I was horrified to find that my mostly classically trained colleagues prided themselves on their total ignorance of science, as also of the arts. It greatly annoys me when my European colleagues assume, as they invariably do, that I had my formal education in England. At such moments I am anything but a semi-detached Australian.

There was no intellectual disadvantage whatsoever in my not having gone to a private school. This was one of the marked differences between the State of New South Wales and the neighbouring State of Victoria. Australians abroad are often to be heard enunciating sentences that begin 'In Australia . . .' where what follows is in fact true only of their own State. Visiting Victoria for the first time in the early 1930s, I was astonished to find that many of the

academics I met had been to private schools, and also that quite a
few of them came from what were, by my standards, relatively well-
off homes.

I encountered this same phenomenon when I went to England.
At least, I then knew enough about Victoria not to say: 'In Australia, private schools are for the most part for country children
who need to board or those who cannot get into the select high
schools', which I should have done on the basis of my Sydney experience. That is not mere class prejudice.

One only has to look through the Australian *Who's Who* to see
this contrast between the two States. Old boys from Sydney High
range from a chemist, Sir John Cornforth, who shared the Nobel
Prize, to four heads of Foreign Affairs, Sir Alan Watt, Alan Renouf,
Sir James Plimsoll and Peter Wilenski. A 1989 investigation showed
that Sydney High School was well ahead of all other schools in the
percentage of its former students who were entered in *Who's Who*,
the third place being occupied by a similar school, Fort Street High.
The situation is now changed, in response to a 'levelling-down'
version of egalitarianism, although Sydney High continues to be
selective; the effect, as in England, has been to drive New South
Wales pupils into private schools, thus increasing inequalities.
There is also now a growing superstition that private schools *must*
be better, merely as being private, not state-run.

In the Australian *Who's Who*, and indeed in the Europa *International Who's Who*, no mention is made of my Manly schooling.
Not only has Manly Intermediate High School ceased to exist; it is
as if it never was. If Manly marked me for life, and not entirely for
the worse, I certainly felt that my education, as distinct from my
schooling, began at Sydney High.

Was this because the teaching was superior? In some areas it
indisputably was, especially in mathematics, although it was only
towards the end of my course that I began to have a glimpse of the
fascination of that subject, and then only in algebra. In moments of
relaxation, the teacher would sometimes talk about what I now
recognise to be philosophical questions, about the role of infinity
and zero and their arithmetical peculiarities. But numerical relationships also fascinated me; I would lie in bed at night thinking about

relationships between, let us say, prime numbers. In one examination, towards the very end of our course, I even did well in mathematics for the only time in my life. Nevertheless, my lack of a ready control over mathematical techniques and my allergy to geometry have continued to be serious weaknesses in my intellectual armoury.

Part of the problem was that most of the time I had no idea why we were doing what we were called upon to do. For example, solving algebraic problems was something I enjoyed, but it was a different matter when I had to represent them graphically, since I hated drawing and my apprehension of spatial relationships was so poor. Not until after reading Whitehead's *Introduction to Mathematics*, later in my career, did I realise that the hated 'graphs' were an introduction to an important branch of mathematics.

I found it hard to learn anything that simply had to be taken as given. Many children, especially the clever kind, do not care about this. Their satisfaction is in doing well what they are called upon to do; it is a matter of indifference to them why they are called upon to do it. I was never interested in coming top for its own sake. What I saw as the irrationality of languages also caused problems for me. I was happy to discover from Goethe's autobiography that he had had the same problem, so this form of idiocy was not unique. Yet I have come more and more to see the world as a very messy place, full of things about which we can only shrug our shoulders and say 'That's the way it is'.

If some of the teaching at Sydney High was very good and in other cases it was at least apparent that the teacher was a genuine scholar—even if he could not control classes, which were often very turbulent—in other cases the teachers were by any conventional standards appalling. Yet it is precisely one such case that justifies my claim that my education began at Sydney High, even if it has left me with continuing doubts about what counts as being a 'good teacher'.

Mulholland taught us English and History in our final year. He was obviously in good repute in some quarters. It was not easy to become head of a department, as Mulholland was, at Sydney High School. Later he was to be selected for a high office in the Army Education Service. But on the face of it his behaviour as a teacher of the honours classes in English and history was unforgivable. He would often profess to forget whether he was to teach English or history at a particular time, arriving with the history books, let us say, only to disappear for some time to get the English books; he did not set us essays to write, which would have meant that he had to correct them; he did not take us through the annotations to *Hamlet*, annotations that we needed for our examinations. At the Leaving Certificate I was the only boy to get first-class honours in English, and I did not get the honours I expected to get in history, as a consequence of facing a paper I knew absolutely nothing about. Yet three years later at Sydney University, three out of the seven Firsts came from that English class. It was also in Mulholland's history class that I developed the lifelong interest in intellectual history on which my reputation mainly rests.

How could this happen? We could say whatever we wanted to say—perhaps asserting, as one boy did, that Edgar Wallace was a better writer than Shakespeare—but we had to be prepared to back up such judgements and to face the vociferous criticism of our fellow students. We did not learn the annotations to *Hamlet* off by heart, but we were introduced to some of the more perverse critical writings of Gervinus or Schlegel, as well as the more obvious Bradley. Mulholland's own contribution to scholarship was a chart of *Hamlet*, placed in the school entrance hall for all to admire, in which all the passages in which Hamlet was melancholy were marked in purple. That year's work on *Hamlet* remains a precious memory. I have *Hamlet* in my bones, which has stopped them from growing brittle.

Principally, however, with little formal schoolwork to do, we read and read, talked and talked. I went up to university with a reading in drama, from the Greek dramatists—in appalling translations through which their greatness somehow shone—through to Ibsen and Shaw and O'Neill, even including such figures as Henry Jones and Pinero. And I was not alone in this: we boys exchanged our literary passions and argued about whether they were justified, which we could certainly not have found time to do in a more orthodox class.

All this was only possible because we were a selective class in a selective school. I discovered that I was not, after all, an utter outsider; my intellectual interests were not a rare disease, or, at the very least, I was not the only victim of it. There is a tendency to suppose that the teaching in schools is all done by the teachers, but in fact much of it in a good school is done by classmates. The idea that pupils might learn at home, or that people might work entirely at home, appals me. It quite misses the importance of the human relationships that play so large a part in what we learn and do and how effectively we learn and do it. Those who take working entirely at home as their Utopia give me the impression that they greatly prefer machines to human beings. Computers in a classroom are a different matter; their use sometimes appears to encourage co-operation. But a crucial element in one's education is listening to other students' questions and the teacher's replies. In a comprehensive school, it might be argued, I could have educated the other boys. But I had certainly not done that in Manly. The other boys might well have finally persuaded me that intellectual interests were 'sissy' and led me to go with the mob.

One particular case in which I learnt from another boy was of special importance to me. I must have talked to him about music, dire though my ignorance of it was. (If a subject interests me, I have always wanted to talk about it. I have often, in consequence, made a fool of myself. But in the process of doing so I have learnt, as a result of being admonished and corrected or laughed at. Being afraid of making a fool of oneself is an enormous hindrance to learning.) In consequence he offered to take me to an orchestral concert at the Conservatorium of Music. There I heard the orchestra, consisting of staff and students, perform the overture to Mozart's *The Magic Flute*. It came to me as an overwhelming revelation, an occasion never to be forgotten.

In our electronic age, when 'she shall have music wherever she goes' sounds like an advertising jingle for a Walkman or a threat of muzak, it is very difficult to realise just how scarce a commodity music was in those days. I have mentioned my principal sources: bands, brass and military, the Serenaders, local church choirs, an aunt who played the piano at the Yass cinema. In my grandparents' house I could hear rather more piano-playing and the singing of popular ballads, including a duet I loved, in which one of the singers extolled the virtues of country life, the other those of the city. I still remember the line 'I love the city, where the girls are very pretty'. There was also, in that same house, one of the earliest types of gramophone with its cylindrical discs and its vast open-mouthed speaker. But to recall that gramophone is to recall, principally, the songs of Harry Lauder.

Even when radio got beyond its early days, in which one spent most of one's time anxiously trying to find the right place to put the catswhisker on the crystal, music of any quality was a rarity. In the early 1930s I would look forward to Easter, even when it had ceased to mean anything to me from a religious point of view, because only then could I hear Bach and Handel. It is easy to understand why *The Magic Flute* came to me as such a revelation. Not until twenty years later did I have an opportunity to hear this opera performed.

There is another point about this concert that is worth a little comment. This was the only occasion, in my recollection, on which I spent time out of school hours with a school friend, except as travel companions on the trip to and from school. The High School had a very large catchment area, but there was more to it than that. The word 'teenager' did not exist—the first reported use in the *Oxford English Dictionary* is 1941—and the phrase 'youth culture' would have been meaningless to us.

Home and school were different worlds; we never spoke of our families at school, and did not visit one another's homes unless we were close neighbours. It is sometimes said that in Australia, and especially in Sydney, men have acquaintances, not friends. This may be related to the fact that most of us were day pupils at school and day students at the university. My wife, a member of a large family, reports the same phenomenon. I played golf and tennis, walked, went to see films, either by myself or with my parents. There were no parties except family birthday and Christmas parties. Even so, birthday parties, except for the twenty-first, usually terminated at an early age. There were no concerts especially designed for the young; at the community singing that was so popular during the Great Depression, young and old knew the same songs. The separating out of the young as a special class has, I believe, been a social tragedy for both children and adults. Interplay between the young, the middle-aged and the elderly is a very important social process. Teachers cannot be expected to bear the whole burden of it.

To go back to school, in history, under Mulholland's regime, there was time to read some of the historical classics, but the crucial thing was that we were now studying European, rather than British or Australian, history and with a remarkable textbook, Robinson and Beard's *History of Western Europe*. Neither Australian nor British history had deeply involved me. In the case of Australian history, there were human interests in the story of exploration, but the bare description of the explorers' trips did not awaken my interest. And the leading ideas that generated conflicts in Australia— whether between Catholics and Protestants, unionists and bosses, whites and Aborigines, landowners and squatters—had their origins elsewhere. The same was true of British history. Again and again there were references to Europe, but one felt rather as if one was working on the edge of a jigsaw with the centre missing. Not until I had studied the Renaissance, the Reformation, the French Revolution, the rise of the concept of nationhood, the birth of socialism, did I begin to understand British history. And now for the first time names like Plato, Aristotle, Galileo, Montesquieu, Voltaire, Rousseau, Luther, Calvin, Darwin, Marx impinged on my consciousness. My Manly teacher's idea of a history course that would avoid controversy looked more than ever absurd.

There are many for whom history is primarily a means for strengthening national consciousness; for me it is primarily an aid to the destruction of provincialism. Was this European history textbook the first step towards my becoming a semi-detached Australian? Certainly I stopped dreaming of a fortress Australia that could somehow put a wall around itself to keep out the wicked world. I am not attacking the teaching of Australian or British history, but I do see them as only intelligible against a background of European history, as something that has generated the primary assumptions of our society, its major conflicts, its Utopian dreams, even if in a manner deeply influenced by local conditions. Without that, history teaching may become nothing but an instrument for reinforcing national prejudices. 'What should they know of England who only England know?', Kipling rhetorically asked. That is dead right, and continues to be right if we substitute 'Australia', or 'the United States', for 'England'.

So much for academic life at Sydney High. When the school was founded it was admitted to the charmed circle of a small group of schools that pretentiously described themselves as Great Public Schools—in fact private schools that would have simply called themselves Public Schools had that title not already been taken over by the state schools, in a way that etymologists could scarcely condemn. At the same time Sydney High was one of the 'combined High Schools'.

Both organisations organised a variety of sporting competitions, and 'High' participated in them all. By the most coincidental of coincidences, it reached a peak in its sporting successes while I was there, winning for once the 'Head of the River' rowing races and having among its pupils an Olympic high jumper, Metcalfe, and a Rugby Union player, Pauling, of more than school-football reputation. (Later, five members of the Rugby Union Wallaby team were to be Sydney High School old boys.) I shared in the school's rejoicings, and am delighted to record that I saw Bradman play his first Sydney game of any consequence, for New South Wales against Combined High Schools.

For a spectator this was all very well, but how was I to perform? In Manly I had taken to playing baseball, not well, but endurably. Sydney High would have nothing to do with such American innovations. Winter was all right; I could play tennis. But summer meant either swimming, in the dreadful Domain baths, or cricket. Cricket it had to be, even if I was the worst cricketer who has ever, with considerable difficulty, put cricket pads on. (The 1991 *Times Higher Education Supplement* article about my work was headed by a drawing of a cricketer hitting a six, to symbolise my tendency to cross intellectual boundaries; no symbol could be more inapt.) Late in life, I discovered that I had a focusing problem that made it hard for me to follow the flight of a ball, but that is not enough to explain my unremitting incompetence, whether as bowler, batsman or fielder. For my first high school game I was allocated to my age-group team, for the second game to a junior team, and thereafter my name simply disappeared. That suited me fine; I had the afternoon free. At that time I knew nothing of Gandhi's 'passive resistance', but I did know that there is more than one way of killing a cat.

Have I suffered physically from playing no game except tennis? Well, to my great astonishment, I am now in my eighties, having lived nearly half a century more than my maternal grandfather, who was dedicated to rowing, and some years more than my sports-loving father, and am still reasonably fit. Astonishment, because as a child I was, as I earlier said, a sickly weakling and as a young man could take out a life insurance only on condition that if I died before I was forty-three only part of the insurance would be paid. A good many of the boys who laughed at my remark that the physical activity I preferred was walking are now dead. Sometimes I feel like echoing Churchill: 'I get my exercise acting as pall-bearer for my athletic friends'.

Game-playing is also said to generate moral virtues, but it is hard for me to believe that this is anything but wishful thinking. Only others can determine whether I fail to 'play the game'. I must confess, however, that these remarks are sour grapes. I should love to have been good at cricket; in my daydreams I often was. But if I still like to see Australia victorious, no particular team now has my allegiance as Manly once did. Nor can I assign to sport the importance that Australians generally do. That by itself makes me a semi-detached Australian.

Earlier I remarked that our Sydney High school classes contained difficult boys. Since student rebellions are often supposed to be peculiar to later times, it might be as well to expatiate on this theme, especially as this unruliness came near to changing my whole life. The innocent examples first. It had always been a privilege of the senior classes, then called fourth and fifth form, to go straight into class without having to line up in the playground first. The headmaster decided that all classes should line up. There is nothing like the destruction of an established privilege to create fury. So we lined up, but in two lines, one containing three boys, the other all the rest. The ex-army gym master—I have spared the reader the horrors of my first acquaintance with a gymnasium—grew apoplectic, and ordered us to move forward into the three-boy line. We did so, but in such a way as to leave only three boys behind in the line we had left. It took the gym master half an hour to bully us into two equal lines. This went on day after day, until the teachers protested that they were losing too much time. 'Twas a glorious victory.

The second example was a little more complicated. There were two travelling Shakespeare companies in Australia at that time, naturally performing, among other plays, the set texts for the year. They differed considerably in quality. We were taken to the Greenaway company and disgraced ourselves by our turbulence. Headmaster's decision, as announced: 'The teachers would not take us to the Wilkie company', which we believed to be superior. We interpreted that judgement literally and made our own arrangements to go. So the headmaster looked out of his window to see the entire fifth form streaming out of the gates. At the theatre we were very well behaved. There were repercussions, but we pointed out that all that we had been told was that no teacher would take us, and this we had accepted. In short, we exhibited just the sort of individual enterprise that was to be held up for our admiration in the 1980s. Pity the headmaster, a man of little imagination, did not see it in that way.

What I found really disturbing, however, was the unruliness in class. One of our classics teachers was a notable scholar, greatly appreciated by the more brilliant boys, who often won classical scholarships to the university. He was not, however, an altogether prepossessing person, gaunt in figure, with two nicknames, 'The Morgue' and 'The Phantom'. The boys were merciless and I watched their behaviour with terror. Would that be my fate? I decided I should not become a secondary school teacher after all: I would apply for a cadetship at the *Sydney Morning Herald*. Shock and horror at home. Teaching, as I said, was regarded as being a secure occupation—it should also be remembered that this was 1930, with the depression beginning to bite hard—and in my type of household security reigned supreme as an objective.

The deputy headmaster, Moore, who lived in Manly and knew my father, warmly supported my decision. Nothing doing. Moore was so angry that he refused to speak to my father. But the decision —no doubt in fact my mother's—was final. So secondary school teaching it was to be, assuming only that I could win a Teachers' College scholarship. And that would depend on my results in the Leaving Certificate. Not entirely so, however, as I would be a little below the minimum age for such a scholarship when the university year began—a few weeks short of sixteen and a half.

A younger boy attending my school once told me in later life that he has memories of my stumbling off the stage at the final prize-giving under a great pile of books. That is one of those legends which often arise about a person who achieves a degree of repu- tation in later life. In fact I should have expected to receive the English prize; after all, I had come first in the honours class. But by what was unanimously regarded as a gerrymander, the prize went to a boy from a lower class, because a section of the paper was marked by his teacher, who marked his own class up and our own down severely. At the last minute I was told, however, that I could choose a second prize and came away with the short stories of H. G. Wells. If I tell this story, it is for two reasons, first to illustrate, once more, my genius for coming second and secondly to destroy any sugges- tion that I was an exceptionally clever schoolboy.

In the outcome I did moderately well in the Leaving Certificate but when the teachers' scholarship results were announced my name was not there. I contemplated with horror the prospect of returning to school to repeat fifth form. It had now been decided that Shakespeare's great tragedies were 'too hard' for schoolboys, so I had to contemplate spending a year on *Richard II* and, worse, on De Morgan's *Joseph Vance*. (One always remembers close escapes in vivid detail.) It turned out that my name had been left off the list of scholarship winners on account of my age. I protested, and was called up for interview. There my reading saved me. We were asked to read passages and then to paraphrase. I quite unselfconsciously began 'Carlyle says . . .' although Carlyle's name was nowhere mentioned. How did I know it was by Carlyle? 'His style', I replied, 'was unmistakable'. The examiner wrote a voluminous report on this interview and I got my scholarship.

I cannot even imagine what my life would have been like had I become a cadet journalist. I know it would have been very different indeed had I gone to university a year later. It is not surprising that I have never believed that lives unfold by any kind of inner necessity, and have always emphasised the way in which the pattern of a life is shaped by accidents. I might not have recognised the style, had the author been someone other than Carlyle. Becoming an academic, and more narrowly a philosopher, was something I never for a moment envisaged. How could I possibly have done so?

5

At University
1931–1934

I WENT TO Sydney University with no particular desire to do so;
going there was simply a necessary condition of becoming a
secondary school teacher. I knew almost nothing about universities. I had occasionally read novels in which Oxford University, in
particular, was depicted as a playground for rich rowdies, scarcely
the kind of company I should welcome. My high school teachers
had been to university, but seldom had occasion to refer to their
years there. No relative, no friend, had ever passed through its doors.

Such ignorance was anything but unusual. Among our group
of some 200 first-year Teachers' College scholarship holders, I do
not know of a single one whose parents had been to university.
Writing about Melbourne University in these same years, the historian Kathleen Fitzpatrick described it as fundamentally middle-
class, the students coming from homes that were well endowed with
books. The Sydney University I knew was not at all like that. Our
accents, our habits, our manners, the character of our households,
did not in any way distinguish us from the bulk of the Australian
public; only our interests did so.

In no other sense did we form an élite. Yet those neo-Gothic
buildings that surrounded us—the quadrangle, even if financial
constraint had left it only partly cloistered, the Great Hall and the
old Fisher Library, built in the style of Westminster Hall—reminded
us that we were in an institution that the community thought of as
being very special. The built-on-the-cheap unimaginative modernism
of so many recent university buildings produces precisely the opposite effect. (Not, I hasten to add, that I should wish architects
to revert to Gothic; in a very different style, the buildings of the

University of Western Australia produce a similar effect of 'being special'. There are some splendid modernist buildings, but very few of any distinction on university campuses. Modernism is designed to display power, not learning.)

So far as we did enter the university with expectations, we soon found that they were erroneous. When we first went to the university to register, the boys among us looked at the taps and water-pumps, fearing watery initiations. Instead, and in a more disconcerting way, we found ourselves ignored as being 'just freshers'. I, for one, did not expect the teaching methods to be so different from school. It took me a little time to discover that I was expected to take notes in lectures, indeed in some cases to write them down verbatim. There had to be a hasty borrowing of notes when the truth dawned on me. I never wholly reconciled myself to the lecture system, whether as student or teacher, but I just had to get used to it. Indeed, with the staff–student ratio that then existed, there was no alternative.

How did university life in Sydney in the 1930s differ from life in a comparable Australian university nowadays? In the first place, the university was relatively small, with slightly more than 3000 enrolled students, about a quarter women and about a third, including many evening students, in the Faculty of Arts. This was the largest number of students since the period immediately following the 1914–18 war, and the lecture rooms were overfilled. The English class where second and third years met in combination had to use the Great Hall. That was perhaps the first time a microphone was employed in a Sydney University lecture course, to the delight of the enterprising Professor A. J. ('Johnny') Waldock, who began his first microphonic lecture by parodying the mannerisms of radio announcers.

The Teachers' College scholarship offered us the relatively generous sum of £50 a year together with freedom from university fees, but it also imposed certain restraints upon us. We were bound to teach for five years after we graduated, or else repay a considerable bond. Once a week we had to undertake gymnastic exercises at the Teachers' College, not then officially part of the university but in its grounds. (The formidable gym instructor, Major Cook-Russell, told me that in later life I would die running for a bus. I hope he may yet be right.) More than that, we had to submit our courses for approval and to concentrate on subjects that were taught in the secondary schools.

There was, however, one striking exception to this: we were to study philosophy. The Principal of the Teachers' College at that time, a remarkable Scot, Alexander Mackie, was a firm believer in philosophy. His son, John Mackie, was to become a distinguished philosopher. With no idea what philosophy was, I would have chosen to study psychology. But that was to be reserved for our postgraduate year in the Teachers' College. Thus accidentally did my study of philosophy begin.

What most annoyed me was that my bond ruled out my taking chemistry, to which I had been more and more attracted at school. Chemistry was reserved for those who were training to be science teachers. In later life quite substantial segments of my work have been devoted to writing about such questions as Darwinism, anti-science and the relationships between science and philosophy. I have read a good deal of the more accessible scientific literature and am now an avid peruser of the *New Scientist*. But, although it has often been supposed otherwise, I did no formal science after leaving school. My training in chemistry, however, has made my conception of science rather different from that of those philosophers who equate it with the higher reaches of mathematical physics.

As matters worked out, I took English and history, which together constituted a single department in secondary schools, along with philosophy and economics. I pointed out to the student adviser that this course, with its total concentration on essay subjects, would not satisfy the requirements of the faculty. He assured me that it did and, innocent as I was, I accepted his judgement, although I could not reconcile it with the regulations as I read them. He was wrong, as I discovered to my cost in my final year.

The structure of an honours degree at that time suited me admirably, but was undoubtedly very demanding. (I ended my degree course weighing only seven stone ten—49 kilograms—on a frame not far short of six feet. A few years later two medical professors whose daughters had undertaken an honours course in Arts protested against its structure on medical grounds, and the system was changed to make it a four-year course.) During the year honours students attended additional classes, much smaller and more specialised than the pass classes; at the end of each year we were examined in the pass work; during the long 'vacation' we wrote a lengthy essay or did some scholarly research; at the end of the vacation we were examined on our honours work; we then began the new academic year almost immediately. There was no provision for joint honours. The few who took honours in more than one subject had to do a full honours course in each.

We were students the whole year around. To study through the summer vacation did not entail any economic loss, as it was difficult to find part-time work during the Depression. Combined with a relatively long teaching year, this enabled us to cover much more ground in three years than undergraduates would get through in North America. Since there were no postgraduate courses, we had to include in our bachelor courses much of what was graduate work in the United States.

What I liked about the structure of our degree was the emphasis it laid on working for oneself. We spent relatively little time in class; we had no tutorials and did not have to bother about examinations until the end of the year. Our teachers were remote beings, except in honours classes and sometimes there, too. My attendance at history classes involved only two hours a week, in other pass classes no more than three. We did not have to face the Oxford chore of writing weekly essays; there would be two or three long essays a year. We were given extensive reading lists, and were expected to show evidence that we had read widely. There seemed to be plenty of time, all the same, for endless talk and for student societies.

The familiar saying; 'in first term only freshers work, in second term nobody works, in third term everybody works' was an exaggeration, but it was not without some ground. Second term was the peak period for student societies; constant assessment, now so widely practised, may have helped weaker students but it has certainly had adverse effects on the general pattern of student life.

Many undergraduates who had excellent results in their entrance examination did very badly at university, whereas I rapidly advanced. This was particularly true if they came from schools that put all their emphasis on maximising results in the Leaving Certificate, standing over their pupils, coaching them, basing their teaching on a careful study of past examination papers and the rigorous use of a textbook. Now called upon to work without a teacher over their shoulder, expected to think for themselves, faced in their reading by a broad variety of conflicting doctrines, they were completely at a loss. It was a sink-or-swim university.

Others found undergraduate life so rich and flung themselves into it with such zeal that their academic work suffered. One such undergraduate, after failing in every subject in his first year, recovered to end up as a distinguished academic at Oxford. More often, however, those who failed were simply not up to university work. The first-year examinations were the normal stumbling block. From my first year on, to make a little money—I charged a shilling an hour, a ridiculous amount even then—I coached one or two students who had come near enough to passing in philosophy to get a 'post'—a second-chance examination held at the end of the long vacation. They passed, and I learnt quite a lot.

High failure rates are often regarded as being shocking, or at the very least 'wasteful'. It was a common view, in England at least, that once accepted by a university an undergraduate should graduate, except in extreme instances. But Sydney had always worked on the 'let them have a go' principle. The quality of schooling was variable, the entrance examinations of uncertain value as predictive devices. More stringent entrance examinations would have reduced the number of undergraduates who failed, but would also have excluded many who flourished under university conditions. Those who failed had at least 'had a shot at it'. Their time was not wholly wasted. They had learnt something, they had grasped what it was like to do intellectual work, and they did not, in my experience, develop a sense of grievance, as they would have done had they not been allowed to try. But academic standards were not lowered in order to 'keep the numbers up', as can nowadays easily happen.

I have been mainly talking about a sub-group of students on Teachers' College scholarships in the Faculty of Arts. But we were, outside the sporting fields, the centre of university life. With some exceptions, the wealthy students and those from the country lived in the colleges. College members had considerable advantages over the rest of us, in the sense that they had tutorial assistance and did not have to face daily commuting. But they went back to their colleges for their midday meal, and that was the time when most student societies met. I have never set foot in a Sydney college and know little or nothing of the life my contemporaries lived there, but I was aware that, had I entered certain of those colleges, I would have encountered both the rowdy well-off I so disliked and the 'initiations' I feared.

It might seem natural to compare Sydney University to an English provincial university. There were, however, important differences. (The Scottish universities came nearer to it.) Sydney University was the only university in New South Wales. There was no draw-off of bright students to a local equivalent of Oxford or Cambridge. Teachers of the classics who came to Sydney from teaching in England used to say that, although the Sydney students knew much less to begin with, they were fresh, enthusiastic, ready to learn, whereas the English students often arrived at universities exhausted by the effort of earning a place there. Certainly we displayed those qualities, even if we were sometimes disappointed by the teaching we were offered.

I remarked that as Teachers' College students our fees were met and we were paid an allowance. We were also lent our textbooks. Too trivial a fact to be worth mentioning? In itself yes. But it was in the unromantic setting of a queue for textbooks in the dingy cellar of the Teachers' College that my eyes first encountered those of my lifetime lover, companion and friend, Doris Sumner, who was to become my wife. Unlike me, she was the eldest of a six-child family. As she relates the story, she had brothers who liked to tell jokes, but these were usually jokes they had read or heard from friends. Here was someone obviously making up jokes as he went along, arousing mirth in the young men around him. (Inevitably, men and women were in different queues.) This is a characteristic that many others, perhaps women in particular, have found intolerable, demonstrating that I was not a serious person. In fact, I am extremely serious, but an enemy of solemn nonsense. Modesty forbids me to report that John Anderson once saw in me an Antipodean Oscar Wilde, but certainly I am too fond of paradox. So it is fortunate, indeed, that I found a wife who actually enjoys my witticisms. For my part, I fell in love—so far as one can ever explain such attractions—with her combination of intelligence and gentleness, at once visible in her face. Others felt the same way towards her; one even tried to separate us by saying that she was 'being talked about'.

At that time such pairing-off was very unusual. I can only remember three other examples, spread over the three years of the undergraduate course. There was a tendency to draw a sharp distinction between university life and 'outside' life. Boyfriends and girlfriends belonged to the 'outside' life. The organisation of the university made cross-sexual relationships extremely difficult. Although women had been admitted as full members of the university in 1881, they could not enter the Union; that was a purely male domain, cafeteria and all. In the same spirit men could not enter Manning House, the women's domain. There was nowhere that men and women could go to have a cup of tea together—coffee was still a relative rarity, known in most households only as a coffee and chicory combination, served out of a bottle—nowhere they could lunch together or play chess together. Inevitably, to pair off, as we did with sandwich-eating in the grounds, was in some degree to be separated from our friends.

Nevertheless our attachment persisted. We wanted to be together as much as we could, and took to working at weekends and evenings in the old Sydney Public Library, in the company of the derelicts who gathered there for warmth and shelter in those Depression years. Depression years they certainly were. My father kept his job, as did Doris's father, a cabinet-maker by trade, although he found himself patching up old trams as distinct from helping to construct new ones. In defiance of our contract, our allowances were suddenly cut from £50 to £26. (This was particularly irritating for Doris, who had surrendered a £40 university bursary, with no commitments attached, for the sake of the extra £10.) In consequence, whenever lecture hours permitted, we took to walking the three kilometres from the railway station to the university, sometimes both ways.

Doris lived on the North Shore line at Willoughby, in a region then still surrounded by wildflowers, so we would meet or part at Wynyard station, some ten minutes' walk from the Manly ferry— although the partings were often so prolonged that it became a five-minute run. Occasionally we would succumb to the temptation of a cup of tea and a biscuit, usually tea-laden after the waitress had slopped the cup down before us with the biscuit in the heavy white saucer. But at the Woolworths lunch counter that only cost a penny halfpenny, still less than the tram fare. On the very rare occasions when we 'ate out', that was a meat pie at Sargent's or a three-course meal for ninepence at a workers' café near Circular Quay.

My mother hated our relationship; my father, in contrast, unconsciously hummed the Mendelssohn wedding march when I first took Doris home. Doris had originally been called Annie, but she had early in life rebelled and insisted on being called by her second name. Unfortunately, that was the name of my mother's eldest step-sister, whom she detested. My mother had felt displaced by that sister when my grandmother remarried; now she was to be displaced by someone of the same name in the affections of her only son. (It was at Doris's insistence that I changed from 'Jack' to my baptismal 'John'.) Not until my mother was in her seventies did she finally concede that Doris had been an excellent wife. If life was not to be wholly intolerable, I had to lie to my mother a good deal, which I hated doing. Fortunately, I have never had an extramarital intrigue; once in a lifetime is more than enough for such lying.

In fact my first romance was to be my last romance; the first person I kissed with passion was to be the last person I kissed with passion. That does not mean that I have never found any other woman attractive. Just a few years ago, in Stockholm, I went into a shop to buy a morning paper and there was a young woman behind the counter so beautiful that my heart seemed to miss a beat. But these are the pleasures of a spectator. Have I left behind me a trail of hearts broken by my relentless monogamy? Not at all. Once or twice, a woman has made it plain that an approach on my part would not be regarded as sexual harassment, but that was in a head-hunting mood after I had become well known.

Yet women have played a very large part in my life. As secretaries, research assistants, typists, coping with a person who can be very demanding, with multitudinous revisions in a handwriting that does not improve with age, they have been indispensable, often well beyond their official duties. I am far from being a misogynist and I hope that I have never treated these assistants in a way that might humiliate them, but always as people.

Oddly enough, as a young man I had the reputation, I am told, of being a super-Casanova. Other legends that have come my way at least had a remote connection with what actually happened. (I did not, at a party in a Melbourne loft, drunkenly recite large slabs of Joyce's *Ulysses*. At the time I did not drink alcohol, and my powers of verbal recall scarcely carry me beyond *Mary had a little lamb*. What I did, the only sober person present, was to read large slabs of *Ulysses* aloud in order to demonstrate that Joyce can be very funny. There could be no better audience for this purpose than a group of drunken Melbourne intellectuals, or any with a greater gift for turning fact into legend.) But when it comes to the Casanova legend, I can only presume that it had its origin with members of the Evangelical Union, convinced that if they had lost their religious beliefs that is how they would have behaved. Unless Doris is so protean that my many appearances with her were taken to be with different women.

Back, then, to the facts. No legends for sale here! What kind of intellectual sustenance did we get in Sydney in the 1930s? That came from many different sources, from our perpetual talk, the lectures we enjoyed or, more often, endured, the work we were called upon to do and our participation in student societies. I shall look first at talk, most often in the south-east corner, under the cloisters near the philosophy room. We called that talk 'quadrangulating'. At that corner there now stands a jacaranda tree where once was an inviolate stretch of lawn, never touched by any human feet except the gardener's. That tree was planted by an administration determined, we thought, to hide the Philosophy Department from the public gaze. It aroused considerable opposition, to the extent of anti-tree violence, but has finally survived. In our time, that covered section of the cloister was a kind of Stoa, even if we were scarcely Stoics.

It was in such talk that I first heard the name of T. S. Eliot, on whom I was to write my first publication. That was from the mouth of Arthur Bishop, one of those young men who never quite came to terms with the university. He entered it with first place in English at the Leaving Certificate. His knowledge beyond that area was considerable; he removed quite a few of the confusions into which my too indiscriminate reading had led me. But his university results did not at all reflect his abilities. In his subsequent career in the public service he did very well. I suspect that he was one of those students who were deeply disturbed by John Anderson's philosophy teachings. Any university teacher who gathers disciples around him is bound sometimes to have that effect. But perhaps there was some other, more personal reason, for Bishop's failure to shine; I do not know. Often enough it was not Anderson himself but Joyce's Stephen Dedalus—to whom Anderson introduced us—who was to prove a fatal model.

If Arthur Bishop was the fellow student from whom I learnt most, there were many others, Frank Bowler, for example, who curbed my streak of intellectual recklessness, my habit of living on the extreme margins of my knowledge, and who sharpened my wits by forcing me to develop my ideas in a more rigorous form. There was one point of difference between Frank and myself. He loved ranking, let us say, the top world poets. I hated it, which later made life difficult for me as an examiner.

Our lively talk was facilitated by the fact that we had very little choice of lectures. If we were taking English, we were all attending the same lectures by the same teachers. These were few in number. Latin, with a staff of four, had the largest complement. English, with hundreds of students, had three, the normal allowance was two, some departments had only one. History had two, whereas by 1991 it had forty-three. In that period the number of undergraduates multiplied by about seven. If there was a choice in essay topics, as there rarely was, it would be very small. Our background, too, was very similar. Discussion could take place against a network of common information.

What did we get from our official teachers? Sometimes, as far as their lectures were concerned, much less than we hoped for. But in many cases their less conspicuous procedures were of particular importance to my education. I shall consider my courses of study in their inverse order of importance in my intellectual development, although in fact I have called upon all of them at one time or another.

The least important of my courses was Latin, to which I had to return in my third year to satisfy the faculty requirements. It was not a subject in which I had ever excelled, and two years away from it had naturally produced a degree of rustiness. There was a real danger that I would fail, which would have been fatal to my hopes of achieving a double honours degree. To make matters worse, my principal rivals, not bound by Teachers' College restrictions, were free to enrol in Oriental History, generally regarded as the softest of all options.

The Professor of Oriental History, A. L. Sadler, was a distinguished scholar; in terms of publication, his record was not matched by anyone else in the Faculty of Arts. I am very sorry that I missed the opportunity of studying under him. I had begun to get interested in Japan—his principal theme—as a result of reading back numbers of the journal *Asia*, beautifully illustrated and sold cheaply by the newsagent on Manly Wharf. (Let it not be presumed, incidentally, that my reading of *Asia* showed that I was already semi-detached. My ferry-boat reading also included such volubly nationalistic journals as *Aussie*, the *Bulletin* or, more occasionally, *Smith's Weekly*.) Perhaps because his background was Oxonian, Sadler did not fail students. I only once knew of his doing so; I was then a member of the Board of Examiners and his recording of a failure was accompanied by 'a very bad student, very bad indeed'. We all wondered to what depths of iniquity the student must have fallen.

His usual attitude is conveyed by what is no doubt a legend. He took his examination papers on a sea cruise, setting them down on a table alongside his deck-chair. A vagrant wind carried the paper that lay at the top of the pile over the rail and out to sea. Sadler went contemplatively to the rail to see the paper floating away in the wake of the ship. Returning to his deck-chair, he picked up the rest of the bundle and dumped them into the ocean.

But I was not to experience either the pleasure or the security of Sadler's course. Latin it had to be. In large part, this was an experience neither delightful nor secure. As matters were then managed, a lecturer could find himself lecturing for years on end on a text that did not particularly catch his interest, to an even less interested class. That was true of a good deal of the Latin teaching. Professor Todd, however, never lost his enthusiasm for Virgil.

I was very much at odds with him as a man. He was an imperialist and in every way a defender of things past. This automatically, for us young Andersonian radicals, put him in the camp of the enemy, but that was not my main quarrel with him. At that time there were university attendants who waited on the teachers, cleaning the board between lectures, holding the door against latecomers, showing slides for such courses as had need of them. These attendants had a semi-paternal relation to such students as liked to talk to them. I remember one of them advising me to leave Australia for California, as a place that valued talent. Todd bullied his attendant, in whom I saw the image of my father. That was enough to arouse my detestation.

My detestation did not stop me, however, from being overwhelmed by Todd's reading of our set text, Virgil's *Aeneid*, Books II and IV. His reading inspired my examination translations, which in turn ensured me a pass of a relatively high standard, to my enormous relief. I drew on Todd's antiquities course, too, on subsequent visits to Italy; it made Rome live. All this is a lesson that 'political correctness', or even common humanity, are not closely correlated with the ability to teach.

I find it hard to discriminate between the next two subjects on my list—economics and history; both of them played an important role in my subsequent intellectual life. I shall begin with economics. If I took only one course in economics this, once more, was for geographical rather than intellectual reasons. After first year, economics was taught only in the evening; it was presumed that it would only be of interest to those who were in business employment. With a staff of three, this limitation was also a way of economising on lecturing resources. But for someone who lived in Manly and was concentrating on other subjects, an evening course would be an intolerable burden.

The three members of the economic staff at this time were each to play a central role in Australian life. R. C. Mills, E. R. Walker and R. B. Madgwick are names that no historian of Australian universities, of the Army Education Service, of Australian diplomacy, of the Australian Broadcasting Commission could possibly ignore. I cannot say, however, that Madgwick's lectures particularly excited me. Except for his forays into economic history, his main intellectual interest, they did not go much further than the textbook he and Walker had jointly written. Nor did the essays we were set to write on such topics of the day as the gold standard and imperial preference excite me greatly—although I felt mildly proud of the fact that I predicted that England would have to go off the gold standard when this was not the received wisdom, and an essay on 'the peopling of Australia' raised considerations that I still regard as being crucial. But it was my reading of Marshall, Pigou, Benham, Jevons that particularly interested me. I did almost no work for the examination, largely relying on what I had picked up from my inveterate reading of newspapers, but performed moderately well. The course left me with a reasonable, but not mathematically refined, knowledge of the basic principles of classical economics, the foundations of today's economic rationalism; the Keynesian era had not yet come into being. It was, however, a very cautious economics; every general proposition was preceded by 'other things being equal'. I wish that this was still always the case.

Two features of the economics course were particularly notable. First, it was the only course in which there was a limited amount of class discussion. That was principally because the class contained a few ardent exponents of the teachings of Major Douglas, the prophet of social credit. They, among other things, supported a measure of inflation, whereas the monetary policy in 1931 was one of sharp deflation. With the 1923 German inflation still in our minds—in the case of stamp-collectors like myself, the

memory of German stamps bearing a value of millions of marks—
we were most of us unconvinced by the Douglas disciples.

All the same, we could not square what we were reading in
our textbooks with what was going on in the world around us. We
had been taught about trade cycles, but as we watched the world
beginning to tumble to pieces it was hard to believe that market
forces, the economist's version of divine grace, would eventually
solve our problems. The resemblances between 1931 and 1991 have
been striking. But Madgwick himself was a very decent man, free
from any kind of fanaticism. We were not bulldozed into self-styled
'economic rationalism'. Rather, we sought a rational economics
that recognised its own limits.

There is a strong element of luck in the time at which one goes
to a university. Accidents of death, resignation or retirement can profoundly affect what one finds there. So I just missed the Renaissance
lectures of 'Jimmy' Bruce, who resigned when Stephen Roberts was
appointed over his head. Roberts had published research to show;
Bruce had concentrated on teaching. At the same time the two-year
course in my beloved European History was suspended. So it was
back to those dreary tribes who cavorted across the British Isles,
back to endless struggles for power. There were some consolations.
It was nice to get the truth about Magna Carta; Roman Britain
introduced me to that philosopher-archaeologist, Collingwood,
whose highly unreliable autobiography was later to fascinate me.
But first-year history was the course in which I came nearest to
failing, out of sheer boredom.

Partly, I must confess, there was also a degree of prejudice on
my part. The lecturer was the son of a famous history professor,
G. A. Wood, who had earlier aroused both the enthusiasm of his
students and some degree of public hostility for his liberal views,
especially at the time of the Boer War. At Oxford he had been
a Balliol man, and so was his son. F. L. Wood was my first acquaintance with the phenomenon of the Balliolised Australian.
Unregenerate Australian as I then was, I found both his accent and
his manner unbearable.

Roberts' second-year course on colonial history was a different
matter, in so far as it was totally unfamiliar. Not everyone is as well
acquainted as we became with French budgetary policy in Tunisia,

knows where Antananarivo is or has discovered that Timbuktu is not just a euphemistic substitute for hell—as in 'go to Timbuktu'. Not everybody can recount the adventures of Abd-el-Krim or has had to confront the Indonesian sufferings described by Multatuli. The conflicts between Spaniards and Aztecs in Mexico, the fluctuation in French policy between 'assimilation' and 'association' in North Africa—these had lessons for Australian relations to Aborigines.

As a teacher, however, Roberts behaved in a way that was quite intolerable. Attendance at lectures was compulsory and in Roberts' case we had fixed seats so that our attendance could easily be checked. Yet week after week he read his lectures from the galley-sheets of his two-volume history of French colonial policy, which most of us had in our possession. He was in many ways a remarkable man, but his indifferent attitude to students was only too familiar. We used to call him the *Sydney Morning Herald* Professor of History, so visible was he in his contributions to that paper and so invisible to his students. The University Senate, a largely lay body, astonished everyone when they elected him later as Vice-Chancellor. Yet Roberts was far from being a failure in that role.

If a committee had been set up to construct the most boring English course possible, they could not have improved upon our first-year course. After the lively arguments of our school days, we were confronted by a term's meticulous biography of Chaucer, another term on Shakespeare's life, and *Victorian Narrative Verse* as a set text. It is no wonder that at the end of my first year I was resolved to abandon English honours. Becoming interested just as I was losing interest, Doris persuaded me to persevere, and she herself joined the class in its second year. She was already a member of the honours course in philosophy. So she unwittingly added to the domestic chores of later life a great deal of criticising, editing, helping to index my publications, although not writing herself on the ground that 'one writer in the house is more than enough'. But at least this work, along with attendance at seminars and conferences, has kept her intellectual interests very much alive.

Yet in retrospect I learnt some important things in that first-year English course. I am grateful for the Anglo-Saxon that I learnt as an honours student and the Middle English that followed it.

What mattered was not the detail, but rather that it left me with the sense of language as something with a peculiar manner of growth, more like a billabong than a regulated stream, so that 'ordinary usage' is always the usage of a particular time and place. I conform to that usage, for the most part, so that my readers can understand what I am saying with the minimum of difficulty. But I do not have the feeling that used to prevail among classically educated Oxford philosophers, that ordinary language was governed by philosophically significant rules. If English reviewers have commented that I do not write as if I had a nanny looking over my shoulder, my historical study of the English language is the reason why. If I grumble about language when it loses, in this case in a sinister fashion, such essential distinctions as that between 'uninterested' and 'disinterested', I could see such relics as 'whom' disappear with no sense of loss. I most strongly complain when American editors— this has never happened to me in England—try to flatten out my style into a graceless uniformity, often by converting Fowler's tentative suggestions into rigid rules.

In later years the English lectures became more interesting as we moved into the Shakespearian comedies and tragedies, away from Victorian narrative verse into a wider study of first the nineteenth and then the seventeenth century. In honours work, *Beowulf* made Anglo-Saxon grammar worthwhile and I was wholly fascinated by the Elizabethan and Jacobean plays we studied. But the lectures were never as exciting as the essays we were called upon to write and the research we were called upon to undertake. There were special occasions, as when the doyen of Shakespearian studies in Australia, Sir Mungo MacCallum, then nearing the age of eighty, lectured to us on *King Lear*, emphasising the importance of the fact that Lear was an old man. But these occasions were rare. Sometimes MacCallum's old lectures were simply read aloud to us by Professor Le Gay Brereton. I thought of MacCallum as being a man of vast antiquity as he tottered, a small, bearded figure, up to the lectern in the steep, smelly chemistry lecture theatre. Yet I am now somewhat older. In a similar spirit, 'Sonny' Holme persuaded us of the importance of the fact that Othello was black, although Holme was not physically black himself.

'Johnny' Waldock could be relied upon to say something interesting, even if the restlessness of the male students sometimes made it hard to know what it was. For we were anything but a passive class; we rejoiced in stamping our feet if any opportunity for comment presented itself. That stamping came to a standstill about 1936. Once students who worked very hard could see the prospect of a job when they graduated, undergraduates became much quieter and duller. We had a degree of recklessness, deriving from the uncertainty of our future. I liked Waldock and we argued quite a lot, in discussions in his room. (We always spoke of 'rooms', not of 'studies' or of 'offices', the last of which we should have found abhorrent. Only quite recently have Australian universities been expected to behave in ways that are in detail, as distinct from in respect to general finances, 'business-like'.)

One year Waldock lectured on Hardy. That was a revolutionary step—to lecture on a writer who had written his major novels forty years earlier, or even less. As a student I fulminated against the fact that our lectures bore not at all on our contemporaries. I now think I was wrong about this. Many years later, in the United States, I encountered an English Department that followed the reverse pattern. It wholly concentrated attention on twentieth-century writers, mainly American, and enveloped them in such webs of symbolic meanings that the students were left with the impression that it was impossible to read intelligently without the help of critics. In contrast we struggled with our near contemporaries—T. S. Eliot, D. H. Lawrence, James Joyce—without the help of critics and were then in a better position to learn from the critics when they later emerged.

I should never have got around to reading the seventeenth-century dramatists—Ford, Webster, Jonson, Massinger, let alone their minor contemporaries and their sixteenth-century predecessors—unless I had done so at university. Yet through having read them, one can more readily understand and evaluate the American baroque writers, from Melville to Faulkner. One of the principal things a university can do is to get rid of provinciality, whether in time or space. Some modern universities, in contrast, strengthen such provinciality, conveying such illusions as that the more modern is automatically the better, that the quest for novelty is essentially modern, that sex, violence and obscurity are peculiarities of the contemporary world. Not to go back beyond the modern is to have no understanding of the modern, against what it is reacting, to what it is returning.

Philosophy lectures were for me, as for so many others, the heart of the matter. Most of these, throughout our course, were delivered by John Anderson. But we did not experience the purely Andersonian course with which later students were to be confronted as Anderson built up his staff with former students—including me. In my first year there was an erratic young Melbourne-educated lecturer called Norman Porter, who was not to last long, as he often did not turn up at all to lecture. When he did turn up, his lectures would commonly last for only twenty minutes, and were then often fragmentary accounts of lecture notes he had borrowed from Anderson. On one exasperating occasion, after having criticised a number of traditional ethical theories, he announced that he would present us with positive views the following week. But we were left next week to guess what they were, Porter being *in absentia.* We were amused rather than angered by his eccentricities in a world where many of the lecturers were distinctly grey. In any case, Anderson was giving us more than enough to think about, whether in his logic course, his lectures on early Platonic dialogues or in the honours course on Berkeley.

Anderson had two subsequent assistants, each for a year. His department, during my undergraduate years, never had more than two teachers, although our class was large enough to fill the rather striking philosophy lecture room, with its murals depicting the great philosophers of the past.

The lecturer addressed his class from a lecterned desk, set between these murals, except when he chose to walk up, down, and around, as Anderson did. The murals made us conscious of the fact that what we were hearing was a contribution to a Great Discussion, in which the living could participate as the dead had participated. To go into this room now is to experience a sense of sacrilege. On an administrative whim, the seats have been turned around so that the student confronts a wall entirely covered by blackboards and plastic sheets for the showing of slides. The entire arrangement suggests that the past is something one should turn one's back on, as no longer relevant. To forget the past is to be doomed to repeat it—this is a maxim worth remembering.

Both of Anderson's assistants were able men, with considerable experience outside Australia. One of them, W. G. K. Duncan, was to end his days as Professor of History and Political Science in the University of Adelaide. He lectured to us on Plato's *Republic*, considered basically as a contribution to political theory. The other was to become, as Sir Alan Watt, one of Australia's most distinguished diplomats. He had gone to Oriel College, Oxford, as a Rhodes scholar and what he taught us as ethics was largely derived from the then very influential Oxford moral philosopher W. D. Ross. These were not negligible minds but they had a minimal influence on us. Anderson swept us away.

Yet by formal standards Anderson was the worst possible lecturer, his influence a triumph of content over style. His accent was thickly Lanarkshire—his father had been a Lanark headmaster —or at best Glaswegian, scarcely intelligible to us in a Sydney where foreign accents were still rare. He stuttered out his lectures, spoken not read, at dictation speed, as he sweated away in his heavy three-piece tweed suits. He used a lot of cant phrases such as 'the position is, then'. My Melbourne friends might ask me, when they heard Anderson talk at a conference, 'How can you, with your interest in prose style, bear to listen to a man who talks like that?' But his style didn't seem to matter.

Anderson kept the exposition of his more revolutionary views for student societies and public lectures. When he attacked 'ultimate realities' in his lectures, Arthur Bishop would whisper 'Why doesn't he say "GOD"?' But Anderson was attacking any theory of ultimate realities—Russell's sense-data, Bradley's Absolute—quite as much as the God of philosophers. He never liked to be called an 'atheist' because that made his disbelief in the existence of God a central fact; it was, to him, a secondary consequence of his philosophical views.

At a time when the principal philosophical battle was between Idealists, for whom Spirit was ultimate, and those Realists for whom sense-data were ultimate, it was exciting to be told that both sides were wrong, since there were no ultimates. Historians of Australian intellectual life sometimes say that in the 1930s and 1940s Australia displayed a cultural cringe, but in fact no Andersonian suffered from cultural cringe. That we differed from the views then prevailing both in England and America in no way disturbed us. We had indeed a sense of superiority.

This is not the occasion to give a general account of Anderson's teachings; I have done that in the introduction to Anderson's *Studies in Empirical Philosophy*, and more briefly in other places. Unfortunately he did not publish a continuous book, could indeed scarcely have done so in the teaching conditions of that time. His articles were usually written at white heat over a sleepless weekend. They are extremely compact, difficult to make out except for those who have his lectures as a background. For all that I have been so profoundly influenced by Anderson and have never concealed that fact, I very rarely find a passage I can quote without a great deal of explication. It was his lectures, not his writings, that so influenced us. What was peculiar about them, apart from their doctrines?

Except in logic and to a lesser degree in ethics, Anderson did not develop his views systematically but rather through a critique of the classical philosophers. There were no courses with such titles as 'metaphysics' or 'epistemology'. He was not a scholar; generally speaking he took his interpretation of a philosopher from some favourite secondary source, especially from such Scottish scholars as Kemp Smith for Descartes, Burnet for Greek philosophy, although as time went on the direction of his views somewhat changed, under the influence of such Cambridge scholars as Cornford. If I have read much more widely in philosophers and scholars than he did, his method of expounding his own views by way of the criticism of other philosophers is one I have largely followed, perhaps too largely.

In a British context Anderson's approach was not altogether surprising. What would have surprised most English philosophers of the 1930s is the range of the writers Anderson referred to in lectures or recommended for our reading. An English reviewer of the Anderson articles collected as *Art and Reality* remarked that we received a much more European education than any we could have encountered in England in the same period. I do not think that many, if any, first-year university students in the England of that time would have been reading, on their professor's recommendation, such philosophers of science as Poincaré and Duhem, as I did with delight in my first year in Sydney; I feel pretty confident that such names as Marx, Freud, Feuerbach, Sorel, Vico, even Nietzsche, would not have found a place, as they did in Anderson's lectures.

There is a legend about Anderson's relationship with Nietzsche that is perhaps worth denying, although it is now probably unexpungeable, having been expounded by Manning Clark in his *Short History of Australia.* Clark invents a Nietzschean group in Sydney, with its leading figures Anderson and the Bacchanalian painter Norman Lindsay. I never recall Anderson so much as mentioning Lindsay—nor does Lindsay mention Anderson. Anderson's artistic theories would have ruled Lindsay out as a painter of any consequence. Anderson's twentieth-century heroes were Joyce and Cézanne, whereas Lindsay was a violent critic of 'modernism' in any of its forms. As far as Nietzsche is concerned, we encountered him in lectures as someone who had drawn a contrast between 'slave morality' and 'master morality', which Anderson went on to condemn. If I sometimes talked about Nietzsche it was to refer to his *The Birth of Tragedy* and the distinction between the Apollonian and Dionysian that Manning Clark himself draws upon. At the time when this group was supposed to exist Anderson was a Marxist, and to reconcile Marx with Nietzsche would certainly have been a remarkable example of an Hegelian 'higher synthesis'. As for Lindsay's Nietzschean leanings, these he acquired in Melbourne, well before he left for Sydney, as his autobiographical *My Mask* makes plain.

More shocking to English eyes is the fact that Greek philosophy played a very large part in Anderson's teaching, although very few of us had even a smattering of Greek. I do not see any reason for apologising for this. Plato is, to my mind, much the greatest of philosophers—although I agree with scarcely anything he said. For it was he who discovered almost all the major philosophical problems, even if it was left to Aristotle to formulate them in a more systematic form, as fields of specialisation. Not to lecture on him to philosophy students unless they know Greek is to cut them off from the roots of what they are studying. Aristotle, however, played a very small part in our education. In this respect, as in many others, we stood closer to Cambridge than to Oxford. As for the pre-Socratic philosophers, what we liked about them was their imaginative daring, a daring that has led them to appeal to modern thinkers so different as Heidegger, Popper and Anderson.

Some years ago at Bad Homburg, I heard the physicist Pirognine give an account of modern physics as he saw it. His account carried me back to Heraclitus as Anderson had described him, basing his interpretation on the fragments that are all that remain of Heraclitus as translated in Burnet's *Early Greek Philosophy*. (Later scholars have translated and interpreted Heraclitus very differently, in the process making him less interesting.) But if it came as something of a surprise to hear Pirognine unwittingly describe the physical world in such Andersonian–Heraclitean terms, it did not wholly astonish me. Anderson had gained honours in mathematics and natural philosophy, i.e. physics, at Glasgow before he turned to philosophy— this was during the 1914–18 war—and he was at least in a position to relate Heraclitus to such physicists as Faraday, thus taking fields of force as central rather than billiard-ball atoms. (One of the more extraordinary legends that circulated about Anderson in Sydney is that he was one of the only three men who understood Einstein!)

My general view of the world derives from those lectures on Heraclitus; when I came to talk about the environment or about political and social life, it was in these terms that I thought about them. I once jocularly remarked that living in Manly prepared me for accepting a Heraclitean world-view. For Heraclitus 'we step and do not step in the same river, for fresh waters are always flowing in'. Equally, I lived and did not live in the same Manly, for fresh tourists were always flowing in, sat and did not sit on the same beach, since fresh waves were always bringing in fresh sand, lived and did not live in the same household, for fresh tenants were always leaving or arriving, went and did not go to the same school, for fresh boys were always arriving—only one boy going through the whole school with me.

I could see, too, that a thing could be in a state of constant change and yet retain its identity over time provided that there was some kind of balance between what it took in and what it gave out. Otherwise it would die of starvation or suffocation, or at least change in character. If no visitors had arrived, Manly would have died as a seaside resort; if no visitors had left, it would have suffocated. If no new tenants had arrived, our flats could not have survived.

My reading of Heraclitus is, I freely admit, highly selective. I would not dare to write about him in a scholarly fashion. My concern is with the ways in which Heraclitus–Anderson influenced my thinking. 'The hidden harmony is better than the open'—that was for me a crucial passage, taken to mean that the attempt to impose order from above is less fruitful than the kind of order that arises when contrary interests achieve a degree of balance without losing their distinctiveness. There I saw the crucial difference between a pluralistic, democratic society and an authoritarian, or a totalitarian, society. Linked with this is Heraclitus's response to Homer's wish that 'strife would vanish from among men and gods'. 'He did not see that he was praying for the destruction of the universe; for if his prayer were heard, all things would pass away.'

There is no room, on this view, for a Great Designer, whether envisaged as a supreme Person or as an impersonal historical force. Things, in the broadest possible sense as including both persons and places, have each of them a history, but that history is determined at different times, in different places, by a multitude of forces, each of which itself is a field of forces, places where events occur. Reaction, neither pure passivity nor pure activity, is a condition of existence. 'Things', that is, are not to be thought of as solid, stable objects, each theoretically capable of subsisting in isolation, but rather as constantly struggling for survival and participating in the struggles of others. In the vast majority of cases these struggles are unconscious, as the sun is unconscious of its effects on the survival of the earth, or, more broadly, of what goes on within itself. Even human beings are far from being fully conscious of what is happening within them.

We are entangled with what lies around us, even if we think of ourselves as spectators, and in some particular respects actually are. Our gaze as spectators can affect the behaviour of others; their glance back at us can affect our behaviour. What we, and they, see as we look will partly depend on our information, itself the product of earlier active experience, partly on the nature of the emotional pressures that have built up within us over time. These in turn are a result partly of what sort of thing we were when we came into being, partly of our subsequent reactions. The complexity of these reactions is such that, to cite another Heraclitean fragment, we have always to 'expect the unexpected'. The search for incorrigible empirical knowledge, as for total security, is a will o' the wisp.

But human beings are not the passive victims of circumstances, not committed to a total scepticism. We can do things that will generally make us more secure, as we do every time we cross a road, although we know that for all our precautions we might be killed; we can take steps that will generally increase our knowledge, as we do when we look up an encyclopaedia, for all that such encyclopaedias will always contain some mistakes. Inevitably, we believe, we predict, we rely on other things and other people, and much of the time we get along all right, very successfully indeed if one thinks in terms of the large number of occasions on which we have to judge, to decide, to act, every day of our lives. Our survival depends on the general reliability of our beliefs; that we survive gives us confidence in them. Nevertheless, prudent as we may be, cautious in predicting, in believing, in acting, we shall sometimes go wrong. There is no way of ruling out the possibility of doing so, no way of wholly avoiding risks.

It might be suggested that this is the world-view of a neurotic, a hypochondriac. Certainly it does not build up confidence in one's power to make the world do one's bidding or in anyone else's power to do so. But this way of looking at the world as I have encountered it has given me a better clue to what is going on than would the classical view that the world is made up of fixed, stable substances, only externally linked to one another, in principle knowable through and through, their operations in principle wholly predictable. That does not prevent me from predicting, sometimes quite successfully. Neither does it prevent me from writing books in which I claim to have knowledge, although it does prevent me from expecting that anything I write will be error-free or from being outraged when people disagree with me. It does not discourage me, either, from trying to make my books as free from error as I can.

Closely connected with what I have just written is the pluralism I also learnt from Anderson. Human thinking tends to switch between the two extremes of monism and atomism, the first thinking in terms of total systems the members of which exist, can be understood, and are to be valued only in terms of their membership of such systems, the other supposing all systems to be simply a collection of individuals, each of them to be understood, valued, independently of their membership of that system. Pluralism rejects both the concept of a total all-encompassing system and the concept of isolated individuals. It thinks of anything whatsoever as being itself a system with constituents that are systems. That is the spirit in which I have approached scholarly, environmental, political and aesthetic problems. I no longer know how far the views that I take myself to have learnt from Anderson are views to which he would have wholly subscribed. But I have no doubt that his lectures gave birth to them and largely shaped their future.

This memoir, thus seen, is about the ways in which a particular self-conscious physical system, itself containing a multitude of reacting activities, interacted with a variety of other systems, ecological and social, and in the process has come to be modified in a wide variety of ways, while at the same time modifying, if sometimes very slightly, as in breathing out, the systems in which it found itself or into which it deliberately entered.

I earlier remarked on the importance of the individual research we did as undergraduates. I shall be content to mention a few examples. In first-year history we were asked to write a long essay on the topic: 'How far was Milton a typical Puritan?' That obviously demanded not only a close study of Milton's works, his prose as well as his poetry, but also a good deal of reading to determine what counts as a typical Puritan. So I was led into the heart of seventeenth-century religious controversy, the effects of which are readily to be discerned in quite a few of my essays, in my first book, *Ralph Cudworth*, on that seventeenth-century Cambridge Platonist, in *The Perfectibility of Man* and in more recent studies of fanaticism. But it also had deeper effects. I found in myself an unexpected sympathy for these small Puritan groups, struggling to interpret the Bible, standing out against state and ecclesiastic power.

These were far from being Roman Catholic sentiments; their appeal was to an Outsider. Particular utterances like Milton's 'New Presbyter is but old priest writ large' and Cromwell's 'I beseech you, in the bowels of Christ, think it possible that ye may be mistaken', I always have in the back of my mind, even if in Cromwell's case I particularly address his admonition to myself. There was much in what I read about the Puritans that I detested but my sympathy for small groups—the Andersonians were such a group—and my distrust of big battalions has remained with me. I have never been a good disciple. For all that Anderson so deeply influenced me, he once remarked that my views coincided with his to a lesser degree than those of any other of those who stood close to him, although he then added, in surprise, that he nevertheless found it easier to talk to me than to those who agreed with him more. For my part, I did not find this at all surprising. If I myself have no disciples, this is for a variety of reasons, the crucial one being that I have never developed any kind of system. But another reason is that, with Cromwell's words ringing in my mind, I have discouraged any signs of nascent discipleship with an 'on the other hand'.

Two of my second-year history essays were also important for quite different reasons. One was on the annexation of New Guinea, the other on German colonial policy. First, there was very little secondary work on them so we were plunged into the historian's 'real world' of archives, documents and correspondence. Secondly, there were notable contradictions in this material. Someone, perhaps everyone, had to be concealing facts, lying, propagandising. When I later wrote about propaganda, this experience was at the back of my mind, as it was when I wrote about the philosophy of history. I had some experience, as many philosophers have not, of what it is like to be confronted by this kind of evidence and the sort of steps one might take in order to come to conclusions under these circumstances.

The feedback from essay-markers could also be important. This could be minimal but in Anderson's case it was meticulous; in this context he was an excellent teacher. So was 'Sonny' Holme, although I disapproved of him for much the same reasons as I disapproved of Todd. Waldock, in contrast, was useless, with nothing but such final comments as 'very interesting', although it was his doing that we were called upon to write an essay on the film as an art form, at that time quite a revolutionary topic. But it was Holme who permanently influenced me by one of his marginal comments. As a young man in love with words, as indeed I still am, I had a tendency to prefer longer to shorter words, the more recondite to the more common. I had used the phrase 'endeavour to eradicate' and Holme asked a question in the margin: 'Why not "try to wipe out"?' Why not, indeed? Ever since, I have sought to write in the simplest language consonant with accuracy. No other single essay correction had so wide-ranging and permanent an influence upon me, but many others pulled me up with a salutary shock.

Of considerable importance, too, was the work I did in the English honours course on Elizabethan and Jacobean drama. We were called upon to have a close acquaintance with five plays, and to be prepared to answer questions on the meaning of particular passages and the state of the text in three of them. This area was the responsibility of R. G. Howarth, who had already made something of a name for himself for his work on the seventeenth century. The chosen plays had been only very lightly edited, if at all. This was genuine research, forcing us to study Elizabethan handwriting and printing, and to consult a wide variety of writings to find clues to the meaning of particular passages.

I took to this work and produced a number of notes of an original character. Howarth wanted me to put them together as a letter to the *Times Literary Supplement*, which was then the normal mode of publication, but I did not take this first opportunity to publish outside Australia. Why so? Was I, after all, a victim of the 'cultural cringe', unable to believe that anything I could do was worthy of publication in an English journal? Or merely a shy adolescent? It is hard enough to be sure about one's present motives, given one's capacity for self-deception. The past is in this respect another world.

I got a number of things out of this research, over and above the enjoyment of an intellectual hunt. The knowledge of Elizabethan handwriting, not exactly common among philosophers, turned out to be very useful when I came to work on Cudworth's manuscripts. More important, however, is that my research forced upon me the practice of close reading. The fact that I could read quickly let me bring to bear on the plays a sweeping acquaintance with just about all the published dramatic literature of that period. Then, however, I had to bring that knowledge to bear on texts that had to be read with intensive care. That combination of two very different types of reading habits made it possible for me to write my best-known work, *A Hundred Years of Philosophy*. In the United States it was suggested that this work must be the product of a group, not of an individual. But if two individuals were concerned, they were my rapid-reading and my slow-reading selves.

What I have just been saying has a certain consequence: if we are judging whether a person is a good university teacher, there is much more to be considered than the quality of that person's lectures, as judged against some conventional scale. The choice of essay topics, the construction of reading lists, the manner of commenting on written work, the power to encourage individual research—all of these are of the first importance. Not many people are likely to find it useful, in later life, to be able to read Elizabethan handwriting. But the capacity to read closely, to sniff out propaganda, to understand the workings of small, fanatical groups, to write clear prose—these are by no means of use only to specialist scholars. And these I learnt, and others learnt, not from lectures but in the process of reading, writing and having what we wrote scrupulously corrected by the teachers themselves, not by some junior tutor.

One other thing was important to me personally. My knowledge of literature, particularly, gave me an area in which I had acquired the values of scholarship. There were things I knew about and could do that Anderson did not know, could not do. And this gave me a degree of independence to set against his overwhelming influence.

6

Education Through Student Organisations and Societies

UNDERGRADUATES HAD TO JOIN two organisations, with compulsory subscriptions: the University Union and the Students' Representative Council. The Union was not a purely undergraduate body. In the pleasantly rambling brick building that still serves as its headquarters, there were two restaurants—one a cafeteria, the other a more formal restaurant—a games room, and a hall. The restaurant had a high table, where the staff regularly met for lunch.

In my first year I frequented the Union a good deal, eating the appalling gravy-covered 'steak pies' with their inevitable accompaniment of hard peas and imperfectly mashed potatoes. We assured one another that the pies were where the cadavers from the medical school ended up. There, too, I began to devote far too much of my time to playing chess. In later life I occasionally beat quite good players, but only as a result of making highly eccentric moves. Most of the time I would lose, as a result of pressing ahead with my own plan without paying sufficient attention to protecting myself. Chess is a great revealer of character. I gave it up many years ago.

Because the Union was a purely male institution, my burgeoning romance meant that after my first year I made much less use of it. In any case, the cut in our scholarships made even cafeteria steak pies too expensive. It was back to the sandwiches of my school days. As in Oxford, the Union held weekly debates, and had done so since 1874. Given my compulsive vocality—thus to describe my habit of talking far too much—and my love of argument, it might have been supposed that I should have found myself at home there.

But debating, I soon decided, was for incipient lawyers, politicians and public-relations officers; I had no wish to become experienced in 'making the worse appear the better reason', as Aristophanes put it. (The most brilliant exponent of this art was 'H. M. Storey, impeccable Tory' in the words of the student song-book.) The Union, after my first year, mattered to me mainly as the publisher of the *Union Recorder*, which printed short summaries of some of the addresses given to student societies.

Equally, the Students' Representative Council was to me important only as the publisher of the student newspaper, *Honi Soit*. I never felt any urge to take an active part in student politics, then largely dominated by the conservative students who constituted the vast majority of undergraduates—particularly outside the Faculty of Arts, but even within it. In 1932, however, the editorship of *Honi Soit* temporarily fell into the hands of the radical W. A. W. ('Bill') Wood, a leading figure in the Student Christian Movement. He appointed a large and miscellaneous group of sub-editors ranging from members of the Sydney University Regiment, through pacifists like himself, to freethinkers, of whom I was one. I cannot remember any particular contribution of mine except a banal article on Hindenburg and Hitler, written just before the April 1932 referendum in Germany. I had a growing interest in what was happening in that country, events which had a permanent effect on my thinking and on my political attitudes.

In the *Honi Soit* office our principal attention was directed towards a more local enemy. The conservative Students' Representative Council, annoyed and alarmed by the controversial material now appearing in its paper, decreed that all copy had to be approved by its Director of Publications. There was no option but to resign, as I promptly did. (Interestingly enough, although the law students had particularly objected to the radical material contained in *Honi Soit*, it was a judge-to-be, Frank Hutley, who most strongly, if unsuccessfully, campaigned against the Council's actions.) Thus ended my career as a journalist, not unwillingly, since I found the constant politicking in the editorial office tiresome in the extreme. This was also my last experience of political activity, narrowly defined, although by no means my last public utterance on political issues.

The student societies, unlike the official, compulsory organisations, were set up spontaneously by undergraduates, often with the help of their teachers, to further particular interests. They were my real concern. They went beyond anything our courses had to offer. They cut across distinctions between years and faculties; they opened up relationships between the university and the world outside; and they provided an opportunity to engage in intellectual activities that formed no part of the university curriculum.

In a way, it was the sporting clubs that most fully exhibited these characteristics. Seldom have I felt such a sense of divided loyalties as when I first saw Manly play University in the Rugby Union competition. But occasional spectatorship, greatly diminishing over time, was to be my sole contribution to the efforts of such teams.

That was true, too, of the musical and the drama societies. Unlike Doris, I did not join the musical society, since I could neither sing nor play a musical instrument. But I still remember with gratitude their performance of a Purcell opera, my first acquaintance with music from that period, except for an occasional hymn. As for joining SUDS—the Sydney University Dramatic Society—it never occurred to me, in spite of my passionate interest in theatre and film. Fancy myself as an actor I did not, and a brief episode as a director did not encourage me to believe that my talents lay in that direction. The performance of plays at a relatively high standard was also very time-consuming—even in an atmosphere where 'in second term nobody works'. As matters then stood, SUDS was an important addition to theatrical life in Sydney, performing classical plays not to be seen elsewhere.

That had its problems in the puritanical Sydney of the 1930s. One year SUDS decided to put on a Restoration comedy—was it Congreve's *Love for Love*? There was a considerable uproar, the ex-Bohemian Professor Le Gay Brereton announcing that the play was 'unfit for public performance'. We thought he had been put up to this by 'Sonny' Holme, but quite likely not. Puritanism ran very deep. That the play was none the less performed was a significant step towards greater liberty of expression, as well as an expansion of our literary horizons.

Freedom of expression was one of the great issues of the 1930s. Political orthodoxy was then easy to define; it could be summed up in our schoolday pledge: 'I honour my God, I serve my king, I salute my flag'. But this was often taken to have a corollary: 'I honour property, I serve my employers, I salute my boss'. In retrospect, I do not know where I got my political heresies from. I remember, at the age of twelve, having to endure the ceremonies of Empire Day —appropriately held on what had been Queen Victoria's birthday —and listening to an appalling speech by the local member, A. A. E. E. V. Reid, commonly known as 'Alphabetical Reid'. 'He will soon be objecting', I remarked to a sympathetic teacher, 'to the red in the Union Jack'.

The prime forms of political heresy were taken by conservatives to be communism—very broadly defined—and anti-war movements. The principal university exponents of political orthodoxy included Professors Holme and Todd, but among the students it was mainly represented by engineering undergraduates, with some help from medical students. Law students, too, were for the most part politically orthodox but the Law School, uniquely, was down town. So that it was not they who broke up student meetings, trying to prevent 'radical' speakers from getting a hearing.

On one memorable occasion, when several student societies were involved in an anti-war meeting, the engineering students got hold of the electrical equipment, and 'God Save the King' came booming over the microphone. The power of that tune at the time was extraordinary. It was invariably played at 'picture-theatres' before the performance began, and not to stand up for it was the most typical radical gesture. The chairman, veterinary scientist Ian Clunies Ross, refused to give way to the protesters by standing, as he would normally have done. A minor gesture, perhaps, but in its time notable.

One of the many important points of difference between university radicals of that time and university radicals in the last few decades lies in the absoluteness of our belief in freedom of expression. We might argue fiercely with right-wing speakers, but we never sought to silence them. Equally, we were never on the side of censorship, on any grounds whatsoever. We could watch attacks on freedom of expression not only in our own society but, much more ferociously, in Nazi Germany and—or so I early decided—in the

Soviet Union. Freedom of expression was the more precious for its rarity as 'the lights went out all over Europe'.

In Australia, radical political writings were regularly seized by the Customs, an organisation in which Irish Catholics played a conspicuous part. Books and paintings of a sexual kind were as severely treated. Anderson used to argue that all censorship was political, that sex was feared as disturbing established relationships of domination. Australia was by no means unique in its prudishness. (As if to lend support to Anderson's thesis, an English magistrate banned the circulation of the cheap Everyman edition of Boccaccio's *Decameron* while allowing the circulation of an expensive illustrated edition.) Few countries, however, could match the inanity of a censorship that banned Aldous Huxley's *Brave New World*. Of course, all English-speaking countries banned *Ulysses*. But a great deal of smuggling went on and in fact many of the major banned books circulated in the university.

I have no personal recollection of *Ulysses* being circulated, as the story runs, in brown-paper covers inscribed 'Book of Common Prayer', but that tale is both plausible and appropriate, considering the reverence in which Joyce was then held. Nevertheless, the unholy alliance of Evangelical Anglicanism and Irish Catholicism that then held sway did seriously limit the freedom to read that runs parallel to freedom of expression. Like all revolutions, the sexual revolution of the 1970s has had serious costs and has fallen in part into the hands of gross profiteers. A return to the 1930s, however, is something I should never advocate but have often, over the last decade, had reason to fear. It is against this background that one has to consider the role of certain student societies in the Sydney University of my time and the extent of the hostility they engendered.

There was a general feeling against the setting up of societies that were branches of the established political parties. In 1932 an attempt was made to revive the University Labor Club, and to shift it in a direction more sympathetic to communism in the manner of the University of Melbourne Labor Club. But it never acquired the prominence of that club. The university's political societies, unlike its sporting and its religious societies, did not provide an obvious link with societies outside the university. Not that this would have worried the political parties too much. University branches have very often been thorns in the side of the parties they were supposedly attached to.

To contrast 'inside' with 'outside' the university is in many ways misleading. We were not isolated from the Great Depression rampaging around us. Teachers-in-training were even less isolated than other undergraduates. Every day we made our way home by public transport or on foot. At home we daily shared the anxieties of our times. On our way there we might well see the queues at the soup-kitchens and we went past the parks where the unemployed slept under newspapers at night. At its height the unemployment reached over 30 per cent, and that fact was obvious enough in the city around us. In the suburbs surrounding the university it went as high as 43 per cent. I daily passed empty shops, silent timber-yards. All this marked us permanently.

How I detest the fashion for torn trousers! For I remember these as something worn out of necessity by men—women did not then wear trousers—who would desperately try to keep themselves as tidy as they could until the effort became too great. I react to middle-class wearers of torn pants as the victims of concentration camps might if it became fashionable to stamp indelible numbers on the wrist. Always a product of the 1930s, I never fell into the 1980s trap of supposing that property had nowhere to go but up, that employment was assured, and that speculation could never meet its nemesis. Like so many of my generation, I still cannot bear to take a taxi except when I am heavily laden with luggage, and as a consumer I rate very low.

In 1918 a Public Questions Society had been established in which leading figures in the university and prominent figures in contemporary Australia would speak on questions of the day. For many, this was the proper style of a university society. Not that this protected it against the rowdies if the choice of speakers was unusually adventurous. Several Andersonians acted on the committee of this organisation. But it was in two of the more committed societies that I was particularly educated and came to be very active.

As someone who was still, although with more and more hesitation, a practising Roman Catholic, I might have been expected to seek out the Newman Society. That did not happen. I had no Catholic friends who might have persuaded me to join it. At that time the church strongly dissuaded the faithful from entering the Faculty of Arts, and especially from attending classes in what they rightly took to be the most dangerous subjects—history and philosophy. When Roman Catholic historians now complain about the fact that so few of the older professors were their co-religionists, they ignore that fact. Only once do I remember attending a meeting of the Newman Society, relatively late in my career, after I had thrown off the last shreds of my Catholicism. I raised philosophical questions about how an eternal unchanging being could, or would want to, create the universe at a particular time, and had the satisfaction of having my rather obvious question referred to an absent theologian, since no one present was prepared to attempt an answer to it.

The most interesting, and the most powerful, of the religious societies was the Student Christian Movement, under the influence of two able figures, Roy Lee—later to make his name both in the BBC and as vicar of the Church of St Mary the Virgin in High Street Oxford—and E. H. Burgmann, whom I got to know better when he became Bishop of Canberra and Goulburn. Both men were associated with Morpeth College, near Maitland in the New South Wales coalfields, then a world of its own with the accent and the attitudes of British coal-miners. They stood far apart from the prevailing attitudes of the local Anglican diocese, which the Evangelical Union more adequately represented. Burgmann was very much what we then knew as a 'fellow-traveller', a warm supporter of the Soviet Union without being technically a communist.

The Student Christian Movement provided a resting place for those who wanted to remain Christian without accepting the narrowness and the conservatism of the Evangelical Union. For my part, I always found it hard to understand why Burgmann continued to call himself a Christian. But no doubt his conversations with me represented a degree of accommodation to my own views.

'Perce' Partridge later suggested that Burgmann never lost hope that he might convert us. Whatever the truth of this, there can be no doubt that the Student Christian Movement in the early 1930s stood for a Christian, pacifist, radical socialism that was attractive to many students in those dreadful years.

The two societies with which I came to be intimately involved were, however, the two societies where Anderson's influence was paramount: the Freethought Society and the Literary Society. How the Literary Society had come to be presided over by John Anderson, I do not know. The University Calendar for 1930 describes it in terms that suggest a very genteel organisation indeed:

> The Literary Society exists for furthering an interest in literature within the university, but outside of lectures and examinations. Various critical meetings, lectures and walking tours are held during the year. It is hoped by means of the critical meetings to help undergraduates with literary aspirations to attain a fair standard of writing.

Although quite a few writers 'with literary aspirations' were to speak at the Literary Society, or at least attend its meetings— to mention two names, Alec Hope and James McAuley—under Anderson's regime there were certainly no sessions of 'creative writing'. The original intent was satisfied only in so far as the society concentrated on contemporary or foreign writers who formed no part of the English course. There was even a small library—kept in Anderson's unsuitably Gothic, perpetually pipe-smoked, room—of writers such as André Gide or Lermontov, who were not otherwise easy to come by. (There was no Russian Department and in the terror-driven French Department, French culture stopped dead at some point in the nineteenth century.) The Literary Society also emphasised criticism, even if in a form its founders would not have appreciated, any more than did the English Department of my own time.

But what was the philosopher Anderson doing as president of this society? It was less surprising that I should have eventually become its secretary, as I was, after all, an honours student in English. One thing Anderson and I had in common, however, was a wide range of interests, perhaps too wide for our own good. My 'power of general comment', he once said, 'was one thing he particularly liked' in me. (Others, I feel sure, have more privately described this as 'opening my big mouth on subjects I know nothing about'.) His interest in the arts, in particular, was quite broad.

He had the advantage over me of possessing a good light baritone voice. Doris and myself were sometimes Sunday guests at his home in Turramurra. There he introduced us to Hebridean melodies, to the songs of Moussorgsky—not only his familiar 'Song of the Flea'—and to songs by Mozart, his favourite composer. His more ribald followers remember him better for his performance of a *Ulysses* song. But that was for beer-parties, in which I did not participate, not for Sunday teas. I did not, however, always share his tastes. He tried to convert me to Duke Ellington's jazz, arguing that one could not consistently admire Bach without admiring Ellington. But I had problems with jazz, arising out of my unusually acute sensory perception. As a boy I could tell what visitors had been in our house by the odours they left behind them, could easily read, from the shore, the names of ships as they sailed across the harbour and could hear conversations from a considerable distance away. Certain pitches I found physically painful, and that included the sounds made by the higher ranges of the saxophone and muted trumpets. Even in later life the higher pitches of the human voice were hard to take. It is only now, with less acute hearing, that I can listen with pleasure to jazz.

Or is this a rationalisation? Arriving at an appreciation of classical music with such difficulty, was I determined to separate myself from the more popular forms of music? All the same, I enjoyed Cole Porter. My alienation from popular music came only with the microphone singers. I cannot really understand how anyone could like a Frank Sinatra or an Elvis Presley, although I can understand the hypnotic appeal of some rock music. Anderson's fondness for tap-dancing did not provoke any enthusiasm on my part.

Anderson's literary tastes and my own were only in partial accord. It was he who introduced me to the great Russian novelists, pre-eminently to Dostoevsky, as to Ibsen, to Melville, to Peacock and, of course, to Joyce. But he also had a bewildering affection for such late nineteenth-century novelists as Marmaduke Pickthall and, of all people, Monsignor Benson, and lacked interest in writers who were to me of great consequence—the poets and the French and American novelists who were my near-contemporaries.

These differences were important, I think, in preventing me from becoming one of those disciples who follow their master on every point, with unquestioning devotion. But even in the field of literature and the arts, Anderson had a profound influence on me, in a manner that greatly complicated my relationships with the English Department.

In those days no one, so far as I know, used the phrase 'literary theory'. It was not just the terminology that was missing. No general utterances of a theoretical kind emerged from the lips of the English Department, although inevitably they worked on certain assumptions. A key assumption was that the biography of an author was central to the understanding of, and judgement on, anything that the author wrote.

Anderson, in contrast, had been greatly influenced by the formalism of such theorists as Roger Fry and Clive Bell, perhaps as percolated through the pages of Orage's *New Age*, a periodical that he read with enthusiasm. In *Art and Reality* he nowhere mentions Bell or Fry, but it is unlikely that he was ignorant of their work, particularly since his favourite painter was Cézanne. The explicit references he makes are rather to the Aquinas-style definition of beauty presented in Joyce's *Portrait of the Artist as a Young Man*.

In some ways, what happened in Sydney is what was to happen in a great many universities in the 1980s. As Anderson wrote in an essay on 'Literature and Life':

> The fact that the artist was himself a critic (of illusions) and the critic was himself an artist (in criticism) would permit of a close co-operation between the two; in fact the establishment of schools of strict criticism would make for improvement in literature, just as literature made for improvement in ways of living.

This paper was not delivered until 1939, but the principal ideas it contains were already familiar to me as an undergraduate, as was the general formalism of his approach. So this is the kind of view the English Department had to encounter in my essays and examinations, along with Anderson's critique of 'expressionism', understood as the view that works of art are primarily to be considered as revelations of the artist's personality. Howarth was very anxious that I should do well; he saw in me a fellow scholar. So it was he who called me into his study to complain that in my examinations I 'had insulted the members of the English Department, individually and severally'.

I still cherish the departmental comment on my final thesis on 'the relationship between twentieth and seventeenth-century poetry' —namely that 'this is altogether too intellectual and too empirical'. Quite an achievement, really, to be both at once. But the trouble did not lie only in my penchant for theorising but also in my habit of challenging received scholarly views—in this instance, by relating Eliot's poetry to Webster rather than to Donne, as the fashion then was. It is quite a tribute to the English Department that I achieved first place in the literature option, even if my thesis was heavily marked down.

Later in life I was to criticise Anderson's aesthetics rather severely, but there can be no doubt that at the time it greatly enlivened my approach to literature and the arts. I had no intention of altering my ways, or concealing my views, for the sake of getting better results in English. It shows what a protected life I have led that I have never had to pretend to hold views I do not hold, although I do not go around advertising my views to all comers.

The Literary Society was also the place where in my first year I gave my first public address. It was on G. K. Chesterton. I recall only some terrible rhetoric about Chesterton as a modern Don Quixote. My choice of subject might be taken to suggest that I was still self-consciously a Catholic and was striking a blow at Anderson. In fact he turned out to be an enthusiast for Chesterton, whom he quite often cited. I might well, however, have been trying to find a Catholic writer with whom I could identify, having completely failed to do so when I read Hilaire Belloc's *History of England*. (In later life, Anderson was also an enthusiast for Belloc's *The Servile State*. One cannot exaggerate his complexity.)

When people talk about 'Anderson' and 'Anderson's views', one has to know to what vintage they are referring. In his general philosophy, it is true, his views were pretty persistent. But in his political thinking that was far from being the case. One has to distinguish three quite distinct stages in his thinking—his relatively orthodox communist years, his Trotskyist years and his virulently anti-communist years. His wife Jenny, a formidable intellect in her own right, granted that these stages are 'hard to define'. This is in her foreword to *Art and Reality*. 'I have often thought of him', she concludes by saying, 'as one who had gone full circle and ended up (now consciously and politically) as he began—one of Gilbert's "little liberals".' This is a rather puzzling remark. Anderson's father was a member of the Independent Labour Party, and Anderson took part in socialist activities as an undergraduate. But after graduation, it would seem, he concentrated on working out his philosophical views until the General Strike of 1926 aroused him from his political lethargy. When I first encountered him he might fairly be described as a 'little liberal' in his insistence on freedom of expression, but otherwise he presented in student societies a straight communist line, or what he took to be that line.

I also participated in the discussion groups of the Freethought Society, where I was glad to study Marx—at a time before the publication of his relatively humanistic Paris manuscripts—and Lenin. Their critique of capitalism I could read, in the heart of the Great Depression, with considerable sympathy. I still admire Marx's early journalism and accept many of his criticisms of industrial society. But one of the first times I intervened at a public meeting was to argue against Anderson that a dictatorship of the proletariat—or, in practice, of the Communist Party—would, like any other dictatorship, ruthlessly repress anyone who threatened its power and would never willingly surrender it.

I nevertheless had, for a very short time, some hopes for the USSR. I read quite a lot of Soviet literature, and my hopes were aroused by a very simple story written by Valentin Kataev and translated in an anthology called *Bonfire*, brought together by S. Konalov. It is about a clerk who is to undergo a political examination. He has learnt off by heart the answers to the questions he knows he will be asked. Unfortunately, he does not realise that the first question he will be asked is his name. So, in his nervousness, expecting the question 'Who is the great teacher', he answers 'Karl Marx' when he is asked his name and when he is asked his occupation replies with what should have been his answer to 'What characterises capitalism?', namely 'Rabid exploitation on the basis of private property'. In the end he is sent to a sanatorium in the Crimea for a rest—an outcome that did not have the sinister suggestions of 'psychiatric treatment' it would have had in later years.

Why did this story, little more than a music-hall turn, so strike me? The monstrous character of the interrogation, with such questions and answers as 'Who is a renegade?' 'Kautsky'; 'Who are social traitors?' 'Scheidemann and Noske', confirmed my worst fears. But the satirical tone of the sketch made me hope that the suppression in the USSR might not be so bad as I had feared. Other stories in *Bonfire* were interesting for the same reason—Zamyatin was one of the names there. But then I read Gladkov's ecstatically received proletarian novel *Cement*, published in 1925, and began to read the documents officially promoting 'socialist realism'. That was enough.

I am glad that I am not an ex-communist. My hostility to Hitler could be whole-hearted from the very first, whereas some ex-communists had a degree of sympathy with Hitler, seeing him as the only person who could bring about the death of the Soviet Union. This was at one stage true even in Anderson's case, to my horror. Again, many ex-communists carried into their anti-communism the vituperative style learnt in their communist days. (The American *Commentary* group is a striking instance.) There are many anti-communists I mistrust as much as I mistrust communists, and for much the same reasons.

What about ex-Catholicism? For an ex-Catholic is what I soon became, deciding in my second year that I could no longer conscientiously attend Mass. This was to the natural distress of my parents, most vociferously of my mother, who explained my behaviour as adolescent suggestibility to the wiles of the seducer, Anderson.

Do I regret having been brought up, to the degree that I was, as a Catholic? No, in the sense that it taught me a number of lessons. It gave me a better appreciation of the most primitive forms of religion. It helped me to understand the structure of totalitarian states, with judgements handed down from the very top, promulgated through the party (the clergy), the senior members of which met at intervals in praesidea (councils) where shifts in policy could be pronounced and set out in forms suitable for the consumption of the laity. There were penalties for those who refused to accept the rulings (excommunications, dismissals from the party and, where the church had sufficient control over the 'secular arm', imprisonment or execution). Reading the witchcraft trials, I came to a better understanding of 'confessions' in the Moscow trials. More generally I began to understand the power of the totalitarian parties and, particularly in the case of the Nazi movement, as in the case of the church, its attraction for women.

More than that, my membership of the Catholic Church convinced me that there was no doctrine of which one can say: 'that is so absurd that no human being could believe it'. A person who can accept transubstantiation could believe anything.

At the same time I am glad that I was not brought up in Catholic schools. I could drop my Catholicism in a quiet way, which did not prevent me from being friendly with a good many Catholics, some of them even members of religious orders, whom I occasionally prefer as persons to others who stand much closer to my views. The people I cannot get on with are those who are dominated by the quest for money and power; the Catholics I have known, inside and outside my family, do not fall within that group. They sometimes engage in unrewarding voluntary work, without using it as an occasion for making converts.

I do not blame members of families with a long Catholic history, often subject in the past to persecution, for remaining in the church. But I do not understand how intelligent people can be converted to Catholicism, unless they are converting from Anglo-Catholicism or from some totalitarian doctrine. So ex-communists often became Catholics and ex-Catholics communists. Neither group readily converts to, let us say, Congregationalism or to a tolerant, sceptical liberalism.

In my case, it was not only Catholicism but God that came to be rejected; under a variety of influences—Anderson, Marx, Freud, Hume and European history—I became a secularist. That is not simply a negative view; it is a positive attitude to human affairs and, beyond that, to human attitudes towards the various natural systems in which human beings live and work. It is sometimes suggested that secularism replaces the worship of God by the worship of Man. That is not true in my case. I have already said there is no doctrine so absurd that we can be confident that no human being would hold it. To this I should add that there is no deed so horrible that we can confidently assert that no human being could commit it. Our daily newspapers constantly remind us that this is so, and nothing of what we know of human history suggests that our age is unique in these respects. In Christian teaching it is supposed that there was a time, in the Garden of Eden, when human beings were very different, and similar myths feature in other religions. This is a consolation that human beings have reserved for themselves, a way of saying 'we are not by nature all that bad', as others have consoled themselves with the picture of a time to come when human beings would not have the defects that led, on the Christian view, to the Fall.

The secularist is not, however, committed to a bland acceptance of such atrocities as being 'just the way human beings are'. Some human beings, most human beings, are not monsters; there have been historical periods, and particular societies, less given to atrocities than others. But as the 1930s went on, I always had before my mind the case of Germany, with one of the best educational systems in the world, rich in philosophers, scientists, writers, artists, advanced social programmes, collapsing into a barbarism the more horrible for its technical efficiency. Where now were the hopes of those who wrote in the first decade of the twentieth century that never again, except in Tsarist Russia, would human beings be imprisoned for their opinions, would books be burnt, would human beings guide their lives by judicial astrology? Gone with the most tragic, the most futile, the most disastrous war in human history, the 1914–18 war, which only a very few—the secularist Bertrand Russell, for one—saw in that light. Yet at the same time one can rejoice in what human beings can and do achieve, often under horrendous circumstances. In the worst days of the 1914–18 war, poetry was being written, courage, affection, kindness, generosity displayed. The men in the trenches had to kill, but they were far from being moral monsters.

If you believe, as I do, that human beings came to be as they are as the outcome of a long period of natural and social evolution—to make a crude distinction, for human beings are social animals—we human beings can rejoice that things have so worked out that at every level of society one can encounter acts that make one feel proud to be human, and occasionally achievements that stagger us by their level of artistic, scientific or technological imaginativeness, without expecting such achievements, such acts of human affection, of self-sacrifice, of courage to be the daily norm.

Similarly, our physical structure opens up wonderful possibilities of intellectual and sporting achievement, sensory pleasure and visual delight. Yet Shakespeare might with more justice have written 'Frailty, thy name is body'. The most brilliant mind can collapse into senility, a minor accident can ruin an athlete forever, our sensitivity to pleasure is also a sensitivity to pain, our senses, like our societies, are subject to decline and fall, we are racked, like other members of the animal kingdom, by cruel diseases—and surely my cat did not die of cancer because she was implicated in Adam's Fall. All these facts are explicable in evolutionary terms, in the fact that we do not matter biologically once we pass the reproductive age, in the fact that our bodies are of use to viruses and bacteria. Once more we can rejoice in what we can do, regard ourselves as lucky in some respects, if unfortunate in others, and see how our luck and our misfortune are intimately intertwined one with another. But there is nothing to suggest that we are made in the image of an eternal, omnipotent and omniscient being or will ever become 'men like gods'.

This picture does not wholly divorce me from what theologians and religious sages have had to say, as I have made clear in *The Perfectibility of Man*—which might better have been called *Human Imperfectibility*. In his earlier years, Anderson had dismissed religion in a Comtean manner, as something that belonged only to an earlier period of human development, as he had dismissed any form of transcendental metaphysics. Anderson, second vintage, did not do this. Rather he went in search of what he called an 'empirical equivalent', taking religion and metaphysics, in certain of their forms, to be misleading ways of saying something of importance about human relations. I found myself blamed for this change by intransigent first-vintage Andersonians. I should explain it, rather, by Anderson's reading of Feuerbach and Vico. But I could wish that they were right.

It was at meetings of the Freethought Society, not in his lectures, that Anderson gave vent to his political onslaughts, although sometimes there was an interplay between the two. The most striking example of this was in 1931, my first year, when Anderson had his most fiery confrontation with state and university as a result of an address he gave to the Freethought Society entitled 'Freethought and Politics'. This controversy has been discussed in some detail by A. J. Baker in his *Anderson's Social Philosophy*. My interest is in how the controversy looked to Anderson's students at the time.

The Freethought Society was like the religious and political societies in having a definite commitment. Anderson always insisted on this spelling, rather than the Free Thought Society, which might suggest a society open to all comers. Membership involved three commitments. The first was to 'the primacy of science', understood as the belief that the way to knowledge lay through experiment and observation—Anderson supposed this to be true even in the case of mathematics and philosophy; the second was to support the extension of such knowledge in all fields; the third was to oppose censorship of every description. The commitment was not to any particular political party or complex of beliefs. We did, however, form study groups on Marx and Freud in 1932, at a time when they were not a serious part of any regular courses—and indeed were scarcely known even in France, where they were to become so fashionable among philosophers after the war. (A little later I reviewed some of Freud's works on the occasion of their first English publication.) So much for the view that Sydney was an intellectual backwater! Since my Freudian and Marxist period, never entirely whole-hearted even then, had been set in the 1930s, I found much of the intellectual life of more recent years surprisingly old-fashioned.

The particular reference in Anderson's talk that created so tumultuous a hullabaloo was to war memorials—mostly memorials to the 1914–18 war, which we then called the 'Great War'. For Anderson these memorials acted as superstitious 'idols'—was he thinking of Bacon's use of this word?—that stood in the way of a critical examination of the causes, conduct and consequences of that war.

He could not have touched a more delicate nerve. That war had a special place in Australia's history and folklore. Its soldiers undertook a dangerous voyage across the world to fight in the Middle East, in Egypt and in France. There was no possibility of home leave; the soldiers were more closely bound together for that reason. They were all volunteers. Mostly young, they were often used as shock troops. The casualty rate was exceptionally high, even by the standards of that murderous war. Almost every family was touched by deaths or serious casualties.

The leader of the right-wing Country Party moved a vote of censure against Anderson in the State Parliament. In the event it never came to the vote, but some parliamentarians who might have been expected to speak out against the motion did not. One of them, C. E. Martin, told me some years later that he felt 'glued to his seat' by the passion the House displayed; he was unable to rise and speak against the motion. (I silently wondered whether what he really feared was the reaction of his constituents.) More seriously, the largely lay University Senate moved a vote of censure.

Anderson would not have been the first professor to be driven out of the university. In the cases of R. F. Irvine and Christopher Brennan, to be sure, expulsion had mostly been on the ground of adultery. But the geographer Griffith Taylor had been refused promotion to a professorship, at least partly because he had attacked another sacred icon, the doctrine that Australia was a country with 'limitless possibilities' that could carry a population as large as the United States'. (The book in which he asserted that Western Australia was 'largely desert' had been banned from circulation in that State.)

The *Sydney Morning Herald* published an editorial on Anderson that began 'It is scarcely surprising that . . .', preceding an account of the parliamentary censure motion. But as Anderson liked to remember, a fortnight later its editorial referring to the same motion began 'It is perhaps a pity that . . .' For the public outcry was astonishing; an evening paper said that it had never received so many letters on any topic—not, as we philosophy students fearfully expected, demanding that Anderson be instantly dismissed, but in favour of academic freedom. That was an important moment in the history of Australian universities. For Anderson was in many ways an extreme instance of the heretic with his attacks on religion, his Marxism, and as one who had committed the supreme crime of attacking war memorials. All this at a time when the Returned Soldiers' League was a powerful political force and right-wing extremists were gathering together to form the New Guard.

It was exciting to be a philosophy student in these turbulent circumstances—the more so, perhaps, as we were at the same time listening to Anderson's lectures on Plato's *Apology*, where Socrates is depicted as confronting many of the same charges as had been levelled against Anderson. In particular, they were both accused of 'corrupting the youth'. Although Anderson did not explicitly refer to his own situation, he could not resist an occasional recognisable cross-reference. Any suggestion that Plato was just a relic from the past was dispelled.

At the same time the whole experience was rather frightening. We were afraid of losing Anderson; I hate to think what the effect of that would have been on my own intellectual development. Those of us who already held radical views, or were moving in that direction, were more than a little alarmed by the torrent of hatred this controversy unleashed, even if we were heartened by the public defence of academic freedom it also brought to light. This fear was exacerbated in the following year when there was another outcry about a collection of articles published as *Freethought*. One of the authors, who had not published under his own name, became so terrified by the response that he wrote a letter to *Honi Soit*, this time under his own name, roundly condemning the article and its author —scarcely an heroic deed. But I do not feel myself to be in any position to castigate him severely.

I remarked earlier that I have never had to write anything I did not believe. But that has been sheer good luck. For all that we may grumble about Australian censorship and censoriousness, Australia has been one of the freest countries in the world. Anderson himself once told me that he could not have spoken out as freely in

Edinburgh—where he taught before he came to Australia—as he did in Sydney. To have been an intellectual in the twentieth century without having had to run the risk of being dismissed, imprisoned, tortured or executed is to have been very fortunate.

I have never been really tested; I simply do not know how I would have behaved in the USSR, in Germany under Hitler, in Occupied France. I hope that I should never have been an informer, but I seriously doubt whether I should have had the courage to join the Resistance. I do not feel that I have any right to throw the first stone at those who lived lives of passive collaboration. Sometimes I have been congratulated on speaking out, as when I attacked the environmental policies of Eastern Europe at a 1973 conference in Bulgaria. The fact remains that, although my hotel room was bugged and my paper was officially condemned as 'highly contentious', I was not running any serious physical risk. My courage, such as it is, has never gone further than sometimes being the first to take the chestnuts out of the fire. If I mention the case of the authorship-denying student, it is simply to bear witness to the fear that reigned in 1932 even if it was, by the standards of most other countries, a fear without foundation. I cannot say that Doris and I suffered in any way from being on the four-member committee that was responsible for the affairs of the Freethought Society; nor was I penalised for leading a study group—as I recently discovered to my astonishment—on 'Class Consciousness'.

There was one other organisation in which I began to take part in 1932 and which played a very important part in my intellectual life for nearly twenty years thereafter. It was then called the Australasian Association of Psychology and Philosophy. This combination was far from unfamiliar. Until a short time previously, psychology in Sydney had fallen within the ambit of the Philosophy Department; Anderson's predecessor, Bernard Muscio, though far from being an incompetent philosopher, had made his name as an industrial psychologist. As late as 1950, as Professor of Philosophy and Psychology in the University of Otago, I was surprised to find myself asked to sign requisitions for 'spaghetti'—which turned out to be a form of tubing needed in the psychology laboratory.

The association was not a student body but, unlike its lineal descendant, the Australasian Association of Philosophy, it did not restrict full membership to those who are 'competent to teach philosophy at a tertiary level', or 'to do independent research in philosophy'. Two of its activities were of great consequence to me. It held conferences at regular intervals, and three times a year it published a *Journal*. That was where Anderson published almost everything he wrote after he arrived in Australia; there I was to publish all my purely philosophical articles for nearly twenty years. Neither of us published anything outside Australia in that time, Anderson never again.

The 1932 Sydney Conference was my first acquaintance with philosophers outside Sydney. Given the size of Australia, the ridiculous character of its then transport system, which required one to change trains at State borders, and the general lack of travel grants, it is scarcely surprising that in practice the Association tended to be a Sydney–Melbourne affair. I never so much as cast eyes on one of the ablest of Australian philosophers, although far from the most pellucid, Sir William Mitchell of Adelaide.

The philosophical disputes at that time were between philosophical idealists of one sort or another and Anderson, uniquely defending an intransigent realism, materialism and, at this time, Marxism. These were to be the lines of battle for many years, until former pupils of Wittgenstein came to Australia in the late 1930s. There were only a few papers, and usually members of the conference attended them all, so that we could discuss them with one another. The numbers attending were also small, so as a student, or a young lecturer, I could speak out without embarrassment. Until I went to England in 1948, the philosophy conferences were to be almost my sole acquaintance with non-Sydney philosophers; the days of regular visitors to Australia and regular visits overseas were far in the future.

One other feature of the congresses that might seem strange by present standards is that they were fully reported by the *Sydney Morning Herald*. True enough the *Herald* then thought of itself as being a 'paper of record' with an eye on future historians. But there was more to it than that; philosophers were thought of as having something to say to the general public. The *Journal* had a greater number of subscribers than it does now, including many who were in no sense professional philosophers. With no university subsidy it could not otherwise have survived. Doris and I—as secretary —wrote begging letters to subscribers who did not renew their subscriptions. We found that this worked much better than a typed circular. With slight, but important, success, I tried to persuade overseas libraries to subscribe, and enticed students to do likewise. With fewer than twenty professional philosophers in Australia and even fewer in New Zealand, there was no other way of keeping our journal alive.

There were papers on such topics as 'A non-hierarchical mathematical logic', which many readers could not profess to understand, but such papers were not the rule. Plato wrote certain dialogues that are inaccessible to any but trained philosophers; neither Kant nor Hegel is easy reading. Neither was Sir Thomas Mitchell. But anyone but a professional philosopher looking at the *Journal* as it is now would simply not know what it was all about; this was not then true. At the same time, it has now established a deserved reputation as one of the world's leading philosophical journals. One can expect to be published in it only after a delay, whereas we often had awkward gaps to fill. Many of my own lengthy reviews and even one article—'Reason and Inclination'—had to be written over a weekend to fill such a gap.

7

Initiation into Teaching
1934–1939

I N DECEMBER 1933 our undergraduate life was coming to an end; the final honours examinations were to be in March 1934. Before they were held, however, not just one, but two, of my friends came to me and triumphantly announced that they would not sit the final examinations. It was not that they were afraid of disgracing themselves; each had a strong chance of being top of the class. Neither was it a rejection of a particular teacher, a particular subject. One was an economist, the other a classicist. Their economic position was not the same. The economist had been very hard hit by the Depression; his father was out of work. A sure sign of poverty, he alone wore sandshoes to lectures. The classicist held a relatively valuable Cooper scholarship and showed no sign of belonging to an impoverished family. Why did they do it?

To try to dissuade them was to encounter a gesture rather than an argument—a gesture against our punishing exam-ridden life but, beyond that, against the hopeless-looking world around us. The economist was awarded a second-class degree on the basis of his work in his earlier years. Classics was less accommodating. In later life the economist, Walter Pawley, became a well-known economic adviser, the classicist, Trevor Martin, a high-ranking judge.

In accordance with my life pattern I did not come top in either of my honours subjects, although first-class honours came my way in both. In English Eric Dobson, taking the language option, was in first place to my second; in philosophy I was third, with first place going to Jim Massie, later to be killed in a plane crash along with several cabinet ministers to whom he was giving legal advice. (In my final examinations, I made the mistake of arguing against

125

Anderson's views about ethics, something it was very difficult to do effectively under examination conditions.) With a double first in what was said to be an exceptional year, however, there was still some chance that the Wentworth travelling scholarship could come my way. But this was never put to the test. The value of the Australian pound was suddenly reduced by a third, and we were warned not to apply for a scholarship unless we had private means and had British relatives with whom we could stay in vacations. Neither of these requirements could I satisfy. The scholarship was awarded to my conqueror in English, Eric Dobson, later to become Professor of English Language at Oxford and the author of a monumental two-volume work on the history of English pronunciation.

Were my results a disappointment? Not so. The double first was a considerable achievement, especially as Latin had taken so much of my time during the year. As for not coming top, that was scarcely abnormal. What about being unable to so much as apply for a travelling scholarship? That, too, produced a feeling of relief rather than a sense of grievance. As I earlier remarked, my experience of Balliolised Australians had not produced in me any desire to be one of them and English university novels, with their wealthy hearties, did not create in me a wish to be their victim.

There was one other consideration. Separation from Doris for two years was far from being a prospect I relished. Alexander Mackie, who always followed my career with interest, placed rather too much emphasis on this as an explanation of why I did not apply for the travelling scholarship. When his son, John Mackie, came to be involved in a romance, Mackie did what he could to thwart it, in case John, as his father saw the situation, followed in my footsteps. In fact, the decision to cut the exchange rate was decisive—there was no question of part-time vacation work during the deep depression in England.

Was my not going to Oxford a pity? Very doubtfully. There was scarcely any provision for graduate work at Oxford; the B. Phil. that so many Australians were later successfully to undertake was a post-war creation. The tradition was to do the last two years of the undergraduate course. Had this been in English, it would have been almost entirely linguistic. It was only by representing itself as a form of philology that English had been able to persuade Oxford that it would not be a 'soft option'. Even so, some colleges were not persuaded. No undergraduates were at that time accepted to study English at Corpus, a college to which I was later to be attached. The English course suited Dobson far better than it would have suited me. As for philosophy, few if any of the philosophers teaching at Oxford in the early 1930s would have excited me as Anderson did. They were clever men but not imaginative. The possible exception was Collingwood, but I should probably not have been ready to learn from him.

Cambridge, with its Leavis and Wittgenstein, would have been a very different matter. But, as *Time* was moved to remark not so very long ago, most Americans do not realise that there is more than one great university in Great Britain. The Rhodes scholarship has been a wonderful advertising device for Oxford. Abstractly, I knew that there was such a place as Cambridge, but it would never have occurred to me to go there.

These speculations illustrate the difficulty an Australian young man could have at that time in making major decisions. Nowadays there would be members of staff with graduate degrees from all sorts of places. In contrast, most of my teachers had no degree except from Sydney or, as in Anderson's case, had a very confined university experience. No one I knew was an Oxford graduate; Anderson had scarcely set foot in England. Informed guidance was totally absent.

It is an interesting reflection that, although travelling scholarships were supposed to weld Australians more firmly to England, most of the leading anti-English political figures in the 1930s had gone to England with such scholarships. That was true of the only communist ever elected, as such, to an Australian parliament, of the secretary of the Victorian Communist Party, of the editor of Sydney's most virulent left-wing newspaper, of one of the very few Australians ever imprisoned on a charge of treason. In order to receive a Rhodes scholarship an undergraduate had to be a Big Man on the campus; at Oxford he found himself very small fry indeed. That must have been very trying. (The best account I know of this phenomenon is in Thomas Wolfe's novel *You Can't Go*

Home Again.) Anyhow, contact with the class-conscious Oxford of that time, with its unique emphasis on accent, its special conception of what counts as rudeness, was bound to provoke reactions. Perhaps it is as well that I did not reside in Oxford until I was forty-one. Well-received though I then was, I can quite imagine that before I had developed such strong anthropological interests, so that I was fascinated by what would otherwise have appalled me, I might well have become anti-English. Manning Clark's memoirs make it plain how easily this could happen.

Thirty years later a person in my situation, bond apart, would have gone on to do postgraduate work culminating in a Ph.D., with the expectation of becoming a university teacher. But Australian universities had no graduate work to offer. The only doctorate in the Arts faculty was a D. Litt. and that was awarded only on the basis of a substantial body of published work. There was a Master's degree, but to acquire that one simply wrote a thesis with minimal, if any, supervision, as I eventually did. As for the idea of becoming a university teacher, getting such an appointment was so much a matter of luck that to have a university post as one's ambition would have been quite foolish.

So there was no option except to continue my training as a high school teacher. There was nothing at all strange in a high school teacher having good honours qualifications, sometimes overseas study as well as a Sydney degree. One unfortunate effect of the rapid university expansion that later took place was that it changed this situation.

I followed, then, the regular path by going to Teachers' College for a fourth year, which would have led me to a Diploma of Education had not Alexander Mackie persuaded us that it was not worth paying the few pounds the university would have demanded to award it to us. It was at Teachers' College, Anderson thought, that I began really to flourish. That might seem surprising, since some of the teaching in the Teachers' College was really abysmal, particularly the lectures on the philosophy of education. In some cases the problem was simply that science and arts graduates were now thrust together; the science graduates often found quite interesting, even exciting, what to the rest of us was boringly elemen-

'Hard work is a fine thing, provided other people do it.' John Passmore's great-grandmother, Martha Crossley

A wedding photograph of Frederick Passmore and Ruby Moule, John's parents, with his grandmother (seated)

John Passmore as a baby

With his mother Ruby

The 'philosophy corner' in the
main quadrangle at the University
of Sydney. 'That covered section
of the cloister was a kind of Stoa,
even if we were scarcely Stoics.'

The young graduate, 1934

John and Doris with daughter Helen on the back lawn at 'Tuncurry', Ashfield, c. 1938

On a walk in the Blue Mountains with friends, 1941

tary. Still, quite a few of the lecturers were able people. Unlike Victoria, New South Wales spent a good deal of money on its Teachers' College—roughly nine times as much. Harold Wyndham, later Director of Education, taught us psychology and the history of education. George Mackaness in English, R. L. Harris in economics, C. H. Currey in history, Ivan Turner in mathematics were by no means negligible figures.

Alexander Mackie himself taught the 'principles of teaching' in an interestingly interrogative fashion. But my clearest memory is of his providing us with our first experience of 'modern' painting, a print of Franz Marc's *Blue Horses*. By the standards of those days, that was a very advanced experience. Robert Hughes has described the great difficulty an Australian painter experienced in finding such a print some years later. How startling we found it! In 1941 James McAuley was to write a poem inspired by it. Mackie constantly encouraged me, as did the motherly Miss Skillen in English.

Meanwhile, while still a student, I began to lecture and even to publish. I was fascinated by twentieth-century American and British poets of the 'modernist' sort, and, at Miss Skillen's invitation, began to lecture on them to students who were training to teach in the primary schools. I had my first experience of lecturing to a more general audience by talking to the Australian English Association on T. S. Eliot. (George Mackaness reported with pride that no one had objected to my accent. He had told me that I could not hope to succeed in academic life with so virulent an Australian accent, and on his recommendation I had undertaken a course with the speech therapist, Gracie Stafford. I still have running through my head such vowel-rich passages as 'Gold, gold, gold/Spurned by the young and hugged by the old/To the very verge of the churchyard mould'.)

How did I find a publisher? Now for the truth behind the *Times Higher Education Supplement* legend that in 1948 I had the run of the drawing-rooms of T. S. Eliot, Sybil Thorndike and Lewis Casson. In 1932 Sybil Thorndike and Lewis Casson were visiting Australia and the Literary Society had the bright idea of asking them to perform on its behalf in the hall of the University Union. The entry fee was one shilling, to see Thorndike–Casson perform a series of what one might call duets from some of their favourite plays. As a result the society had money and put it into publishing pamphlets. The first of these was Anderson's *Some Questions in Aesthetics* and the third was my *T. S. Eliot*, published in 1934, at a time when the literature on Eliot was anything but voluminous. The only thing I can remember about it is my prophecy, before Eliot had written any plays, that his best work might well be in that medium. I was later congratulated on my foresight. Unfortunately, when the plays did appear I concluded that I had been wrong.

The publication of this pamphlet undoubtedly helped me to develop a reputation. Meeting Thorndike and Casson many years later in Canberra, I told Sybil Thorndike that she was responsible for my subsequent career. Delighted, she called Lewis Casson over so that I could tell him the story. Eliot I never met, in spite of at one stage in London living near the church where he functioned as churchwarden and seeing him in the street. So much for my having the run of the Thorndike, Casson and Eliot drawing rooms!

When 1934 came to a close, it was obvious that there was no work available for us in the Education Department to which we were bonded. At the same time, it became apparent that the sharp rise in university numbers was no transient phenomenon. If at minimum cost, additional staff had to be secured. So new grades were set up, tutor and assistant lecturer. 'Perce' Partridge had become an assistant lecturer in 1934. In 1935 a tutorship came my way, at a nominal salary of £200, reduced to £180 as a result of all-over cuts. The theory was that a tutor would help with logic teaching by taking tutorials and doing some correcting; in fact I gave four lectures a week and corrected all the logic exercises.

Anderson's logic courses were, for their time, rather strange. He operated with a revised version of traditional 'Aristotelian' logic, but developed it so that it could deal with sentences that Russell had claimed traditional logic, as distinct from his own mathematical logic, could not deal with satisfactorily. Anderson incorporated into his logic such Russellian concepts as propositional functions but took everyday arguments rather than mathematics as the object of his inquiry. That suited me fine; I developed a good many complications that made his logic somewhat richer, invented new types of exercise and took great delight in exemplifying fallacies by taking as examples the utterances of politicians. Or sometimes colleagues. On one later occasion there was a 'post' paper to be prepared. These were not published, so it seemed safe enough to give as an example for analysis a beautifully straightforward logical fallacy uttered by one of my colleagues, Professor Bland. But it so happened that a *Herald* journalist in the class was so taken by the example that he reproduced it in a newspaper column, giving its source as being from the examination paper. I could only hope that my colleague's memory for his own utterances was not of the highest order.

The tutorship had one advantage. R. G. Howarth had been asked to write a short history of English Literature for use in the schools, and suggested that I should write it. Thanks to my tutorship it went unwritten. It would have been quite a task in later life buying back copies in order to burn them. There was, however, no reason to believe that my appointment would be anything but temporary. Doris, meanwhile, was teaching six subjects in a private school for thirty shillings a week.

While I was still a tutor my first philosophy article, on 'The Nature of Intelligence', was published in the *Australasian Journal of Psychology and Philosophy*. At the Teachers' College I had encountered for the first time not only intelligence tests but new-style examinations consisting of filling in such forms as 'ideas are to mind as furniture is to . . .'; both made me furious. I found myself having to give answers that I knew the examiners expected but that I believed to be false. There was no way of arguing the point. My reaction was not unique; somewhat paradoxically, those who were most sceptical about the reliability of intelligence tests were precisely those who did best in them.

The paper on intelligence is characteristic of much of my later work in that although nobody but a philosopher—and indeed nobody but an Andersonian—could have constructed the general line of argument, it nevertheless looks in some detail at the actual structure of intelligence tests and Spearman's related psychological theories, in a way that philosophers do not normally do. It argued that it was impossible to construct intelligence tests that succeed in abstracting from environmental influences so as to estimate pure, genetically based, intelligence. That is scarcely an unorthodox doctrine nowadays, but in 1935 it caused great indignation among local psychologists.

Oddly enough, although I had laughed at the description of my English thesis as being at once 'too intellectual and too empirical', the examiners might have been on to something. For this article raises philosophical questions that are too closely reasoned and too abstract to be readily accessible to psychologists and yet, as I said, its detailed criticism of intelligence tests is not the sort of thing philosophers usually go in for. Something similar might be said about my later writings on the environment, education and art. They are argued at too high a level of generality to suit environmentalists, educators, art critics, they are too concrete in their references for philosophers. And, one can add, too historically minded for either, although not enough for historians. It is sometimes said that I mysteriously turned aside from philosophy proper in the 1960s to address a wider audience. But from my very first writings much of my work has had in mind an audience more empirically minded than are most contemporary philosophers. (Horror from a French philosopher when I said that I was writing about the environment: 'None of us would dream of writing about such a thing'.) Nevertheless, I can claim in this respect to be following in the footsteps of most philosophers until the present century.

There were special problems for Anderson's pupils in writing about what are regarded as the central problems of philosophy, as there were for Wittgenstein's pupils—who, however, often responded by total silence. Few of Anderson's ideas were published, except in an extremely sketchy form, and he strongly objected to his pupils summarising them in print. It is not surprising that I began by writing about T. S. Eliot and the nature of intelligence.

When my year as a tutor was completed, I was appointed to teach at a central school in North Sydney—a school of a practical bent, for boys who could not get into, or did not want to go to, academic high schools. Here I was called upon to teach English, mathematics, history and economics, all to students in their final year, facing public examinations.

A few weeks into term, however, Anderson told me that he was negotiating to have me appointed as an assistant lecturer. This had to be kept confidential. But I felt that I had to go to the headmaster and tell him what was likely to happen, since it would be unfair for the final-year pupils to face a change of teachers relatively late in the year. So, to the gratifying dismay of my former pupils, I was moved to teaching the bottom class.

That indirectly created another decision point. I met Professor Mackie in the streets of Sydney, as one quite often did meet people casually in those days when Sydney was still a large small town. He asked me what I was doing and I said that I was teaching the bottom class in a central school. I could not tell him that I was hoping to get an assistant lectureship. He, too, said nothing. But just as I was informed that I was to get the assistant lectureship, I received a telegram from the Department of Education, offering me an appointment as Lecturer in Education in the Teachers' College. This was totally against the rules; to get such an appointment one had first to teach for three years in the schools. Mackie must have moved heaven and earth to get me appointed. Prudence would have advocated acceptance. I should have been paid more than the £300 the university was to pay me. Unlike the university post, it was not a one-year appointment only. The Education Department had given me a year's leave, but the bond still hung over me. Nevertheless, I accepted the university post.

This was decisive in another way. Unofficially, Holme had told me that I should be appointed to the next vacancy in English. I was still torn between English and philosophy; I had been doing a good deal of informal lecturing on poetry and continued to read literature voraciously. My interest was in American literature, and in such movements as Imagism, which conjoined theories about poetry with a sometimes wishy-washy poetical practice. In contrast, my only public philosophy lecture had been on Hegel's philosophy of rights, even although none of our lectures had been on Hegel.

Once again what Joyce calls an 'epiphany' affected me powerfully. I was talking to Howarth in his room. Holme came in and spoke to Howarth, in front of me, in a way that I can only describe as 'bullying'. That, I decided, would not do for me. Yet in fact Holme was much better than Anderson at advancing young members of staff, getting them overseas leave and so on. Anderson was so critical of others on selection committees and the like that he could not, in consistency, advance the claims of his own people.

Was my appointment a racket? I do not see how any modern-style committee could have appointed me. I had not come top of the year in philosophy, ranking behind Massie and W. H. C. Eddy. But Anderson once told Doris that I would be a late developer—I was only nineteen when I graduated—and he thought that this late development had come into being at Teachers' College. There I had secured the Jones medal and the Walter Beavis prize, and could now at last buy the lamp that Mr Whitlam took to be essential, although I still did not have a desk or a room of my own, either at home or at the university, where I spent most of my days and a considerable part of my nights, though allergic to tobacco, in a corner of Anderson's smoky room or in the library. (The desk finally came home for my twenty-first birthday. Farewell, rickety portable bridge-table!) Frank Hutley told me two years later that he had thought my appointment had been a piece of gross favouritism, although he was good enough to add that he had now changed his mind. Others must have felt the same way. But such appointments were common in the university of that time, when professors had something more like the absolute powers of a German professor than they now have.

Anyhow, racket or not and with however tenuous a tenure, there I was embarked upon a career, at the age of twenty, as a university teacher of philosophy. I was glad that university lecturers then wore gowns; since I was thin, and in some ways young-looking for my years, undergraduates would otherwise have seen no reason to let me pass through them on my way to the lecture dais. I was still far from confident that I should spend my life as a university teacher. My appointment was for only one year and the dreaded bond still hung over me. But two things happened: first the Education Department, in a rare burst of generosity, decided that for the purposes of the bond university teaching should count as teaching and, secondly, my appointment was renewed. So I found myself on a ladder that led to my being successively lecturer and senior lecturer, eventually reaching in the late 1940s £600 per annum, by then with a wife and two children.

Being a lecturer in the period 1935–39 was very different from what it now is, and in a way that suited me well but that many university teachers of a later age might find deplorable. We were not specialised; there were no two consecutive years in which I was set down to give exactly the same courses. I lectured at one time and another on every branch of philosophy and a great variety of individual philosophers ranging from the Ancient Greeks to the logical positivists, giving a total miss only to the medieval period. That was made easier than it would now be—not that it was ever easy—by the fact that the total number of publications in any area was, by present standards, minuscule. Nowadays, 'keeping up with the literature' even in a specialised area of a specialised field is a full-time task. The multiplicity of bibliographical tools makes it easier to find out what has been written, but not what is worth reading. One can no longer presume, either, that if a writer comes from a minor university or writes in one of the lesser-known journals the resulting article is unlikely to be particularly useful. As a result of cut-backs good young innovative philosophers may be able to obtain positions only in once-negligible colleges and publication in major journals may be so delayed that they may feel it necessary to write for lesser-known journals.

I am quite sure that philosophers—and this phenomenon is by no means peculiar to them—now give a much more professional training to their students than anything I could possibly have provided. Still, there were some advantages, particularly for the vast majority of the undergraduates who would not become professional philosophers, in having lecturers who could bring out cross-connections, over time and over different fields of philosophy. I hope that in some measure I was able to do this and have done the same sort of thing in most of my writings. But I do not claim that any lecture I have given or anything I have written has been technically sophisticated. In many ways I am a very old-fashioned figure, even if I cannot be accused, as the author of *Recent Philosophers*, of wholly neglecting the work of my contemporaries. In the United

States, in 1960, philosophers first asked me, 'What is your field?' It quite flummoxed me. Indeed, it still does. The only question I like to be asked, and the question I like to ask, is 'what are you working on now?'

Thanks to the reputation Anderson had established, the classes in philosophy were rather special. Almost every student in the Faculty of Arts except those who were committed to the study of languages took at least one year's philosophy—often, as the relatively flexible degree system permitted, in their third year. Every year there were interesting students, a surprising number of whom ended up as poets, as judges, as diplomats, as academics in various fields, even as magicians like the well-known 'Dexter', who once, meeting us by chance in the Blue Mountains, performed extraordinary tricks for my family, with no props except what he could obtain in the bush environment. There was a brief period in which scientists were allowed to take the course on logic and scientific method; among those who came, one was to share a Nobel prize, four others ended up as Fellows of the Royal Society.

Partly because philosophy was so widely studied, my first year as an assistant lecturer was more than a little embarrassing. The members of my class included John Mackie, along with the sons of the Vice-Chancellor and of the Professor of Psychology. I managed, more or less, but the Vice-Chancellor was moved to ask Anderson whether so young a lecturer should be given so much responsibility.

The students showed no sign of adoring me, but large numbers of students did attend my classes, even when they were under no obligation to do so. Attendance at pass lectures was legislatively compulsory but I hated the idea that undergraduates could be forced to listen to me and got around that rule by asking them at the end of each term to write down the number of lectures they wished to be recorded as having missed—they were officially allowed up to three. The gratifying thing was that very many more undergraduates came to my honours lectures—particularly on, of all things, Plato's later dialogues—than were taking honours degrees. In later years, too, former students have often approached me to tell me that my classes had meant a good deal to them. A reasonably good teacher: that is the most I could claim. It was not from a sense of failure but rather out of a conviction that my teaching could no longer be reconciled with my writing that I finally abandoned undergraduate teaching in 1955. Although, as well, I hated examining.

Why was I not adored? Quite early in the piece a woman student, like so many of my students a little older than I was, told me that I 'lacked dignity'. Much later John Mackie wrote a series of wittily malignant verses about members of the Philosophy Department. He rhymed 'Passmore' with 'played the ass more'. They were both right; dignity has never been my strong point. And I could not resist joking in my lectures. I have already referred to this unfortunate habit of mine, taken over from my father. I largely give it up on visits to Cambridge, whether of the British or the New England variety, although not in Oxford.

Joking is often a form of defence mechanism. One asks for laughs because the alternative is to howl in fury. Professional comedians are notoriously melancholic. But in my case it arose, rather, out of a sense of discomfort at the position in which I found myself —standing behind a desk, lecturing to students most of whom would regurgitate what I said in their examinations whether they understood it or not. I did lay down one condition; examinees who regurgitated not only what I had said but the very examples I had used would be severely dealt with. Many failed this test.

The word 'regurgitate' has popped up rather often in my last paragraph. In fact it was often I who did the regurgitating, or came very close to it. For I felt, have continued to feel, so nervous before every lecture that vomiting was never out of the question and lesser physical reactions were almost invariable. People have often said that they wished they could be as relaxed as I am. This is sheer deception on my part, as Doris can fully testify. The joking was, in part, a way of concealing that nervousness. But it went deeper than that.

When I was still quite young Anderson said to me: 'You could be a leader of men but you don't seem to want to be'. Half a century later when I addressed a very large audience at McMaster University, on the occasion of my being awarded an honorary D. Litt, one of my Canadian colleagues said to me: 'I had not realised that you could have been a leader of men'. I do not know whether the 'could have been' is correct. Certainly I very seldom have reason to complain that an audience is restless or inattentive. And I have often swung the body of opinion at meetings where I supposed myself to be in a minority of one. Anderson was right, in any case, when he said 'But you don't want to be'. To want to be a leader of men, you need a self-assurance I have never possessed although, I can, it would seem, appear to possess it.

It really troubled me that an undergraduate who went to Sydney normally became an Andersonian, whereas one who went to Melbourne became a Wittgensteinian. It was not that at any stage I felt myself to be saying things I did not believe or employing arguments I did not regard as being valid. But my awareness of the history of philosophy made me very conscious of the fact that it would have been nothing short of miraculous if all the propositions I asserted were true and all the arguments I used were valid. My 'playing the ass' has been, I suspect, a way of sending a rather complex message: 'I believe what I am saying but please don't take me as a guru'. Not adoration from a captive audience of suggestible adolescents, but discriminating admiration is what I should like to be able to claim.

This is not an apology for sometimes writing in a comic spirit. Comedy can often be the best way of cutting through illusions, bringing pretentious solemnity to court. Shaftesbury once remarked that 'ridicule is the test of truth', that what cannot stand up to ridicule is thereby revealed as being false. Certainly Hitler feared Chaplin more than he did those who fulminated against him in a solemn fashion. But a lecture is scarcely the place for ridicule; my 'playing the ass' did not take that form. It was intended, simply, as a prophylactic against too ready acceptance. People who want to be adored never laugh and never seek to arouse laughter. Remember Jesus, remember Heidegger.

I was happier, really, in working over the essays students wrote, with the complication that these were also read by Anderson. I early resolved that the best thing was to try to teach first-year students to write plain argumentative prose. In that, I could claim some success. At the lecturing level, I preferred the evening students to the day students. They already had careers, they were older, more resistant. They often wrote interesting essays but did not have enough time to excel in their examinations. Later, I found it much more satisfying to supervise Ph.D. students who had been trained elsewhere and already had firm views. My object was to get postgraduate students to formulate their views in a better way, more clearly, more concisely, and I generally succeeded.

Quite unexpectedly, the thing I found it hardest to cope with in my earlier lecturing years was my relationship with Anderson. In personality, in habits of life, we were poles apart. Even our internal time schedules ran contrary to one another. I have always been an early-morning person. Anderson was the reverse. His favourite time for discussing serious administrative issues was at night after the evening lectures, when I wanted to get home after a long day. But that was not all. He thought of the department as being rather like a German Institute, in which we should all work out ideas that, as he granted, he had only sketched. I wanted to see philosophers appointed who came from a different school of thought, he did not. I disliked the fact that he read my comments on essays and, in general, his degree of supervision. More than that, we quarrelled over a great many issues, in a way that was not always productive.

Some of these will seem absurd to an uncommitted observer. There was a particular passage in Plato's dialogue *The Sophist* that Anderson regarded as anticipating one of his own views; I said that Plato's view was quite different. This may seem strange but, quite unlike Descartes, Wittgenstein and many other philosophers, Anderson was as far as could be from putting up a sign that read 'Philosophy begins here'. He once said to me, indeed, that he did not write books because he felt he 'had nothing new to say'. Even in his extremely unorthodox ethical lectures he would point to the most tenuous of links between his own views and, let us say, Bishop Butler's in relation to the centrality of 'the spirit of inquiry'. Anderson's habit of mind remained with me; I have always laughed at the 'philosophy begins here' attitude, along with corresponding political and social slogans. In my book *Ralph Cudworth*, I saw Cudworth as a predecessor, somebody whose thinking was still alive, to the indignation of those scholars who wanted to relate him simply to the times in which he lived. One such reviewer described my book as being excellent of its kind, but of an awful kind.

There were other disputes of a more fundamental sort. Anderson had carried over from his Marxism a rejection of the concept of heredity. When, interested in Darwin, I complained that sociologists ignored biology, his reaction was that this was an excellent thing. I was bothered by his talk of 'social forces' and emphasised individual differences more than he did. This was part of a more general conflict of attitudes. He vehemently protested against my view that the discovery of a distinction that had not previously been recognised could be as important as the discovery of a new general relationship. When he was criticising a philosopher, he would normally do so by trying to bring him under some general rubric. In contrast, my approach was to look for what was exceptional.

So, lecturing and writing on the logical positivists, my concern was with their principle of verifiability, the positivist critique of metaphysics, the linguistic turn. Anderson, as he told me, would have concentrated on their subjectivism, one of his familiar targets. The first article of mine that was in obvious opposition to Anderson's views rejected the possibility of generalising across works of art in a theory of aesthetics.

Many philosophers, most scientists, would be on Anderson's side in his passion for generalising. Without denying that there are general laws about abstract objects that hold good under idealised circumstances and are capable of being applied, when modified in particular ways, to concrete circumstances, I am very wary of empirical generalisations. My mind immediately turns to exceptions. Some would see in this one of my leading intellectual weaknesses.

We were a very small department when I first joined it. Apart from Anderson, there was only Partridge, four years older than I was. We saw a great deal of one another. Indeed, we three came to be known as 'the three Marx Brothers'. Partridge was always a much wiser, much more confidence-inducing, less erratic person than I have ever been. Although he did not write a great deal, he was an exceptional teacher with an enviable range of reading. Unlike me, he concentrated for the most part on political and social theory.

Having already developed a capacity for keeping his views to himself, he left the battling with Anderson to me. Much of that battling took place in the nearby Grace Brothers store, in the tea-room that served as our nearest equivalent to a Left Bank Parisian café—if oh! so different.

Why not a pub? Here again I was an Outsider. I was an Australian who did not like beer, who was in fact upset by its chemicals, even in small quantities. Years later, in Germany, I found 'alt' beers that I could drink, but nothing of that sort was then available in Australia. As for Anderson, he shared the Celtic tradition, so he once told me, that the reason for drinking is to get drunk. He also thought that to appeal from Phillip drunk to Phillip sober is to get things quite wrong; Phillip drunk was the better authority. 'In vino veritas', then, except that Anderson did not care for wine. He never had an opportunity to test his hypothesis on me. But much later at New College, Oxford, when I was no longer a teetotaller, the philosopher A. J. Ayer once deliberately sought to get me drunk— unlike Anderson I drank only because I liked wine and generally in moderation—in order to make the rough, boisterous Australian of the British stereotype come to the surface. Happily he failed, as he confessed to Doris; all that came out of this occasion was a very cheerful evening followed by a headache.

It was not, however, differences in opinion, drinking habits or even temporal habits that made me feel in the later 1930s desperate to get out of Sydney. The crucial things were my dislike for the way Anderson was constantly peering over my shoulder and my desire to engage in discussion with philosophers who were not Andersonians. There were very few opportunities for moving, but a post was advertised in Melbourne. The salary was even worse than in Sydney, with an increment of £25 every five years, but there was a considerable variety of philosophical opinion there. The Professor of Philosophy, 'Sandy' Gibson, decided to offer the post to a man from Birmingham, but he refused it. Gibson then wanted to appoint me, but his staff reminded him that he had agreed that if his favoured candidate did not accept, the post should go to a Cambridge graduate, George Paul, a pupil of G. E. Moore and Wittgenstein.

That was in many ways a fortunate failure on my part, as it was a success on Melbourne's part. There Paul had an influence I could certainly not have equalled. I had discovered the earlier Wittgenstein when I picked up a very tattered second-hand copy of his *Tractatus Logico-Philosophicus*. It entirely fascinated me. Another Cambridge graduate, Douglas Gasking, who also made his way to Australia, was perceptive enough to write an article comparing Anderson's views with the *Tractatus*. Both Anderson and Wittgenstein had a principal source in the doctrines of Bertrand Russell, even if they then deviated from Russell in opposite directions, Wittgenstein developing, Anderson rejecting, logical atomism. I was faithful to the way Anderson had moved but saw in the early Wittgenstein an alternative to Anderson far more interesting than the varieties of Idealism that characterised Australian philosophy outside Sydney.

Paul and Gasking were products of a later Wittgenstein, whose writings were to remain unpublished until 1953, and they brought with them those notes of Wittgenstein's lectures that circulated as the 'Brown Book' and the 'Blue Book'. These I was finally allowed to read. Paul and Gasking had come to Australia in part because pupils of Wittgenstein were then largely ruled out in British appointments. One effect of their coming to Australia was that I was at a relatively early stage in my life put in touch with what were to be leading tendencies of post-war Anglo-American thought. My discovery of the *Tractatus* led me to explore logical positivism, my encounters with Paul and Gasking prepared me for what came to be called 'linguistic philosophy'. There were no longer simply battles with Idealists to be conducted. Now I had my own opponents. Anderson despised the new tendencies, but I came to feel more reconciled to being in Sydney. It helped, too, when Alan Stout arrived in Sydney in 1939 along with his father G. F. Stout, now in his eighties but still philosophically active. Here was my first encounter with a philosopher the world had actually heard about, whom I had lectured on.

Alan Stout arrived under unusual circumstances. The University Senate was by no means reconciled to Anderson's teachings and influence, so they decided to set up a Department of Moral and

Political Philosophy and appointed Alan Stout to it. (No doubt these were the areas in which they were particularly afraid of Anderson's influence.) There was to be a common first year and after that a choice between morals and politics or Anderson's courses. Partridge eventually joined Stout's department. I was somewhat aggrieved at being no longer able to teach moral philosophy, where I had done a great deal of work on the 'British moralists'. But Alan Stout had a considerable influence on my ways of life, making me, some of my critics might say, more bourgeois. The Senate, incidentally, failed in its objectives: Stout came greatly to admire Anderson.

One remark that Alan Stout made particularly influenced me. In his *Republic*, Plato is caustic at the expense of what he calls 'the lovers of sights and sounds', comparing them adversely with those whose minds turn towards the Platonic 'forms'—towards ultimate general principles that are only imperfectly exhibited in what we sensorily perceive. Anderson had taught me to reject ultimates. As an empiricist—even though one who rejected the view that experience consists in the apprehension of ideas, sense-data, impressions or sensations as distinct from complex states of affairs—one might have expected him to be on the side of the lovers of sights and sounds. But in fact when Alan Stout said 'I've never been able to see what is wrong with being a lover of sights and sounds' this came to me as a revelation. From Anderson's aesthetics, formal in its approach, one would never have guessed that the arts could be sensually exciting. But I suddenly realised that I, too, was a lover of sights and sounds. Was Alan my Mephistopheles? Or my liberator?

So far as contacts outside philosophy were concerned, Sydney University was an excellent place to be in. As an assistant lecturer I was at the bottom of the hierarchy. At first, assistant lecturers could not attend faculty meetings; later we were allowed to attend on condition that we spoke only when we were spoken to. This was a rule to which it was difficult for me to conform. I had very strong views on many of the matters that came before the faculty, even drawing up plans for the reform of the University Senate, designed on the one side to circumvent the government's moves to increase its degree of control, and on the other side to get rid of the predominance of lawyers and doctors among members of the Senate elected by graduates. Although my plans were published in the *Union Recorder*, the only change that occurred was that undergraduates were granted the right to elect a member who, however, had to be of five years standing from graduation. (No one expected that the eventual result might be the election of someone who was still an undergraduate, in medicine, although it was more than five years since he had completed his first degree in arts, having spent the interval in studying law. That was one of the most extraordinary people I have ever known, Alf Conlon.) Seeing me near to bursting at a faculty meeting on one occasion, the Professor of Economics, R. C. Mills—the academic to whom I should most naturally apply the epithet 'gentleman' in the best of its senses—urged me to talk. I did so, and the barriers came tumbling down.

Outside such administrative occasions, the atmosphere was completely non-hierarchical, partly as a consequence of the university's relatively small size, with a little over 4000 students at the end of the 1930s. The number of staff too was still very small. As for the senior administration, that was tiny by contemporary standards. There was a Vice-Chancellor, a Registrar, a Deputy Registrar and an accountant who, since the Vice-Chancellor was an English Language scholar with no talent for finance, exerted a very considerable influence on university affairs. We all had lunch together, with no fixed places. So I could well find myself sitting next to the Vice-Chancellor, to a mathematician, a scientist, a member of any department in arts or economics or engineering or medicine and of every rank. The cost was one shilling for my glass of milk and a cheese salad, which I supposed to be the ideal meal until a doctor persuaded me otherwise. A doctor, because I had begun to suffer from that scarcely mentionable disorder, a spastic colon, although it was a long time before I knew that this is what it was.

My favoured food as a child had been, in retrospect, abominable. It included bread spread with tomato sauce and soup with large quantities of Worcester sauce poured into it. As well, there were the customary cleaning-out routines of castor oil, cascara sagrada, even calomel. So it is scarcely surprising that my bowels protested. But also feeling anxious on social occasions and talking

With Helen, February 1941

As a young man

John Passmore, his family (foreground) and students at the Workers'
Educational Association house, Newport, early 1940s

From left, John Passmore, Gilbert Ryle, Perce Partridge and John
Anderson together at the Australian National University, about 1956

Helen and Diana in front of the Norwegian Christmas tree,
Trafalgar Square, on Christmas Eve 1947

too much while I ate did not help. An Oxford doctor later described spastic colon ('irritable bowel') to me as a 'Don's disease', as common among academics as ulcers are among businessmen. In later life, it produced miserable aftermaths to official dinners; if I have sometimes appeared to be unsociable that has been the reason. A gastro-enterologist I once had to consult had on his walls 'Bowels are more important in a man than brains'. I have sometimes been tempted by that motto.

To return to more cheerful matters. Nowadays, a young lecturer —who will be older than the 20-year-old I was—is likely to be almost wholly confined within a single relatively large department. That will probably not be a source of regret to such a lecturer in these highly specialised days, when even philosophers often seem to prefer to talk only to other philosophers. The senior professors in other departments the young are now unlikely to have a chance of talking to. They are scarcely likely so much as to cast eyes on the Vice-Chancellor, except perhaps at a graduation ceremony. What is much worse, the Vice-Chancellor is most unlikely to talk informally to the young lecturer. While it is generally agreed that a secondary school should not grow to such a point that the headmaster no longer knows the teachers, that is now the regular situation in universities so far as the relationship between Vice-Chancellor and teachers is concerned. The large universities indeed are more like states where one does not expect to know, as a citizen, the rulers except through the media, where one's personal relationship with them is confined to filling in forms for statistical consumption, than they are like the community Sydney University was in the 1930s.

There were plenty of senior people—scientists, humanists, economists, engineers, medical professors—it was worth listening to or discussing with. Eric Ashby, later Lord Ashby, the Professor of Botany was one of them. Amusingly enough, when he decided to return to England in 1946, he told me that this was because he had become too involved in university administration and wanted to get back to research. Ashby, who was to become one of the best-known university administrators of our time! My experience has been that academics who become heavily involved in administration can seldom happily return to the cloistered life of a scholar or a scientist. But Ashby had a breadth of interest, a liberality of mind, that attracted me, although Anderson remained suspicious of his Englishness and we were both critical of the 'fellow-traveller' attitudes he shared with so many English scientists at that time.

Anderson was a great puzzle to such people; many of the causes he defended they thought of as being ultra-conservative, even when he would still have described himself as a Marxist. So, for example, he was a warm defender of the traditional classical education, suspicious of educational reform. In his *Short History of Australia* Manning Clark identifies Sydney with an attack on philistinism and puritanism, preaching culture for 'great souls', whereas Melbourne, he writes, stood for 'providing happiness, culture, and material well-being for all'. In Sydney, the scientists were on the Melbourne side, and expected Anderson, as a Marxist, to be on that side, too. In fact Anderson saw Marxism, as Trotsky did, as looking towards a future in which producers generally, not just the fit but few, would be 'great souls'. He stood far closer to Matthew Arnold than he did to Nietzsche.

A genuine Nietzschean, however, came to Sydney in 1937 as Professor of Greek, Enoch Powell. At that time he was still very much a follower of A. E. Housman, even in his attitudes to women. He ate at the university in the evenings, as evening lectures, not celibacy, forced me also to do. We talked quite a lot in these evening hours. He was then far from being the married, Anglican, secretary of the British Conservative Party that he later became but I can easily envisage the wartime career that culminated in his becoming a Brigadier. Eventually he reverted to his natural role as a one-man Opposition. When I heard him deliver a speech on Northern Ireland to a British House of Commons reduced to utter silence as soon as he stood on his feet, I could still see in him the same person who had addressed our Philosophical Society on Nietzsche's 'will to power'.

The same person, too, who, when I approached him about a difficult passage in Plato's *Phaedo*, replied that it was an 'obvious interpolation'. No wonder his students called him a 'textual pervert'. But he was an extraordinary person and I was sorry to see him go after less than two years, even writing one of my rare poems on this occasion. He fitted Manning Clark's description of 'Sydney' far better than John Anderson did.

I did not spend all my time talking with senior people. There were plenty of able young lecturers, with many of whom my paths were also to cross in later life. In German, there was Ralph Farrell, to whom I owe a double indebtedness; he introduced me to the Mahler song cycles and to wine. In French, it was Derek Scales who greeted us on our first family trip to Paris, finding hotels and restaurants for us. The names roll on. Jim Nicholls in classics with his exceptional generosity of spirit coupled with a wry humour; Trevor Swan in Economics; Ian Hogbin in anthropology; Noel Butlin and Max Hartwell in economic history; Cecil Gibb and Bill O'Neill in psychology; 'Mick' Borrie, then a social historian, later a demographer; Harold Oliver, Alec Mitchell and Wesley Milgate in English; Gordon Greenwood and John Ward in history; 'Roberto' Shaw in Italian; (Sir) Rutherford Robertson in botany; Frank Lyons, who led one of the most productive scientific groups in the history of Australia, including Alan McColl, John Cornforth, Arthur Birch; Jack Still in biochemistry. Many of these will be familiar names, at least to specialists, outside Australia; some of them were to be leading figures in Australian university life. No doubt I have overlooked some individuals, and am dismayed to realise that so many of them are now dead; I always assumed that I would be the first to go. But my roll-call illustrates what a wide range of discussion was available in the Sydney University of my time. We were not a bad lot, really, even if most of us were appointed by methods that would now be frowned upon.

I was sustained during the 1930s by the belief that at the end of that decade I should be eligible for study leave. Anderson had been abroad in 1938, characteristically avoiding England except for participating in the annual philosophy conference, held that year in Durham, where he caused a sensation by speaking in the discussion on every paper. He had returned through the United States and had been particularly taken by the Philosophy Department in Berkeley, San Francisco. There, he thought, I should go. Since I by this time had a wife and a small child and the fare to San Francisco via Vancouver would be cheaper than the fare to England, that suited us fine. (There were no study grants then, although I would be paid my salary.) So we booked a third-class passage to Vancouver, which entitled us to a cabin with bunks and the right to share with other third-class passengers deck-space roughly the size of a back-yard swimming pool. All for nothing. My leave was to be approved by the Senate on a Monday morning. But on the preceding Sunday evening, 3 September 1939, we were listening to a radio perform-ance of *Turandot* when we were informed that Australia had joined England in declaring war on Germany. That was that.

Not until 1948 did I finally travel outside Australia, not until 1960 did I finally give a lecture at Berkeley, a lecture that aroused an exceptional degree of hostility by arguing that the nature of philosophical problems could only be understood by looking his-torically at the intellectual circumstances in which they had arisen. I was never invited back to Berkeley. Would my life have been very different if I had gone to California in 1939, finally following that advice an attendant had given me when I was still an under-graduate? Who knows.

8

Living in Sydney
1930–1939

UNIVERSITIES HAVE OFTEN been described as 'ivory towers'. This is intended as an insult. Yet it is certainly not to be read as such in the Song of Solomon when the neck of the beloved is compared to a tower of ivory. Poetry aside, the dictionary description of ivory as 'hard, elastic, fine-grained' surely makes of it a substance to be sought after rather than spurned. Imagine a great white ivory tower, in contrast to the dreary concrete towers of commerce, casting its shadow into the sparkling waters of Sydney Harbour, glistening in the sunlight, still faintly visible on the darkest of nights. Or transpose the dictionary definition into a description of thought. Then it becomes a description of the best kind of mind—'hard' in its demand for evidence, 'elastic' in its capacity to change in the light of fresh evidence, 'fine-grained' in its sensitivity to subtleties. What more could be wanted in any sphere of life where thought is in demand, as distinct from blind habit or ruthless brutality?

As for towers, whether ivory, stone or red brick, looking from such a tower at the crowds below we see much that the members of the crowd cannot see. From a tower one can get a glimpse of what lies around the corner, can come to understand the patterns of movement that members of the crowd create but cannot perceive.

The Sydney University of the 1930s was certainly in these respects an ivory tower, beautiful in the sense of being what H. G. Wells called a 'great, good place'; exhibiting, and trying to create, minds that were hard, elastic, fine-grained; encouraging the long, sweeping view. Not always—there were shallow thinkers, narrow pedants—but sufficiently to make 'ivory tower', in the sense in which I have just employed it, a not inadequate description.

If, however, being in an ivory tower means being wholly isolated from what is sometimes preposterously called 'real life'—as if artists, scientists, scholars were imaginary beings living imaginary lives rather than real beings living imaginative lives—we certainly did not inhabit such a tower. Oxford University in the early nineteenth century tried to isolate its teachers and its undergraduates by imposing celibacy, by compelling teachers and pupils to live in colleges, by prohibiting the railways from coming nearer to Oxford than Didcot, thus reducing the temptations of London. Even then everyday human passions could not be wholly excluded. 'Hath not an academic', Shakespeare might have written, 'hands, organs, dimensions, affections, passions?'

As contrasted with nineteenth-century Oxford, Sydney was a mid-city university with most of its undergraduates living at home. The trams stopped at the entrance; to make our way home was to struggle through the crowds, not to look at them from on high. If by living at home we could just survive on our £26, our budgeting had to be as tight as that of the now-prized 'lean and hungry' managers. If we did not have to sleep under newspapers or queue up at soup kitchens, it was still difficult to meet fares, meals, the purchase of books, entertainment, on ten shillings a week.

There were those, like Doris, who sought temporary work in the pre-Christmas period but that was abruptly terminated when they reached an age at which they would have to be paid an adult wage—as Doris's brother, Bob, had been dismissed from a 'permanent' job once he reached the age of eighteen, to be replaced by someone younger and cheaper. In recent years we have often been told that employers could be relied upon not to exploit workers who were unprotected by unions. No one who lived through the 1930s could believe that, just as no one who lived through the 1970s and 1980s could believe that unions will never exploit their power. An English academic once said to me: 'I don't know why you describe the Depression in such dismal terms; we have never been so well off as we were in those years'. Everything depends on whether you had a secure, relatively well-paid job. Professors were very well off, living in spacious houses in expensive suburbs with gardeners and domestic help. We students certainly had no chance of experiencing the freedom of choice that comes with affluence. Every penny had to earn its keep. Doris supplemented her Teachers' College allowance by constructing artificial flowers out of wood-pulp, something she continued to do after our marriage. I remember particularly the elegant white camellias. The returns were meagre, but every little helped.

If 'real life' is extended to mean things other than money-juggling, there was plenty of that, too. Living at home meant sharing the routine problems of our households—households that had no academic experience, so that to some extent we shared their problems without their being able to share our problems. Beyond that, too, there were the 'real life problems' that arose from the deep concern I felt about what was happening in the political and economic life of my own country and abroad—particularly in Germany and in the USSR. And then, too, I was in love, which created problems of its own, in a world often censorious and hostile, rarely sympathetic to young love.

From the top of a tower, I said, you can see more clearly the general shape of movements in a crowd than any member of the crowd can do. I have no intention of going back on that remark, feeling unmitigated hostility to those who would like to pull down the ivory tower and replace it by a one-storey workshop. That still leaves me free to criticise those who, in a modern version of Platonism, are so perturbed by the ebbs and flows they see from above that they withdraw from watching the crowd in order to con-sider how wholly rational persons with perfect information walking along a level path, not confined by such rules as giving way to the elderly or the cripple, could find the best route to their destination with a minimum of effort. They then proceed to construct math-ematical models of the ways in which this best route would vary if the road followed a particular curve or confronted particular obstacles, without any longer interesting themselves in how the crowd actually behaves. (So, when I asked a mathematical econ-omist whether in England policies based on neo-classical economics had been successful I got the response: 'I'm an economist: I am not interested in facts'.)

My weaknesses lie at the opposite extreme; I am too interested in the particulars of life. And yet I am fully aware that the move-ment away from concern with particulars to very generalised universal relationships is often the sole path to understanding the particulars. My objection is only to those who become so fascinated with the ideal worlds they construct that they come to treat them as if they were the actual world, what we normally call the real world being for them nothing but a messy entanglement of appearances.

The 'commonsense' for which I have sometimes been praised can in fact be an obstacle to a deeper comprehension of the world; it worries me less when I am told that something I have written is wrong—anyone can make mistakes—than when critics condemn it as 'trivial' or 'shallow'. This is because I fear that my critics may have pointed to a really serious weakness. I can only console myself by reflecting that what these critics call 'depth' is often pretentious nonsense and that truth does not always lie at the bottom of a well; it can be hardest to see what is there for everybody to see if only they will look more carefully. The boy in Hans Andersen's fairy story who called out 'the Emperor has nothing on' is one of my principal culture heroes. I am not ashamed of my fascination with much that one can only see in the streets: the sidelong glances, the tacit negotiations for position, the alternations of habit and decision, fashion and individuality, every kind of diversity. (A question to another economist: 'What value does economics give to diversity?' Answer: 'None at all.')

At a certain point, however, there is no difference, from the point of view of detailed observation, between looking down on a crowd from above and being part of it; if the crowd is too closely packed, individuals are reduced to the particles of classical atomism —indistinguishable from one another, their relationships simply that of pushing and pulling. The central Sydney streets are now like that. But even in the 1930s, when one could still spend long periods on the footpath talking to friends—to Frank Hutley, let us say, on the intricacies of a law case he had just encountered, a far from hurried conversation—the streets were still busy enough for one to seek out places of refuge that were yet not devoid of opportunities for spectatorship.

For me that refuge, everywhere it is available, is a coffee-shop. Not one of those places where customers sit on high stools at a counter, let alone stand, gulp down a cup of coffee and leave. And certainly not one of those sit-down cafés where a waitress hovers around to clear the table, looking as if she would like to clear you off your chair with the same dexterity. There the impatience of the street is simply transferred indoors. What I have in mind is a genuine coffee-shop where one can sit reading newspapers and periodicals supplied by the proprietor while keeping an eye on those who sit entranced with one another, or can busily write away, or engage in animated conversation, or dreamily watch the crowds flow past—for in an ideal coffee-shop one should be able to do all these things.

In Sydney, as I earlier hinted, we philosophers repaired for our most animated conversation to Grace Brothers, making our way to the tea-room through merchandise that perpetually reminded us of human eccentricities, talking over the 'woosh' of the miniature railways that ran beneath the ceilings, conveying payments one way, change the other.

That Grace Brothers tea-room scarcely accorded with my picture of an ideal coffee-shop. Its model, rather, was the tea-room in one of the less elegant English department stores, in food—sandwiches, scones and cream-cakes—as in all other respects. But it was the best we could do near the university. In the city, too, there was little to offer in the way of coffee-shops.

There was one important exception, Mockbell's cafés. The one Doris and I frequented was in a basement, completely cut off rather than partially cut off from the passing crowds. It did not offer any reading matter but it did supply draughts and chess to be played on its marble tables, in what I later recognised to be its vaguely Middle-Eastern atmosphere. If finance permitted, we would sit in one of its alcoves, sometimes discussing our work, sometimes our lives. It, too, was to fall a victim to Sydney commercialisation. But it set for me a pattern of behaviour that has later persisted, whether under the chandeliers of Poland and Hungary, in French or Viennese cafés, in German conditorei or in Tokyo's fantastic contributions to the coffee-house genre. Everywhere they have served both as refuges and as centres of observation. A time and motion study would show me to be a time-waster on a grand scale. Yet somehow things have got done.

If coffee-shops were hard to find in Sydney, the same was true of those great contributions to diversity, the arts. One must not, however, exaggerate. If it is not wholly unjust to say that Sydney was a cultural desert, it was by no means devoid of oases. Nor is it true that what culture it had was a pale imitation of England.

Consider what I have before me as I write: the programme for the 'Seventh Annual Music Week, 1936'. 'Music Week'—that sounds absurd in a modern Sydney where music is often harder to escape from than to find and performances of the highest order are perennial. But let us look more closely at the programme before allowing its title to determine our judgement.

It begins with a tribute to Signora L. Ferrari-Passmore, the 'Honorary Organiser'. So far as I know, she was not a relative even by marriage; I mention her simply to indicate how much depended on the voluntary efforts of a few people, as often as not women. Although the official patrons set out in the programme were mostly men, the General Committee consisted almost entirely of women and they were prominent in all the executive roles. 'So music week was just a social diversion!' For some it no doubt was, but the organisation of the week must have been very hard work.

The 'Inaugural Ceremony' was for, and by, what we then called 'youngsters', with school bands, school choirs. Even so, there was some Mozart, some Schubert. And on the Australian side a song by Edgar Bainton, the Director of the Conservatorium. Turn another page and one comes to the Sydney Symphony Orchestra, conducted by Sir Malcolm Sargent, performing in the majestic if scarcely comfortable and acoustically unreliable Sydney Town Hall. That orchestra, the visit of that conductor, was the work of the Australian Broadcasting Commission; one can scarcely exaggerate the importance of the Commission in Sydney's musical life.

But what did they perform? Simply muck? Let us look and see. The overture to Weber's *Oberon*, Brahms's first symphony, the suite from *Coq d'Or*, Chausson's *Poème for Violin and Orchestra*, with Ernest Llewellyn as soloist, the *Hungarian March* of Berlioz. Not a tremendously demanding programme, but also not the kind of programme Sargent would have hesitated to conduct before any but an unsophisticated Australian audience.

On the Sunday evening we find what had to be described in those Sabbatarian days as a 'Sacred and Classical Concert', largely consisting of familiar war-horses but surprisingly hymn-less. Then there was a by no means patronising concert conducted by Malcolm Sargent for children (Weber, Delius, Berlioz, Mendelssohn, Richard Strauss), a chamber-music concert (Chausson, Beethoven, Tchaikovsky), a surprisingly international folk-music concert, although with no Australian songs, and what I still recall as an overwhelming performance of Verdi's *Requiem*. But also there was an evening at the Conservatorium entirely devoted to Australian composers, two of them—Dulcie Holland and Mirrie Solomonn—women. I suspect that I should not have warmly appreciated R. H. McAnally conducting the New South Wales Tramways Band in such of his own compositions as 'Triumph of Industry' and 'Vita Triumphalis', but other local compositions by Hill, Hutchens, Evans and Agnew were of a different order, if scarcely world-shattering.

Then there were the rare cultural events that permanently enlarged my concepts of what was humanly possible. Those that had the profoundest effects on Doris and myself, I can quite briefly set out: the J. C. Williamson Italian Opera Company; the Australian Broadcasting Company's tours of Lotte Lehmann, Elizabeth Schumann, Dorothy Helmrich and, above all, Ezio Pinza and Elizabeth Rethberg in duet; the visit, under the same auspices, of the Budapest String Quartet; the seasons by various ballet companies, inheritors of the Diaghilev tradition; the Benjamin Fuller Opera company; the *Herald* exhibition of twentieth-century French and British painting and sculpture; the opening of the Savoy cinema as a showcase for foreign, particularly French, cinema.

The special attraction of some of these is obvious. The lieder were not only a delight in themselves but led us into the world of German poetry. If we could only afford one visit to the 1932 Italian Opera, even the now somewhat despised *Pagliacci* and *Cavalleria Rusticana* offered us a point of entry into a world we had so far known only through the physically imperfect gramophone records of the day, those in my possession mainly second-hand. (I say *physically* imperfect for the second-hand records—some of them, by a curious chance, bought from that Lionel de Noskowski who had taught me at school, when I responded to an anonymous advertisement—were by the great singers of the past.) The colour, the melodramatic force, of these operas were a revelation.

So was the Sir Benjamin Fuller Opera Company, in 1934–35, presenting us with *Siegfried, Tristan and Isolde, The Flying Dutchman, Samson and Delilah, The Pearl Fishers*. The audience was at first small, and we sat in quite reasonable seats in the back of the gallery for our three shillings admission—by now Doris and I were both earning and could therefore afford such luxuries. As the season went on, however, its popularity increased and, in defiance of fire regulations, we sat uncomfortably on the steps, with our minds inevitably turning towards the end of the longer operas on the question whether we should succeed in catching the last transport home. (Fortunately, in the Sydney of those days women had little hesitation about travelling home late at night by themselves on a train.)

No doubt, by later standards, these would seem tatty productions. But we were both as deeply moved by *Tristan and Isolde* as we have been by any opera performance we have seen since. Why the initial slow reaction of the Sydney audience? Opera in Australia had meant Italian opera; this was a company associated with Covent Garden, all of them either British or Australian, so far as I recall, and mainly singing French and German operas. The 'cringe' in this case was towards Italy, not towards England.

For sheer enjoyment, nothing surpassed the concerts by Ezio Pinza and Elizabeth Rethberg—this is one of the few occasions on which Manning Clark's personal memories coincide with my own. Their Mozart duets, especially, caught my heart. But four of the events I particularised had a very special importance; they took people like myself into the twentieth century, in its modernist aspects.

In literature I was already there and by lecturing and writing on T. S. Eliot, by lecturing on other contemporary poets and contemporary American novelists, by talking about Joyce, I was even contributing to a wider public knowledge of what had been going on. But in music and the pictorial arts, even in film—although I was modernist enough to lecture on the film as an art form and had read the leading theorists—I was far from being in a position to act as such a guide. If Bartók, Prokofiev and Hindemith, as introduced to me by the Budapest String Quartet, were by no means disciples of the Schoenberg–Webern school, they still stood as foremost representatives of modernity, reacting against the Romanticism that in Australian concert halls was largely identified with serious music. (Consider the Sargent programmes cited above.) The combination in Bartók of genuine folk music and fresh tonal experiments, too, gave body to Anderson's classical aesthetics.

Painting was one area where it was difficult to be enthusiastic. In the principal galleries there were neither old nor modern masters. The emphasis was on nineteenth-century painting, both pre-Raphaelite and French. 'Modern' art was something we were acquainted with only in rare and imperfect reproductions. There was no way of following up the Marc reproduction we had been shown at Teachers' College.

In this atmosphere the three great ballet companies who performed in Australia each year between 1936 and 1940 were a revelation, not only as demonstrating to me that the Serenaders' version of *Les Sylphides* was scarcely a fair sample of the art of ballet—I succeeded in not seeing that ballet again for a surprisingly long time, so horrendous were my memories of it—but by the brilliance of their costumes, their settings, to which so many modern artists had contributed. Then there was the music by a variety of modern composers, Stravinsky in particular, but going much further in *Icare*, where Lifar invited Sidney Nolan to paint the decor and costumes for a ballet set to minimalist music.

While the ballet companies were visitors, their influence was a permanent one. They had created not only an appetite for ballet but some capacity for satisfying it. A few members of the ballet stayed in Australia, including the beloved Helen Kirsova, who founded in 1941 the first professional ballet company in Australia. Edouard Borovansky established the Melbourne-based company that made Melbourne the home of classical ballet in Australia. It was visitors, then, collaborating with local talent, who made possible the later achievements of Australia in classical ballet and, as an offshoot, the contemporary dance theatre of the classically trained Graeme

Murphy. One nice thing is that the emergence of such companies upset British stereotypes about Australia.

Towards the end of the 1930s the position in respect to painting began to change, with the emergence of some of Australia's leading modern painters. Sydneysiders, however, were scarcely conscious of this fact. This was a time during which many painters lived in exile. So my namesake, John Passmore, was out of Australia between 1933 and 1950. And some of the most interesting painters were at work in that still distant city, Melbourne. We went to what exhibitions there were in Sydney, but the only painter I should have liked to buy was Roland Wakelin. It took a great exhibition, perhaps the most important in Australian history, to destroy that isolation. It was brought out in 1938–39 by the Melbourne *Herald*, then owned by Sir Keith Murdoch. In Sydney, its patron was the *Daily Telegraph*. (Let it not be said that the newspapers of that period were wholly philistine.) Here were no fewer than eight paintings by Bonnard, four by Braque, seven by Cézanne, eight by Gauguin, nine by Picasso, five by Rouault, six by Signac and Utrillo, eight by van Gogh, five by Vuillard, and two or three each by many others, such as Chirico, Chagall, Dali, Derain, Dufy, Ernst, Gris, Laurencin, Léger, Modigliani, Seurat, Soutine and Valadon. Oddly enough, there was nothing by Renoir or by Degas, who were later particularly to capture the Australian fancy.

The impact of such an exhibition on a young man who up to this time had not seen a single work by a single one of these artists is so easy to imagine that I need not pause to describe it. There was a representative collection, too, of the best-known British painters. I was certainly attracted by Paul Nash, Stanley Spencer, Edward Wadsworth. Indeed, the first print I ever owned was by Nash. But it was the Continental painters who revolutionised my way—and not only *my* way—of looking at painting. There were a few interesting sculptures, too, but at that time sculpture meant much less to me than it now does.

The Sydney exhibition opened on 20 November 1939; the Second World War was under way. It would obviously have been too dangerous to send these paintings back across the sea. Unfortunately most of them were packed away until well after the war—

in the basements of Sydney and Melbourne art galleries under the surveillance of curators who were hostile to every form of modern art. But some were put up for sale. There was one we particularly wanted to buy, Léger's *La Bicyclette*. It was on sale for £34. But my salary had still not reached £400, almost the sole income coming into the household, there was a wife and a daughter to keep and the ominous uncertainties of the war hung over our heads. Generally speaking my later regrets attach to what I have not done rather than to the positive actions I have undertaken; this is a striking instance.

The last of the great events I mentioned was the opening of the Savoy cinema to show Continental films, beginning with the splendidly rambunctious French depiction of sixteenth-century Flemish life, Feyder's 1935 film *La Kermesse Héroique*. So far as time and money permitted, I had continued my cinema-going. I was far from alone in this; in the Great Depression the new and splendid cinemas —no equal magnificence was to be seen in Sydney—were refuges from the horrors of the times. The first time I took Doris out it was to the most elegant of them all, the Prince Edward—long years ago destroyed to make room for yet another anonymous office block. The film we saw was called something like *Viennese Nights* —anyhow it was full of Strauss waltzes in Hapsburg Vienna. No masterpiece, it was immensely popular as an anti-depressive. (Why were we not dancing rather than looking at other people dancing? No one, I said, could ever succeed in teaching me to dance. Doris, in contrast, was an excellent dancer. Giving it up was for her a real loss. Every such relationship involves sacrifices as well as gains. But it is hard for me to point to anything I sacrificed.)

To return to films. The ordinary programme was made up of at least two films, generally preceded by a newsreel. There might, as well, be a musical interlude, often performed on a Wurlitzer organ, sometimes accompanied by community singing with the words on the screen and a little ball bouncing over them to indicate just where we were. Community singing was a bond in those desperate years.

The 1930s was the period in which the United States largely took over the world of popular entertainment. It witnessed the decline of Australian film-making. There were some good English films but we used to groan when the first of the two films turned out to be of British origin. As in so many other British ways, British films were either first-class—rather rare—or third-class. The Americans had a much greater talent for making the B-grade action films that commonly made up the first half of the programme. What the Continental films did, however, was to introduce us to quite new ways of looking at human beings and the world at large, a world where sensuality could be comic rather than sinful. It must be remembered that we were still a basically Anglo-Celtic society.

No doubt when Australians in the 1930s boasted of being '98 per cent British' that was genetically speaking a gross exaggeration. Yet apart from the Cantonese of the Chinese market gardeners, I never heard a foreign language in the streets until, quite late in the 1930s, I heard to my astonishment an interchange in French in a grocery store.

That remark ignores sailors. Sydney still had something of the atmosphere that Joseph Conrad described, an exceptionally maritime city, as the name of the 'First and Last' inn at Circular Quay made plain. Great liners from all over the world pulled into wharves at that same Circular Quay from which the local ferries departed; timetables were sometimes disrupted as tugs pulled the liners away from the farewelling crowds. Other boats moored in the harbour; close at hand were still more wharves at Darling Harbour and Woolloomooloo.

On my first visit to London, I was surprised by an absence, almost never seeing a sailor in uniform. In Sydney one might see them anywhere. Making their way in groups through the streets, the sailors spoke a great many different languages, Eastern and Western. But they were exotic visitors; the men in the grocer's shop were perfectly ordinary-looking citizens. That was why the experience of hearing them talk French was so memorable. The few, mostly German, refugees whom our government reluctantly admitted undoubtedly made a difference, particularly to the size of audiences at concerts and theatres and in such minor ways as introducing us to briefcases. But we did not experience the cultural and scientific surge that grew out of their arrival in much larger numbers to a more generous United States. Our failure in generosity was as tragic as the failure of our galleries to buy the French paintings.

'Continental ways' suggested to most of our parents nothing but sexual wickedness and the eating of strange foods, certain to make one ill. If we intellectuals were too advanced wholly to acquiesce in the first of these views, the second largely held sway. To be sure, in country towns there was usually a milk bar that was generically known as 'the Greek's', but one did not go there to eat moussaka; its menu was steak and eggs, with fruit salad and ice-cream to follow. There were a few very simple Chinese restaurants, and an occasional restaurant, generally expensive, that called itself 'French'. But into none of these had I ventured until the 1930s had drawn to their end. Almost no native-born Australian would have known what moussaka was; I ate a pizza for the first time in New York as late as 1960. In short, in culinary matters, as in so many other ways, one looks back at the 1930s as a world apart.

To return to the arts. I have said nothing about drama except for passing references to Shakespearian companies and to the Sydney University Dramatic Society. It is the harder to remember what went on in the theatres of those years because not a single one of the eleven theatres still survives, although there are two that have taken over the names of the theatres I once knew. There is perhaps no city in the world where such destruction has taken place; even in the bombed cities of Germany the old theatres were substantially rebuilt.

My theatrical recollections do not stretch far beyond the operas, the ballets, the Gilbert and Sullivan operettas and the music halls. I did not scorn any of them. My theatre-going has never been confined to 'serious' work. If Cole Porter's musicals delighted me, so did many works of much less quality. Once, in Melbourne, I was asked how I intended to spend the afternoon before a Wednesday evening lecture. When I replied 'at a second-class musical, if there is one on', my philosopher-interlocutor was deeply shocked but I was unrepentant. Sometimes I act like a 'tired businessman'.

There was certainly some drama to be seen, most of it as a result of the efforts of that heroic woman Doris Fitton, eventually at the Independent Theatre in North Sydney, with productions that were technically professional—400 of them in all, in half of which she acted—but did not approach the quality of the imported opera and ballet. Still, there were performances of such American dramatists as O'Neill and Tennessee Williams that came nearer to the heart of the matter than did the too-brisk productions I later saw in London. The visit in 1932 of Sybil Thorndike and Lewis Casson in *Saint Joan* and *Ghosts* had no similar successors that I recall. There were a few Australian plays, largely thanks to Doris Fitton, but only the musical *Collitt's Inn* won any popular favour. The combined effect of 'the talkies' and the Great Depression diminished people's interest in any but spectacular entertainment. Along with the entertainment tax (or so the entrepreneurs argued) this led to the widespread closing down of theatres or their transformation into cinemas. It was, indeed, as others before me have said, the worst decade in the history of the Australian dramatic theatre.

Reading, then, had to be our recourse. Reading was aided by the emergence of Penguin books, so far as our pocket went, and, as far as availability went, by the arrival of the Roycroft bookshop in Rowe Street, which made possible my excursions into contemporary poetry, and the nearby bookshop in Martin Place devoted to books in European languages. There is no street in the mid-Sydney of today comparable to the old Rowe Street, with its bookshop, its little theatre, its café. Now nothing more than an undistinguished lane at the back of a large, equally undistinguished, bank building, it was then the place one was most likely to meet the Sydney intelligentsia. Most of my purchases nevertheless were made in the secondhand shops of Castlereagh Street; there were many who had been forced by the Depression to sell quite extensive libraries at sacrificial prices.

If there was not much drama on the stage in the early 1930s, there was more than enough of it in the streets. The poverty, the unemployment, were more obvious than they are sixty years later. It is no doubt true that even an exceptionally severe Depression is not so devastating to endure in a relatively warm seaside city like Sydney as it is in colder climates. The young unemployed could make their way to the beaches. Older people did not die of hypothermia; even in winter it was possible to sleep in the parks under blankets of roped-together newspapers. (How wonderfully versatile the *Sydney Morning Herald* was! A blanket, a lining beneath linoleum, a stuffing for wet shoes, a window-cleaner, a shelf liner, toilet paper. It made me feel at home, decades later in Moscow, to find *Pravda* equally versatile.) One could fish, too, with some hope of success in waters much less polluted than they now are.

For all that, there was in the first half of the 1930s a smell of fear and misery in the air, most marked in those who blamed themselves, or had wives and children who blamed them, for having lost their jobs. With so small an income oneself, it was hard to know how to respond when approached by someone who assured you that for a few shillings he could make his way to a possible job. John Anderson, in those years still a convinced Marxist, opposed all welfare efforts as ways of obscuring the class struggle. Nonetheless, in Turramurra where he lived he had the reputation of being a 'soft touch'. On my £26 a year, as compared with his £1200, I could certainly not be that. But it was a miserable business saying 'No' or 'Sorry', without really knowing whether this was a genuine case where even the little one could give would help. How to choose between such cases and 'stings'? Sometimes I was certainly stung.

I have carried over from those years a detestation of any situation where people are forced to beg, a situation at once demeaning to the beggar and giving rise in the rest of us either to ruthlessness or to a complacency that is equally dreadful to observe. (A woman in Trieste rises from a seat in an outdoor café to bestow a few coins on a beggar and returns to her seat with an appalling look of self-satisfaction; I continue to sit there, feeling guilty but not willing to do anything to encourage a demeaning practice. Or have I simply become mean after long years of straitened circumstances?)

One thing we did not have to worry about was crime; in that respect there was less street drama than there is now. Of course there were areas of Sydney into which no sensible person penetrated after dark. In his novel *The Dirty Half-Mile*, Lance Peters has described these areas as they were in the early 1930s with the special relish of a New Zealander. For the ordinary suburban citizen, however, crime was not a problem in the Great Depression as it has been in the 1990s depression. I went through most of my life without personally knowing anyone who had been a victim of even minor forms of crime.

There were various reasons for this. First, the only drugs in wide use were relatively inexpensive: nicotine and alcohol. Secondly, few of us had anything portable that was worth stealing, especially at a time when, with so many forced sales, second-hand prices had fallen to a very low level. Until relatively late in life, I never carried more than ten shillings in my wallet. We, and the people I knew, possessed no jewellery, no car and nothing corresponding to the videos, portable stereos, microwaves, television sets that are now the favourite booty of housebreakers. Thirdly, houses normally had people in them at varying times of the day, and an array of trades-men and pedestrians passed through the streets.

Public transport, too, was relatively crowded at all hours but not to the degree that made pickpocketing easy. It was largely true that petty crime did not pay. (As I write these words I hear an alarm ringing. Almost certainly a false alarm, but I had better go and look. There have been so many burglaries in this quiet street that people are taking precautions.)

The drama in the streets, then, was not of the violent sort. With its repertoire of beggars, soup kitchens, unemployment, anxiety, boarded-up shops, people with holes in their clothing, it resembled one of Beckett's plays. Fortunately, as in the case of those plays, it was often relieved by a touch of mordant Australian humour, in the manner of Lennie Lower or some of our cartoonists. The caption of one of the most famous of these cartoons, 'Stop laughing, this is serious!' reflects the way in which people did manage to laugh, however serious the situation might be.

In the political sphere, however, there was drama of a more threatening kind. In retrospect it might be described as theatre of the absurd, but as lived through it was rather seen as a narrative that might prove to be the first act, perhaps even the second act, of a tragedy. The details of this narrative have been described by many historians: how the New South Wales Labor Premier, Jack Lang, was converted by the pressure of events from being a moderate social reformer into a passionate rabble-rouser who decided to repudiate the payments due to English investors; how the federal government intervened; how the British governor dismissed him from the premiership in May 1932 and called a new election in which Lang was defeated.

At Sydney High School I had already encountered an earlier stage of this drama. Lang was determined to abolish the Legislative Council, the house of review. It was an appointed, not an elected, body and Lang appointed several members who were supposed eventually to vote for their own abolition. One of them was my fourth-year English and History teacher, D. M. Smith, who was universally known as 'Deadfish', from the glazed look in his eyes. One day I picked up my evening paper and found a rhetorical headline splashed across the first page: 'I came into this House to scorn; I remained to admire.' Naturally, then, he voted against the abolition of the house as, to Lang's fury, did his co-appointees. It was this sort of frustration that changed Lang's approach.

There is certainly, with the wisdom of hindsight, something absurd in the fact that Sydneysiders, generally so sceptical of politicians, could be seen wearing badges with such slogans as 'Lang is Right' or even 'Lang is greater than Lenin'. (Fortunately, T-shirts had not yet been invented; the doctrine that every area of space is a place for an advertisement was not yet widely held.) Those who proclaimed Lang's superiority to Lenin were not setting him up as a super-communist, although his conservative opponents often described him as such. A fierce nationalist, he saw socialism in general as a foreign doctrine; in his first term in office, he was a typical welfare reformer of the old school, sometimes increasing state control, no doubt, but with the relief of the poor and the ill a major consideration.

No less absurd in retrospect is the notorious official opening of the Sydney Harbour Bridge in March 1932 when Captain de Groot, mounted on a horse, cut the ribbon before Lang could do so, Lang being unworthy, in his view, to undertake such an historic task. De Groot, to his indignation, was temporarily taken off to an asylum. The stuff of comic opera, surely. One can readily imagine a musical accompaniment to De Groot's cavalier deed, preferably performed by a Bavarian band.

We were at the opening. How could we not be? Doris had daily travelled under the bridge in the ferry on the way to the university; I had daily watched its construction from the Manly Ferry for four years past. (The arch was built first, held up by cables until, to our immense relief, the two sides finally met. It was amusing to hear tourists wonder how cars were going to cope with what then looked like an extremely steep hill to the top of the arch.)

Every now and then mysterious tickets came my way through my father. So I had once found myself on board an ocean liner, moored in the harbour, to watch the harbour event of the year, the Anniversary regatta, although I found exploring the ship much more fascinating than watching the unintelligible races; at another time Doris and I had tickets to the grandstand of the Royal Agricultural Show. This time it was to an enclosure from which we could walk out on to the roadway of the bridge when the opening ceremony was completed. We did not see the gallant captain's cavalry charge; we were on the wrong end of the bridge. But it is amazing how rapidly the news spread. Anyhow we were among the first to walk across the bridge—if not in total solitude. Indeed all Sydney seemed to be there.

'A Bavarian band'—it is not by accident that this came to my mind. For it was precisely what was happening in Bavaria that led these events to terrify me. As the badges illustrate, Lang was a charismatic figure. John Anderson had rather a weakness for such persons and once told me that Lang was 'the only real politician that we had'. In contrast, I was terrified of charismatic leaders, rabble-rousers of any kind, and saw in Hitler's rise a striking case of what I feared. 'Lang is right' badges naturally aroused my mistrust. 'Lang is right about X' would not have troubled me, but nobody is right all the time.

The Bavarian band I imagined was, all the same, to accompany De Groot, not Lang. For Captain De Groot was a member of the New Guard, a quasi-military organisation. It was impossible not to think of the New Guard—which was said to have something like 100 000 members, no doubt an exaggeration—in terms of what was happening in Europe. As it happened, my sense of alarm was unjustified. Lang took his departure peacefully; there was none of the 'maintain the rage' attitude that followed Whitlam's dismissal by the Governor-General in 1975. Conservative governments came to power both at the State and the federal level; despair began to lift as Australia gradually made its way out of the Great Depression. The years that followed were exceptionally stable even if also exceptionally philistine.

But my political anxieties were by no means assuaged. By 1934 I was already predicting, or so friends have told me, that war would break out before the decade ended. Not for a moment did I see Hitler as a clown. Reading *Mein Kampf*, I did not dismiss it as a rhetorical exercise. A Nuremberg rally was broadcast and filled me with chilling horror.

There was only one reason for doubting the stories that were beginning to filter out of Germany. This was a time when exposés began to appear of propaganda in the 1914–18 war. My favourite example was from Germany: 'In England young women are cutting to pieces young men who do not enlist'. The evidence was a threat in *The Times* personal column: 'If you are not in uniform by the end of next week, I shall cut you dead'. But there were equally weird examples on the British side. This aroused a sense of unease.

Were these stories about anti-Semitic atrocities mere propaganda, spread perhaps by communists? Some said so because it suited them to believe as much. After all, others argued, Germany was famous for its cultural achievements, in science, the arts, the humanities. Many of their greatest figures had been Jewish. Surely these stories must be false. I did not believe that they were. But one could excuse those who thought otherwise.

I cannot recall exactly who said that the primary duty of every democratic government is to ensure that when it loses power it will not, by its actions while in power, make it easier for its successor to govern in an anti-democratic manner. But I thoroughly agree. One of the main points I should make against the Labor government in the 1980s and 1990s is that it did not govern on that principle; it is now much easier for an authoritarian government to exercise power of such a kind that dissidents could not possibly oppose or evade it, so many are the computer lists on which we all now find a place.

The need for personal budgeting of the most careful kind persisted through these events, as it did in the case of most other people whose young adult life was passed in the Great Depression. This need was accentuated when Doris and I decided that we could no longer postpone marrying. Life in our respective homes had become more and more difficult. In Doris's case, as her brothers and sisters grew up, working at home was more and more of a problem. My culture clashes with my mother, as she became ever more absorbed in astrology, numerology and all the rest, became even more frequent. She really worked at these activities, making use of astronomical Ephemerides, and became an expert in the eyes of many of her friends. It was difficult for the same household to contain an Andersonian secularist and a mother so prematurely 'New Age'. I regarded her with a mixture of affection and intense exasperation, never failing in later years to write to or telephone her weekly, although our daily encounters could be quite maddening. Taking evening lectures, as I had to do thrice weekly, was also a strain, with night-time public transport back to Manly infrequent and wearisome and the dimly lit ferry not conducive to reading.

Doris and I had our doubts about marriage, both moral and financial. On the first front we disliked the relationship between marriage and contract, as if we were assuming property rights over one another. As for finances, the rule in the Department of Education at that time was that as soon as a woman married, she had to resign. Furthermore, the period of Doris's bond was not yet ended and if we married there would be a considerable amount of money to repay, although the department did agree that its arbitrary reduction in allowance and its inability to provide jobs for us had slightly reduced the amount of the bond.

Why did we not simply live together? That was not so easy then as it has since become. It would have provoked moral outrage in a great many quarters, involving dismissal rather than resignation if the fact had been discovered. And we certainly did not want to have an illegitimate child, at a time when that carried with it real disadvantages for such a child. So we married as quietly as we could in a registry office with witnesses off the street, letting our family and close friends know but hoping that the department would not find out. But the baby did come along and, although Doris kept her secret as long as she could, resignation was inevitable.

That was a great loss to the Education Department. She had rare gifts as a teacher, being able to take a class full of children whom other teachers had dismissed as impossible, in whom indeed they produced a breakdown, and make something of them. What she liked about this was that she was given a free hand, with no anxiety about results in public examinations. But she found teaching very tiring. Later in life she did a little individual tutoring, again very successfully, but never faced a class again. The Education Department did finally abandon its ban on married women teachers but that was not for some time to come. They did not offer part-time work. It was quite enough for her to cope with our children and a demanding husband, more and more needing assistance as he settled into a dual role as lecturer–writer.

Where were we going to live? Our first choice was Kings Cross. That will no doubt sound surprising to those who associate that region of Sydney with strip shows, prostitution and drugs, but Kings Cross did not assume its present condition until after it became a favoured rest and recreation centre for American troops, especially after the Vietnam war. We were charmed by its leafy streets and its strangely 'village' atmosphere. That atmosphere has still not wholly vanished; one can still experience it if one goes shopping for food or a newspaper in Kings Cross in the early morning. The friendly atmosphere, just a kilometre or so away from the centre of the city, makes me nostalgic for its past. Its proximity to the life of the then less febrile city and to the Botanical Gardens was something we looked forward to. Our feelings were by no means unique; 'the Cross' was the chosen residence of several writers and painters, although I doubt whether any of my university colleagues lived there.

Alas, the £2 5s rent for the furnished apartment we wanted was somewhat beyond our means. We discovered that it would be cheaper to take a flat in the largely working-class suburb of Ashfield, west of Sydney and only about twenty minutes away from the university by public transport. That would be unfurnished, but we could buy furniture on time payment. We should then still be paying somewhat less than the cost of the Kings Cross apartment. The rent was £1 12s 6d; the furniture cost in all £72, which we could repay in instalments over two years. We persuaded ourselves that this furniture, with its shiny veneered surface, would soon be replaced in better times. In fact, these better times were not to come until twenty years later, after the furniture crossed to, and returned from, New Zealand.

We took up residence, then, in 'Tuncurry', close to the railway station and the nearby shops. I do not know when people stopped naming houses. The replacement of names by numbers was one of the first stages in the war against individuality that has been so notable a feature of our century. I gloomily anticipate a time when people will be introduced to one another by their tax-file number. The choice of a name for a new house used to be a family affair, demanding more imaginative effort than the naming of a new-born child. In his *Kangaroo* D. H. Lawrence comments on the passion for such names as 'Wywurrie' and 'Torestin'. In contrast, Lawrence hoped to find himself in a house with an Aboriginal name. 'Tuncurry' was such a name, although I suspect that it was more immediately a nostalgic reference to a northern coastal town thus denominated. Its meaning, 'plenty of fish', certainly did not apply to the surroundings of our Ashfield flat.

Living was cheap in Ashfield, although the food was of poor quality. Yet we would push the baby in her pram up the low, rolling hills in search of still cheaper food. Super-economising was the order of the day. They were, however, by no means unhappy years; I did my university work conscientiously, preparing lectures at home since I had no room at the university, and began to write more consequential articles, but I was not the work-machine I sometimes became in later years. There was more time for living and loving, for my wife and our daughter Helen.

Doris had been respected in her home as a 'scholar' and was by no means, when we were married, an expert housekeeper. I hated the idea of her having to spend all her life in 'domestic duties'. But Doris again displayed her capacity to learn. It was off to the gas company demonstrations for cooking lessons, pushing the child in a stroller. In sewing and knitting she went her own way, making a suit, overcoats for herself and our children for use when we finally went to England—so well that they were condemned as 'too posh' by the schoolchildren there. Then there was her coaching. As a result of all these efforts we managed to cope with our budgeting. At our lowest point we still had ten shillings in the bank. I was paid once a calendar month. Some months had five weeks in them and they were really tough.

Living in a flat was a strange experience for Doris; it took me back in some ways to my boyhood. These flats, however, were a cut above Manly's 'Wentworth'. Only the laundry had to be shared between the four flats and we had a gas hot-water device above the sink. The bath heater, too, did not have the shocking explosiveness to which I had been accustomed; in short, the flat could truly be advertised as containing 'all mod. convs'.

Socially, however, it was rather more like 'Wentworth' than like a modern, anonymous apartment building. Although we only lived there for two years, we had several changes of tenants; with some of them we became very friendly, with others considerably less so. Indeed, when we decided to move, it was partly because new tenants arrived who were disturbed by a baby's crying and unwilling to make concessions in laundry-sharing during bouts of wet weather.

Baby-crying. Helen was not a difficult child and had a notable capacity for amusing herself with toys. But in retrospect it astonishes me that we so religiously followed the instructions of the Tresillian baby clinics to which we repaired each week. The clinics were not American, but they were profoundly influenced by Watson-type behaviourism. We were not Watsonians and had read our Freud but this did not prevent us from accepting, at least in the case of the first child, such stringent rules as 'don't pick the child up when it cries'; in fact we followed all the rules with a fidelity worthy of a better cause. So helpless do young parents feel.

To a degree, then, we were driven out of our flat by an intransigent neighbour. But also we were alarmed by the steepness of the concrete steps that led down to the laundry, although Helen always managed them with great aplomb. We consulted an agent who suggested that we might like to rent a flat he had available in his own sprawling house, 'Glenara', on a rising hill with a double-decker bus to the university. This was one of the miniature mansions that wealthy merchants, some of them Chinese, had built in Ashfield in the last decades of the nineteenth century, when Ashfield was a gentleman's distance from the heart of the city. It was set in very large grounds. When we left it in 1941 one reason for doing so was that we saw the grounds being pegged out by a surveyor for the erection of six apartment houses. There were some splendid fruit trees on which we could in some measure draw and a tennis court we were allowed to use, provided only that I did the line-marking.

The rooms, if very few in number, were huge in size, with beautiful cedar doors. I could ensconce myself at a desk looking out on the garden through a great bow window and still leave plenty of space for the room behind me, which also served as a sitting room. It is a very pleasant experience to look out on a large garden for which one has absolutely no responsibility.

Further up the hill lived Gaius Mackintosh, one of Anderson's first-generation pupils, a strong supporter of his philosophical but not of his political views. At that time single, he lived with his mother and ran a small coaching college, which allowed Doris to do some coaching, but devoted much of his attention to chess. He taught me billiards, which I played with my usual incompetence, terrified that I might tear the green baize surface. Once I beat him at chess with my unorthodox moves. In retrospect, with its tennis court, to which we could invite friends, its great garden, its nearby friends, Ashfield was the calm before the storm.

In some ways life was financially easier for us than it would now be under similar circumstances because there was so little we 'simply had to' buy. No car, no washing machine, no television, no refrigerator. A mangle through which clothes had to be pushed, which did something to strengthen my muscles, a simple radio (which I bought by dashing up early to Winn's in Oxford Street to be first in the queue at a sale), some second-hand records, an ancient wind-up gramophone, a distinctly odd second-hand ice-chest, a bookcase full of second-hand books—these were what we counted as necessities.

All this detail might seem to be unnecessary, but the details marked me for life. If I am now afraid of a burglar breaking in, this is because he might be so angry at finding nothing to steal—no video, no television, no compact discs, no stereo, no computer, only a pre-transistor radio—that he might vent his anger in vandalism. To be sure, we now have a car, but a 15-year old Subaru is not particularly attractive to thieves. Even when I have been in Paris on my birthday, I could not bear to meet the cost of eating in a one-star restaurant. If I visit Sydney, I take with me *Cheap Eats*, not the *Good Food Guide*.

Our early furniture-buying is one of the last times, house mortgage apart, we have ever been in debt. Then surely I must by this time be quite rich? Not at all. I could just about buy a mediocre house in a reasonable suburb of Sydney. Simply, I have not spent my income on things—books and occasional low-priced works of art excepted—but rather, as soon as we could afford it, on going to places and seeing things. But that has been possible only by staying in low-priced hotels, eating at cheap restaurants, as we got used to doing in the Great Depression. We managed in the long run to live a very rich life without ever being rich. Fortunately, I have never thought of myself as a Great Man whose dignity would be injured by travelling economy class.

I give credit to the Depression for this. But sometimes I uneasily remember a story my mother used to tell about the circumstances in which she first met my father. He was serving behind the counter; when she ordered lollies, he would give her the precise amount she paid for, never more. She nicknamed him 'Mingy Passmore'.

9

From Anti-War to War
1935–1941

I
N THE MID-1930S, especially in universities, anti-war movements reached their peak. If in Sydney University there was
nothing quite so dramatic as the Oxford Union resolution: 'This
House will not fight for King and Country', anti-war was the only
cause that could bring together on a single platform university
societies otherwise deeply divided in politics and religious beliefs.

Memories of the 1914–18 war were still fresh, constantly re-
vivified by such occasions as Anzac Day and Armistice Day and by
the activities of the Returned Soldiers' League. The military hospi-
tals were still overflowing with victims of the war; one could see
cripples, mutilated men, being wheeled through the streets. The
cousin who showed me his bullet wounds was by no means unique.
Such novels and films as *All Quiet on the Western Front* helped
to destroy the sentimental–heroic vision of trench warfare. At
the same time war could no longer be dismissed as an eventuality
too remote to be worth considering. The Japanese invasion of
Manchuria, films of the Nanking massacre, Mussolini's invasion of
Abyssinia, Germany's move into the Rhineland made it plain that
the League of Nations was far from being a secure prophylactic
against militarism.

An anonymous article in *Freethought* May 1936 illustrates
how the Andersonian circles in which I moved saw the situation.
It bore the capitalised title: 'THE RHINELAND CRISIS: THE
COLLAPSE OF THE UNITED NATIONS'. The League of Nations,
it argued, had ceased to be what it professed to be. The powers had
failed to act together in Manchuria, in Abyssinia and now in the
Rhineland. 'The structure of international relations from now on',

so the author tells us, 'will be based on a confused system of pacts and treaties between groups of two or three states'. 'On every side', he went on, 'there is feverish activity in armament building, on every side the fear of war'.

So far this could serve as a reasonably representative expression of the way in which a great many students saw the situation. A fundamental error the article contained—the belief that the Maginot line guaranteed that Germany would not invade France—was also very widely held. Poring over diagrams in the *Illustrated London News* had led me to accept that conclusion without hesitation. (This was a lesson in scepticism for the years to come.) The differences between students arose when the question was what should be done to prevent war from breaking out. There were some who put their faith in united prayer, some who saw the only hope in a strengthening of the League of Nations, still others who advocated parallel disarmament.

None of this satisfied the intransigent Andersonians. They saw peace as being realisable only after the dissolution of capitalism and the creation of 'an international working-class movement to set up a world union of socialist communities'. Only such communities, it was argued, could be relied upon not to make war on one another as capitalist countries regularly did. One finds a similar ascription of blame for war to capitalism, of hope for peace to the international workers' movement, throughout this *Freethought*. It begins with Anderson's initial explanation of the political thrust of these articles. Freethinking, he tells us, is a defence and promotion of freedom of inquiry and therefore freethinkers must criticise whatever institutions they see as being hostile to free inquiry, capitalism in particular. Such criticism is exemplified in articles attacking Christian Socialism and that favourite target, the New South Wales Education Department.

If it was natural enough in the Australia of the 1930s, with its preposterous censorship, to identify capitalism with hostility to freedom of inquiry, was it not absurd to appeal to socialism as the alternative? Were not socialists notorious enemies of free inquiry? Stalinists, yes, the reply would have come; true socialists, as exemplified by Trotsky, not at all. For it was Stalin who was seen as having betrayed the revolution. Stalin's 'socialism in one country', it was freely granted, would by no means remove the risk of war; it might indeed intensify the risk.

To most academics outside the Andersonian group, all this was very puzzling. That anyone should happily describe himself or herself—for there were women contributors—as a communist and yet dissociate him/herself from Stalin, how was this possible? Trotskyism was far from being the household word it was to become in post-war England. Indeed, it never came to be a familiar concept in Australia, although some Trotskyists were later to play a conspicuous role in the battle against communist leadership in the Australian trade union movement.

The comings and goings of the Trotskyist 'Workers' Party', the ruptures and coalitions of its eight or so members, are extensively described by Susanna Short in her biography of her father, Laurie Short. I was sometimes present in Anderson's room during his meetings with Short, and admired this vigorous young trade unionist who was subsequently to play a large part in Australian political life. (This was never in positions of direct political power, which he always refused to seek.)

Where did I stand in all this? My relationship with the Workers' Party never went further than, under a degree of pressure, making a financial contribution to their lively publication, the *Militant*, and I was not a leading figure in anti-war activities. In both cases my position was an awkward one. So far as Trotsky is concerned, I was on his side in his attacks on Stalin and I found him more interesting to read than were most communists, although I did not believe that everything that had gone wrong in the Soviet Union was Stalin's fault or that the Soviet Union was still, for all its defects, a workers' state. There were many features of capitalism to which I was hostile, then as now, on moral grounds. To be thus critical of capitalism, to be thus hostile to Stalin, that is about the limits of my Trotskyism. Difficult as it will be for my friends, or even acquaintances, to believe this, my memory is of sitting silently through the discussions between Anderson and Laurie Short.

My position in relation to the anti-war movement was even more difficult. Detesting war made my detestation of Hitler still more profound, but my detestation of Hitler made it impossible for me to be unreservedly anti-war. If I had no doubt that Hitler would invade other countries, I had no doubt, either, that if he were at no point resisted such Western civilisation as existed would be totally destroyed.

Anderson disagreed with me right up to the end about the inevitability of war with Hitler. A statesman's task, he argued, is to find compromises reasonably satisfactory to both sides; there must, he thought, be some way of achieving such a compromise with Hitler. He was one of the many distinguished philosophers who welcomed the Munich agreement, although I by no means stood alone in seeing Chamberlain's 'peace in our time' as wishful thinking on a grand scale.

If I could not wholeheartedly support disarmament, since I had no doubt it would be one-sided, I did not want to find myself on the side of jingoists, armament manufacturers and the like. That is not the last time that I have had to face this kind of problem, liking and sympathetically understanding people who took a position I regarded as intellectually untenable, finding myself intellectually on the side of people I did not like and whose motives I did not share.

There was another reason for my not being inclined to speak out. Close to Anderson, even sharing his room much of the time, I could see how emotionally wearing public controversy could be, for all that he enjoyed the fray, and how time-consuming. I resolved never to be, on any serious scale, a 'public intellectual'. For I was determined to write, and writing demands unbroken periods of quietness. In later years I secured some measure of praise as a 'public intellectual' but that was when I formally retired, had no teaching or administrative responsibilities and had abandoned the idea that I might some day write the kind of book I had wanted Anderson to write.

It also had to be a condition of my intervening that nobody was saying what I felt had to be said. For there again Anderson unintentionally taught me a lesson. In faculty meetings he weakened his influence by so constantly being the first to speak, often at length and against a motion that would obviously be rejected. The time to speak up, I early decided, was only when enough discussion had ensued to make it plain there was a real risk that on a serious question a decision would be made to which I was strongly opposed.

My attitude to Hitler was by no means unique. It consoled me to listen to 'The Watchman' (E. A. Mann), a commentator on the Australian Broadcasting Commission, who managed to sustain his independence in the face of governmental hostility. He was sometimes rambunctious, imperialistic, but he refused to take the official line on the Spanish Civil War or on Munich, and attracted a large popular audience.

An important factor in the general underestimation of Hitler was an unwillingness to believe—to believe that a country whose culture was so advanced could have fallen into barbarism, to believe that such an obvious mountebank could be anything but a puppet for behind-the-screens political figures who would surely be accessible to rational argument, to believe that a civilised world could once again embark upon the unmitigated savagery of war. At the same time there was a willingness to believe that the more horrifying stories that came out of Germany were propaganda or were deliberately circulated by armament manufacturers with a view to selling their wares.

To this it must be added that there were those who admired the dictators, and more particularly Hitler. One can quote as an example a speech made by Australia's Foreign Minister, Henry Gullett, as late as 1938, lamenting Hitler's territorial ambitions, but extolling him for having restored Germans' 'pride and their power' and offering them 'a future of great glory'. As for Mussolini, Gullett praised him for 'his genius, his patriotism and his irresistible stimulus and almost superhuman capacity'. Then, too, there was anti-Semitism. That was rarely blatant. When the Melbourne philosopher Paul Edwards told me that Australian anti-Semitism was one of the reasons why he moved to New York, I was surprised and complacently took this to be a Melbourne peculiarity. But Leonie Star's biography of the jurisprudentialist Julius Stone makes plain the extent of 'Establishment' anti-Semitism in Sydney, taking much the same form as it does in England.

As well there were Australian right-wing farmers who took Mussolini as their ideal figure. Many others saw Hitler as an economic miracle worker. Still others, who by no means supported Hitler, nevertheless cried 'Cassandra' when I forecast war—to which

I would not unnaturally reply that, after all, Cassandra turned out to be right. These were particularly the Melbourne philosopher-communists.

Doris and I ventured to Melbourne in 1936. That was an historic moment for me: the first time, so far as I know, that any member of my family had deliberately travelled interstate. Doris, in contrast, had visited relatives in Queensland, from which her parents had moved to Sydney, and told stories of tropical fruits, of houses on stilts, and even of cattle swept downstream in the great 1918 Rockhampton flood—exotic memories to which I could only feebly respond by saying that it once snowed when I was in Yass. But she, too, had never visited Melbourne. After a thirty-six-hour journey in hot weather with no air conditioning and windows that could only be opened at the cost of admitting particles of coal, Doris was strongly inclined to the view that her first visit would also be her last.

The journey to Melbourne led us through Yass and up to that point was familiar to me. We stopped at railway station after railway station that was simply a shed, often with no sign of habitation, leaving us time to meditate upon the wide spaces of plain, littered with the white corpses of ring-barked gum trees, undulating towards the distant 'Australian Alps'. But once we changed trains at the border we seized upon every discernible difference—in the colour of trains, the shape and size of public notices—that persuaded us we were indeed in a foreign land.

To see that Melbourne was very different from Sydney required no such attention to minute detail. Its straight broad streets, laid out in the classical Roman fashion, its compactness, the deciduous European trees, the long summer days, all made its distinctiveness clear. I made it plain that I liked Melbourne, a statement that won general approval, although the reason I gave, that it was like a large country town, was not always received with total enthusiasm.

What I did not at first perceive was that Melbourne differed from Sydney in the range and intensity of its fanaticism. That came out in its football, a strange game with, I am told, a lineal relationship to Gaelic football, which aroused in its supporters a degree of intensity I had never experienced. I gradually came to realise, too, that the Irish Catholics were both more Irish and more Catholic, the Orangemen more Orange, than anything I had encountered in Sydney. So, too, the academics were far more likely to be ultra-conservative or fervently communist than their Sydney analogues.

Most of this only fully sank in on subsequent visits to Melbourne. I became conscious of Melbourne University communism and its relative optimism in 1938, at a Melbourne congress of the Australasian Association of Psychology and Philosophy. Anderson was abroad, distancing himself still further from communism in talks with Sidney Hook and Max Eastman. Acting as a surrogate, I found myself subject to a cross-examination on Andersonianism that lasted, unsupported, until 3 a.m. So far as that involved a debate with the Wittgensteinism that Paul and Gasking had brought to Australia, I could both enjoy and profit from such an interrogation. What startled me, however, was to find that Paul and Gasking had also brought with them a Cambridge communism that ran far deeper than what I had already encountered in Sydney from Cambridge-educated scientists who were rather to be described as 'fellow-travellers'.

These I admired as scientists but found naive in their admiration of the Soviet Union. They belonged to an organisation, the Fellowship of Scientific Workers, which from time to time issued statements. In my youthful aggressiveness, I criticised one such statement in a radio programme, and received from the secretary of the Fellowship a quasi-threatening letter. He had been informed, he wrote, that I had said their document was 'theoretically feeble' and he proposed to take corresponding action. I could only reply that he was inadequately informed; I had said that it was *both* theoretically feeble *and* factually incorrect. Silence. I had not been bullied at school for nothing.

But in Melbourne I was dealing with full members—although I did not realise this at the time—of the Communist Party, experienced in its intrigues and confirmed in their faith to a degree that made my pessimism seem nothing short of ridiculous. I was amazed to meet very intelligent philosophers who were optimistic not only about the remote future, but even the immediate future—in 1938! They must have been convinced that any further advances would bring down upon Germany the irresistible forces of the Soviet

Union, backed by the united workers of the world, provoking a workers' revolution in Germany. Or something like that scenario, in my eyes totally incredible. Still, I must in justice add that when Germany invaded the Soviet Union, I heard John Anderson and Stephen Roberts agree that the Soviet forces would crumble before the German forces, and I had no idea whether they were right.

The ex-Cambridge philosophers did not take orthodox communism to Melbourne. Although the official centre of the Communist Party of Australia was in Sydney, its intellectual centre was in Melbourne, especially after the appearance of the journal *Proletariat* in 1932. There Anderson had published his early pro-communist articles. The rejection of one of his articles was a factor in Anderson's break with the Communist Party. But it was in the Cambridge or Cambridge-influenced members of the Philosophy Department— which also contained the very respectable figure of Professor 'Sandy' Gibson, already embarrassed by having a communist brother—that I first encountered full-blooded communists.

I could scarcely expect to have any effect upon them. Manning Clark makes it clear in his autobiographical *The Quest for Grace* that Anderson was regarded in Melbourne as the devil incarnate, and people like myself as the devil's emissaries. Nevertheless, Paul and Gasking were prepared to sup with the devil's emissary, thus exhibiting, I suppose, communist charity. Some of their disciples, I suspect, would neither have accepted our hospitality nor offered it. Notoriously, disciples are likely to be more fanatical than their masters.

I felt myself fortunate to be able to share the company of the slow-moving but warm-hearted Douglas Gasking and his wife Betty, an historian of biology. The rather withdrawn, introspective George Paul and his wife Margaret, bringing with her the aroma of the Ramsey family, fertile in philosophers, theologians and archbishops, were not so immediately accessible, although Margaret could be quite maternal, thrusting food before me on the ground that I had the reputation—then quite justified—of being rather absent-minded about eating.

It was in our closer contacts that Doris and I discovered how little proletarian Melbourne University communists could be. As guests they made it apparent that they had been used to having servants. But the matter of my cap was more significant. I liked my cap, especially in the chilly mountain air of Katoomba. I had observed, to be sure, that when I wore it suspicious-looking characters would hastily move to the opposite side of the pavement. That scarcely troubled me. But the Melbourne communists argued me out of it, saying it made me look like a manual worker. So much for the solidarity of workers and intellectuals in the communist ranks!

A second incident illustrated the degree of political participation of the Melbourne University communists. It must have taken place in 1940–41, when the Communist Party had been banned. The Pauls were our household guests. Margaret Paul returned to our house from an outing in a somewhat panicky state. She had lost her purse and could not remember quite what it contained; she was afraid that it might contain incriminating documents, which the police would find when the lost purse was taken to the police station, as we in those days expected to happen. There was a degree of alarm and confusion when the police rang, but relief when the supposedly incriminating document was uncovered; it turned out to be the constitution of a newly formed Melbourne University Conservative society, which Margaret had noted down for later controversial reference—or perhaps infiltration?

How far Security was in fact interested in them I do not know. It is quite likely that in Security's eyes Andersonians and the Melbourne philosophers were in the same basket, even after Anderson had become hostile to the Soviet Union, with all the bitterness that comes from disappointed hopes. I have it on excellent authority that Security had a considerable file on Anderson and not, I suspect, as the man who had destroyed communists' hopes of infiltrating Sydney University as they had infiltrated Melbourne.

When it came to serious work on Marx and Marxism, Sydney, not Melbourne, was the centre. Paul wrote an admired article on Lenin's theory of perception but the major writings on Marx and his followers, critical but not dismissive, came from Anderson and his pupils Harry Eddy and Eugene Kamenka, whose explorations of Marx's ethical thinking have a classical status. Melbourne University Marxism was by no means a learned Marxism; it was Marx as read by the Communist Party, describable rather as Leninism and, what Anderson had come to think of as being much the same thing, Stalinism.

Melbourne University communists broke away from the party at different times, but always with the conviction that anyone who broke away before them did so on inadequate grounds and was therefore intellectually suspect, and that anyone who broke away later was morally blind. When, in later life, I was involved in discussion with a Melbourne philosopher who had remained attached to the party until as late as the Hungarian intervention, he defended his faithfulness on the ground that not until then had the true colour of the Soviet Union been revealed. To my exasperated response that well before that time much had been written that exposed the character of the Soviet Union, his contemptuous reply was 'Oh, you people read'. He was dead right.

In all of its forms, the anti-war movement proved unavailing. Neither prayer nor negotiating skills nor the 'international working class' called a halt to Nazi ambitions. The Civil War in Spain was rapidly followed by the Australian declaration of war on Germany and, after Pearl Harbor, on Japan. How did the anti-war movements react?

The Spanish War had sharply divided Australia, bringing home the fact that Australia was only in theory a monocultural country. Some Catholic school-children were told to clap when Franco appeared in newsreels or even to offer up prayers for his success. Their symbol of the war was the violation of nuns. Others, including myself, favoured the Republicans. The symbol in our case was the bombing of Guernica. But most Australians, whatever their sympathies, accepted the official policy of non-intervention, even when, like myself, they detested the hypocrisy with which it was surrounded. Only a few went off to join the International Brigade.

It has to be emphasised how little we knew about what was going on in Spain, reliant as we were on what the cable companies let us read. Not until the publication of George Orwell's *Homage to Catalonia* (1938) did we have any real conception of the internecine warfare within the Republican ranks. One can scarcely exaggerate Orwell's influence on my generation, from *Down and Out in Paris and London*—published in 1933 but having its most powerful effect in the uncensored Penguin edition of 1940—which left many of us with a permanent mistrust of the Salvation Army, through to his better-known post-war writings, although they came as less of a shock to long-time critics of the Soviet Union than to those whose admiration for the wartime courage of Soviet citizens misled them into a general enthusiasm for the Soviet Union.

When it was announced that Australia had declared war on Germany, Australia was much less divided. There were some who resented Menzies' assumption that if England was at war so, automatically, was Australia; there were Irish whose hostility to England was intensified by its declaration of war; there were communists who, after the Soviet–German pact and until the German invasion of the Soviet Union, were obliged to attack the war as another example of bourgeois adventurism; there was the small 'Australia First' group. But there was a notable absence of anti-war demonstrations at the outset of the war.

Equally, however, there was a lack of public demonstrations in support of the war. So far the anti-war movement had been effective. The war was seen as an unfortunate necessity, not as anything to arouse enthusiasm.

Why did not the horrors of Hitlerism provoke a more positive reaction? It had been official policy to play down, or even to censor, critics of what was happening in Germany. The dread of war was so intense that it found expression in hypocrisy and censorship. Very few realised how dreadful life was for Jews and dissidents in Germany; indeed none of us did so, although I read everything about Germany I could lay my hands on. One could see Germany as having lapsed into barbarism, without realising how deep that barbarism ran.

Another thing that distanced Australians from the war, in its first phases, was the immediate ground for it, the invasion of Poland. It was not until the collapse of France and the Battle for Britain that Australia was seriously at war, not until Pearl Harbor and the subsequent fall of Singapore that the war penetrated the entire society and set it on paths that would transform its subsequent history. That war temporarily anaesthetised the anti-war movement until the threat of nuclear war revived it.

10

Relatively Difficult Years
1939–1947

WHAT A HYPOCRITE you are! Difficult years—what non-sense! Did not the Commonwealth government reserve all university teachers, so that the nearest you got to the armed services was a medical examination, which, to general surprise, declared you fit for service? While other Australians fought, you could safely skulk in the Upper North Shore suburb to which you prudently moved. Millions of people were bombed or massacred or died from disease and starvation while you were discovering food and wine. The correct title for this chapter would be 'Lucky Years'.

This is the voice of conscience speaking. Although I cannot deny what it says, I still stand by my title. By any ordinary standards these were for me very difficult years, even if they were by no means as calamitous as what others all over the world had to endure. I still feel a sense of guilt that I was not physically engaged in the war. Yet as a soldier, sailor or airman, I should have been more of a menace to those I fought alongside than to the enemy, as my one attempt to shoot rabbits lamentably displayed. At no stage did anyone rebuke me for not being in uniform; somehow I did not look the part. I could have entered what I thought of as the civilian part of the army with the rank of a major, but I was uncomfortable at the thought of wearing a uniform without doing any actual fighting. I soon found, too, that I could be more effective with my observations, quite unhampered by considerations of rank, than I should have been from inside the army.

To begin, however, with what was relatively fortunate. It is true that we moved in 1941 to rent a house on the 'wrong side' of the marginally Upper North Shore suburb of Roseville, with a distinctly middle-class reputation, even if 'Upper' was technically a geographical rather than a class description. That move was far from being totally advantageous. Our colonial house in spacious grounds—it is difficult to describe a house without falling into the language of a real-estate agent—with its proximity to the university and to familiar friends, was left for a very ordinary bungalow, saved from being totally banal only by a veranda with an extensive view across the Lane Cove National Park to the now less readily accessible Blue Mountains. But we could rent only a very small segment of the Ashfield house, and with a second child would have been pressed for space. Why not simply move houses in Ashfield? The houses available were for the most part very dreary. Yet I must confess that class consciousness played a certain part in our decisions. The public schools in Ashfield were rather tough, and we could not afford private schools. Doris had been to school in Roseville; that would be all right for the children.

Alexander Parade, Roseville, was physically a dead-end, on a hill, separated from the railway station by still more hills and terminating at its lower end in the wilderness park. As often in such cases, it formed a community. At Ashfield we knew none of the five neighbours whose houses backed on to ours; in Roseville we came to know them all. Such suburbs had a reputation for stuffiness, but we did not find that so.

Our neighbour on one side, Charles Magee, was an expert on the diseases of banana and hemp, in demand for his expertise in countries as exotic to me as Borneo, Egypt, Ceylon. Given to hunches, to seizing opportunities, he was impatient of routines. In our garden the banana passionfruit fought for supremacy with a rampant convolvulus and the dreary but prolific choko. Magee decided to try out genetic crosses between our fruit and ordinary passionfruit in order to protect the ordinary sort against a disease that dried them up. It did not come off, but he thus introduced me to biological techniques.

Another neighbour was a businessman named Hill. At one stage his wife was taken to hospital with pneumonia. She was given sulfa drugs, but they did not work, so the doctors resigned themselves to awaiting the perilous climax. That was not enough for him. He made his way to the Public Library and read everything he could find on pneumonia, discovering in the process that a patient with anaemia might not respond to sulfa drugs. The doctors were not pleased when this layman demanded a blood test. Mrs Hill did have anaemia and recovered once it was treated. I have had little reason to complain of my doctors but have always, after that experience, checked their decisions. It showed me, too, that a man I could well have dismissed as uninteresting could have an admirable tenacity and independence.

If human beings in Alexander Parade turned out to be more interesting and varied than we had expected, so was nature. A ridge cut us off from the sea breezes. At our nearest beach, Balmoral, we could find ourselves driven off the beach by a chilly breeze, but would arrive home to a heat only slightly mitigated by the height, a few hundred feet. In this local climate, fauna could flourish. It turned out, too, that the house we were renting had been built over a rubbish tip, a dwelling-place for a variety of insects and spiders. The wilderness park was only a few houses away.

On the good side were the parrots, the honey-birds, the kooka-burras, the wrens, the boobook owl we found one evening contemplating us from the clothes line, or the occasional families of flying foxes. We could cultivate a wide variety of tropical flowering shrubs—poinsettias, frangipani, gardenias. The *monstera deliciosa*, now often to be seen imprisoned between the glass walls of office buildings, flourished and fruited against the hot brick walls of our front veranda, so that we could understand both the *monstera* and the *deliciosa* of its Latin name. The citrus fruits also flourished, yet so did roses, even during the terrible drought years when we were not to have more than three inches of water in our baths—I did not understand how this law could be policed—and the gardens could be watered only by buckets of soapy water from the bath, the laundry or the sink. This was until ferociously heavy rain washed most of the back garden around to the front, to be laboriously replaced.

If in this drought and these storms nature showed its less benign face, the case of the large blue-tongue lizard that found its home in the rough space at the top end of the garden was more ambiguous. Harmless enough in itself, it could look at a rapid glance disquietingly like a snake. Definitely on the negative side was the nest of bull-ants just outside our back door. A bite from one of them severely challenged my enthusiasm for nature. Then there were the spiders. The garage swarmed with poisonous red-back spiders, with their knack for concealing themselves. In later life I never picked up a watering can without checking the handle or grasped a stone or brick except in a gingerly fashion. One can add the ticks. Resting one hot afternoon after pruning, I awoke to find one had penetrated the lower lid of my eye. Above all there was the epic battle between my wife and the most dangerous of our local spiders. I have asked her to describe it:

'John was away for long hours during this period, teaching both in the morning and until relatively late at night. So I had the children on my hands alone and often became exhausted. One night when John was still not home from University, I began to prepare for bed. Taking off my glasses, I went into the bathroom. Seeing what I thought was a button on the floor (I was short-sighted) I went to pick it up. Fortunately it began to move, stretching out the long hairy legs of what I knew to be a dangerous funnel-web spider. It ran into the hallway. I just did not know what to do. There was no weapon near by and I dared not let it out of my sight lest it go into either the children's bedroom or our own. I spied an insect spray in the linen cupboard—grabbed that and began to send spray towards the creature, although I knew full well that it was not supposed to be effective against such spiders. It began to fight, jumping towards me regularly. But I persisted until the contents of the can were gone, with the spider still alive. I then threw the can itself at it, unsure whether I had hit it. It ran into the main bedroom and vanished, completely out of sight, much to my discomfort. I switched on the light, looked into slippers—nothing. There was no use going any further—there were no lights on the adjoining veranda. So, uneasily, I went to bed. Next morning the spider was found on the veranda, dead. It had managed to climb up the wall and almost out into the garden but the effort was too great. I had killed it somehow, be it by spray or by can.'

There are some questions likely to be asked about this statement. Why was I out of the house both morning and night, sometimes for as long as thirteen hours? The answer to that question will have to wait a little. 'Sole care of the children'—surely there was some kind of child-minding arrangement? In fact, American-style child-minding was still unknown. In Ashfield unmarried friends would sometimes give us time off, but in a city as spread out as Sydney is and with wartime transport problems they could relieve Doris only by staying overnight—during the day they were working —in an already crowded house. Our neighbours were amiable enough but none had babies and some of them thought it immoral for us to have had a baby in wartime 1941. Doris could occasionally visit a sister during the daytime, but it was a long push with a pram or stroller up and down steep hills.

If I say nothing about cultural life in Sydney during these years, it was because theatre, films, concerts, galleries were all closed to us. Our sole artistic resources lay in playing our antique gramophone, or reading critiques of what we could not attend, or, pre-eminently, listening to our radio, for all its wartime limitations. From the radio we had music and, to a lesser degree, plays. For critiques there was Neville Cardus, combining cricket and music commentaries for the *Sydney Morning Herald* from 1941 to 1947. It is easy to laugh at his plush style, but his passionate denunciations, his equally passionate enthusiasms, greatly enlivened the critical scene. I remember his fulminations against the ABC Symphony Orchestra for putting on an all-Tchaikovsky concert—something, he said, that could only occur in the most provincial of provincial cities. It was amusing to see such a concert advertised in London when I arrived there in 1948. But I also found that, thanks to his advocacy, I had heard over the radio in Sydney much more Mahler than was performed in London in those years. There was no tendency in the Second World War, as there had been in the First, to ban all German music. The doctrine was that we were fighting the bad Germany represented by the Nazis, not the good Germany of Goethe and Beethoven.

To return to neighbours. Many of my colleagues had taken refuge from Sydney's summer humidity in the Upper North Shore, with its leafy streets and relative height. Several professors, including

Mackie and Anderson, lived in what was indisputably the Upper Upper North Shore. So did the Professor of German, Eben Waterhouse, famous rather for his success in growing and breeding camellias than for expertise in the cunning ways of German syntax. He and his wife had a spacious home with gardeners and domestic help, the sort of thing now confined to 'executives'. (One has to add that a limited amount of domestic help was not expensive. I hated seeing Doris do nothing but housework and for a while we managed to get help for a few hours a week.) Three other academics lived nearer to us and more modestly: G. F. Stout, Julius Stone and Ralph Farrell.

Rotund, cynical, Ralph Farrell, disciple of the bohemian poet and scholar Chris Brennan, has already been introduced as a benefactor, bringing us to consciousness of Mahler's song cycles, Berlin life in the early 1930s, and, above all, wine. It was in Roseville, where he lived with his sister, that these momentous events occurred. The wine was German, sweet in flavour, but it was through sweet wines that those relatively few Australians who then drank wine made their way to wine-drinking. The name of the then favourite, Rhinegold, says it all. We would cheerfully drink, winning cries of approval from our guests, a wine, Porphyry, which is now labelled 'Sauterne'. Even the wine we finally settled on as our favourite, Penfold's Trameah, was scarcely notable for its dryness.

If I say we became wine-drinkers, it was only on those rare occasions when we had guests or, more rarely still, if there was something special to celebrate. The days when we would regularly drink a glass of wine with our meals were still far away. Licensed restaurants were quite beyond our reach.

Julius Stone, the second name on the list of relatively near neighbours, was Professor of Jurisprudence in the University of Sydney, at this time writing the book that was to make his name: *The Province and Function of Law*. He was a very different kind of person, distinctly self-important and very conscious of the fact that he was a professor and I was only a lecturer.

An anecdote will illustrate our relationship. He asked me to read his chapter on logic and law. Finding it very unsatisfactory, I wrote a note suggesting changes to get rid of such extraordinary views as that every non-fallacious piece of syllogistic reasoning is a demonstration, ignoring the fact that the syllogism can be valid even although the premises are false. As it happened, I went down with influenza, as I tended to do in the August vacation. Since there was some haste, Doris telephoned to suggest that he come around to pick up my note. Impossible; fever or not, I was to take it around to his house. I have rarely heard Doris get so furious. I did not go. Stone gave somebody else the task of picking it up.

Discussing other chapters with him, I would sometimes tell him that some particular writer had held the view he was defending or criticising. That immediately became a footnote. If our relationship was reasonably amiable, that amiability was always tinctured with wariness. The footnote episodes left me less inclined than others to speak with admiration of the depth of his scholarship—without abating my admiration for other aspects of his work.

My relationship with the third near-neighbour, G. F. Stout, was very different indeed. Here was a man whose reputation as a psychologist and philosopher was firmly established. He had taught both Russell and Moore and was for a long time editor of the leading philosophical journal *Mind*. I was a nobody, aged twenty-seven when he was eighty-one, but there was not the slightest touch of condescension in his relationship to me; we were friends, for all our difference in age, reputation and beliefs. The Cambridge philosopher McTaggart once told Bertrand Russell that Stout was an 'acquired taste'. I found it exceptionally easy to acquire.

Alan Stout had found for him a kind of retirement home in Killara, attractively placed in a spacious garden. We would visit him there for talk and perhaps a short walk. There was some difficulty in the discussion. He was notorious both for his unusual shortness and the lightness of his voice. 'Stout retreated behind the desk and for the next hour became invisible and inaudible'—that is one contemporary account of him as a lecturer. He had also developed with age a selective variety of deafness. If I put forward what I regarded as a strong point against some view of his, his hearing failed him; if he had a ready answer, it miraculously recovered. But he was quite interested to encounter fresh ideas, largely Andersonian, and was immensely generous and tolerant.

One might have supposed G. F. Stout to be wealthy, since some of his books had been for many years the standard textbooks in psychology. But on that point he issued a warning. He had sold his *Manual of Psychology* for a very small sum—Doris remembers it as £50—with the proviso that he would revise it at intervals, as he did until finally rebelling in the fifth edition. I was warned never to sell outright. If not wealthy, he was also not poor. On a holiday with him in the Blue Mountains in 1940, Doris and I, along with our elder daughter, found ourselves being driven around in a chauffeured car. This was still during the great drought, and Stout was fascinated to find sheer cliff-faces with seams of coal and shale alight from bush-fires. Although he gave the physical impression of being very old, much less able to move about than I am at the same age, he was mentally alert until the very end—his last article appeared just a fortnight before his death in 1944. His death removed from my life not only a friend but the only internationally known figure I could call upon to support me for a longed-for overseas appointment, longed-for because it seemed to be the only possible way of going abroad.

In fact, just before his death, a post was advertised in Johannesburg. Stout refused to act as a referee. He told me that he would support me for a position anywhere else but South Africa. A friend of his who had gone there, the philosopher Hoernlé, had become so politically involved as a liberal that he wrote nothing later except on political issues. Indeed, looking at the University Calendar, I found that the professor of classics was writing articles on the Kaffir click. Obviously too interesting a country.

Shortly after his death a position was advertised in Glasgow. I did not get it; the response was that 'they could not say that I would have been appointed if I had been available for interview, but my not being available made it impossible to appoint me'. (That very British belief in interviews did not work very well; the appointment they made was catastrophic.) It began to look as if I should never get abroad, particularly in the light of the special circumstances that made these years so difficult.

I have still not explained why these were difficult years. The difficulties were first medical, secondly financial. Our first medical ordeal occurred when our 7-year-old daughter, Helen, developed a rather unusual mumps, which turned into meningitis, the second when my father showed signs of senility at the age of sixty-two, the third when our second daughter was diagnosed as having melanoma—a disease of which we had not even heard. Each of these events affected our life profoundly.

Helen was taken off to hospital by ambulance. She was in a coma. The next morning, when we rang the hospital, we were told that her condition was unchanged and that we were not allowed to visit her 'since it might disturb the children whose parents did not visit them'. In our tight little world, fortunately, our worries got through to a neighbour who happened to be a nurse in the same hospital. It turned out that, not knowing what else to do, the hospital had given her a newly discovered drug, which they did not expect to be effective. She had immediately recovered from her coma and was progressing well. This left me with two convictions: first that there was something wrong with hospital priorities when parents would be so badly misinformed about the condition of their children and, secondly, that there was something seriously wrong with any form of egalitarianism that worked on the principle that we should all be equally miserable. Helen naturally felt that her parents had deserted her just when she needed them most, which could have—fortunately has not—ruined our relationship for life.

My father's senility was first evidenced through a decline in his sight. At the age of sixty, playing in a competitive tennis match, he appealed against the light. The *Manly Daily* accused him of bad sportsmanship, an accusation he took very much to heart. It soon became apparent that his eyes were at fault when he had to give up playing golf, no longer being able to see where the ball had fallen. The Gas Company dismissed him at the age of sixty-two with a small pension. Characteristically, my mother was furious, refusing to admit that he had anything wrong with him, talking ominously about suing the company for wrongful dismissal and pushing him to take another job. For the first time in his life he had to commute to Sydney, to smelt lead for John Sands, the printer. The smell of the lead, he told me, made him feel ill. It is possible that he was suffering from his years as a painter, in the days of lead-based paints.

He lived for another ten years, with no decline in neatness and character, until he suddenly turned violent and had to be taken to an asylum, where he seems to have been maltreated and died twenty-four hours later. My mother never forgave herself for having let him be taken to the asylum but there did not seem to be any option in those pre-drug days. I, too, felt guilty for having been out of Australia when these things happened. All my life I feared that I would experience the same fate, particularly when, in my fifties, I suffered from depression with alarmingly similar symptoms. This fear influenced my life-plans in many ways.

The third medical catastrophe was that at five years of age our younger daughter, Diana, was diagnosed as suffering from a malignant skin cancer, melanoma. One of my most searing memories is of Doris returning home from our local doctor with this diagnosis. My visual memory is usually rather poor, but every plant in the garden where I was then working is etched in my memory. The melanoma was quite untypical in its form; the doctor said that 'you could have knocked him down with a feather' when he heard the diagnosis. I could be sure of one thing, so the surgeon told me: the pathology was unquestionable. Not until twenty years later, picking up a medical book in Blackwell's bookshop, Oxford, did I find that a researcher had noted that children diagnosed as having melanoma never died from it. Back to the pathology, to discover a minute difference that had previously gone unnoticed. For twenty years, however, we had to live with what we had been told: that any illness, however minor and in whatever part of the body, could be a sign that the cancer was on its destructive course.

This was not an easy diagnosis to live with. John Anderson observed that I ceased at this point to be a 'Weltkind', someone who feels completely at home in the world. I doubt whether in the full sense I was ever that, conscious of evil and suffering as I always was. In a weaker sense, I am still a 'child of the world', finding hell, heaven and purgatory in this world, in no sense other-worldly. What I did lose was a certain kind of youthful exuberance, becoming middle-aged before my time, if after that ageing only slowly, so that people who knew me half a century ago still readily recognise me, helped perhaps by the fact that I was prematurely bald, like both my father and my mother, and never went in for any kind of hirsute facial adornment.

Doctors have always tended to talk to me as to an equal. It was disconcerting when the surgeon described melanoma, on account of its complexity, as 'a beautiful disease'. On the other side, although we dreaded the bills, all the doctors involved made only nominal charges. They knew that university lecturers were very badly paid. That was the second factor that made life in the period 1939–47 more than ordinarily difficult.

When university teachers were reserved from military service at the beginning of the war, this was conditional on their not receiving any increase in salary for the duration. That was reasonable enough. We did not anticipate, however, a very severe inflation, rising to 25 per cent, so that our real income sharply declined. Neither did we expect the salary to remain at the pre-war level even after the war had ended. Not until 1946 did the *Daily Telegraph* draw public attention to the fact that we were being paid less than bus drivers. Only after this revelation did I finally rise from the £400 per annum where I had been stuck since 1939 to the giddy heights of £600.

The only way of surviving and at the same time continuing to save for travel abroad was by finding additional employment in such areas as adult education and radio, while at home Doris relieved boredom by what little coaching was available, enlarged her skill at the sewing machine and learnt to make gloves and hats. Adult education fell into two classes: university tutorials, conducted in conjunction with the Workers' Educational Association, and university extension lectures, usually consisting of only a single lecture.

During the war years my concentration was on the tutorial classes. My suggestion that I should offer a set of lectures on Early Greek Philosophy received a lukewarm response from W. G. K. Duncan, then Director of Tutorial Classes, and Dave Stewart, the (normally) benign dictator who was secretary of the Association. It was finally decided that the course should be listed and allocated a small seminar room, holding no more than fourteen people. In the outcome ninety turned up, involving hasty readjustments. In subsequent years I taught a wide variety of courses, eventually two a week. Couple that with another two nights a week teaching at the university, along with truncated public transport and the difficulty of making my way home in a world of black-outs or brown-outs, and it will be obvious why Doris had to face such solitary days and, partly, nights. Although I do not know how I got through such long days, I at least had the consolation that the adult students were an interesting lot: refugees, perhaps, who while by no means uninterested in the topics of the classes were primarily intent on mastering English, or sometimes American soldiers who felt the need for some intellectual stimulation. It was wonderful to be teaching classes without having to examine them, without any feeling that they were a captive audience, and to get so wide a variety of responses.

I adopted a special technique: the lecture part of the two-hour meeting was devoted to an exposition and defence of the philosopher or point of view to be discussed. The next half was devoted to criticism from the class, with me acting as the Counsel for the Defence, whatever my own position. The effect was always lively, sometimes comically so. One member of the class was a factory-owner. A few days after a lecture in which I had staunchly defended Zeno's paradoxes, he rang me to say that he had got his engineers to work and they had solved the paradoxes. A member of another philosophy class had been fascinated by Berkeley and my defence of him. She worked in a large store, David Jones, and told me that the next day business was disrupted by arguments about perception. Managing director and shopgirl—that will illustrate the membership range of my classes. In an evangelical spirit, I recall with particular pleasure the case of a plumber who had announced that he could find nothing worth reading in novels. Persuaded to read Dostoevsky's *Crime and Punishment*, he was wholly entranced.

The Workers' Educational Association owned a rambling house at Newport, not far north of Manly, with extensive verandas that could serve as lecture rooms and dormitories. Newport was an entrancing mixture of beach, trees, flowering shrubs, birds and marsupials. By lecturing there at the summer school, I could provide my family, who were allowed to accompany me, with a holiday we should otherwise not have been able to afford. The people at the summer school were often interesting. We met the scholarly

Trotskyist Guido Baracchi, along with three of his wives. At that time I cannot recall knowing a single divorced person, so the impact of meeting three of his wives under the one roof was not inconsiderable. They seemed to be on good terms with one another, united in their hostility to his first wife, whom they accused of having been a financial disaster.

The teaching at Newport could, however, be very hard work. On one occasion the subject was propaganda and the audience included a large group of coal-miners, who became impatient with my attempt to draw distinctions between propaganda, publicity and education. Rebellion threatened until an idea emerged. Why not a dramatic reading of Plato's *Euthyphro*, in which the importance of definition becomes obvious? I was careful to choose the role of poor Euthyphro, flummoxed by Socrates, leaving the role of Socrates to be read by my co-adjutor from the Department of Tutorial Classes. We did, I confess, cheat a little; what we read was not quite 100 per cent Plato, but varied only slightly to make its relevance plainer. There was no further problem with the coal-miners. They saw what I was trying to do and co-operated, illustrating once more the Greeks' capacity to illuminate the contemporary scene. Still, six pounds in weight vanished from my body during that week.

There was plenty of nature around us at Newport. It was wonderful to see the koalas in the magnificent eucalypts that surrounded our simple dwelling-place. Yet the noise of their nocturnal wooing, surprisingly like a blocked water-pipe, made sleep difficult at a time when I needed it. The picturesque native shrubs contained ticks on an unprecedented scale and, as some of my colleagues found to their cost, they had a special fondness for the more tender parts of the human anatomy. All in all, however, Newport was a pleasant, if scarcely restful, interlude in difficult times.

Apart from lectures, I also wrote a number of courses for groups scattered throughout New South Wales. The procedure ran as follows: a cyclostyled lecture was sent out, followed by a set of questions for discussion. The group would read the lecture and respond to the set questions or make any other comments they wanted to. Their responses were summed up by the discussion leader and sent back to the lecturer, who would respond in turn. If possible, the writer of the lectures would pay one visit to the group. In consequence, I visited a number of country towns, always with interest, if with a good deal of discomfort. To my regret I was unable to visit a very intelligent group in Tibooburra in a remote corner of New South Wales. I felt a real sympathy for these small groups, usually led by a teacher or librarian, who wanted to go on thinking in sometimes barren physical surroundings and under social circumstances in which, inevitably, the emphasis was on the physical.

The extension lectures were mainly given to Rotary Club meetings. The American-style ritualised bonhomie I was unenthusiastic about, but individual members took me around and gave me a sense of Australian diversity. There were the Cessnock coalfields, where I heard nothing but Welsh and Scottish accents; there was Tamworth, a substantial country town, particularly memorable for the dam being built there. In every country town that had a dam, it would be shown off as a mark of human creativity, a conquest of nature about which we still had no qualms. This was, however, a conquest in the making, with equipment I had never seen before. It was uncanny to see bulldozers doing work that would previously have employed dozens of men. Being driven around in a jeep across steep slopes was alarming, but contributed to a growing sense that we had turned a technological corner, that things would never be quite the same again.

My involvement with broadcasting was a more complex matter. I was not only a performer but also an object. On 2SM, the Roman Catholic station, Father Rumble and the more sophisticated Dr Ryan, with whom I had some acquaintance, would occasionally deliver a diatribe against something I had said or, more often, something they wrongly interpreted me as saying. When it came to performances, some were more than a little weird and not calculated to encourage confidence in the medium. There was a time when the programme was supposed to be a discussion between myself and a local notable, summed up by a leading Protestant preacher. When the time came for him to sum up, he pulled out of his pocket a sheet of prepared remarks that paid no attention to what either of us had been saying but must have sounded impressive, considered as an impromptu address.

On another occasion I was to engage in a discussion with Brian Penton, then editor of the *Daily Telegraph*. I had read his novel *Landtakers* and had heard a good deal about him from others. He had taken on several young people who had done very well at university in the Faculty of Arts. Very few, however, survived beyond the twelve-month trial period and many stories were retailed about the difficulty in satisfying him. I was scarcely prepared, even so, to find him arriving for the discussion with everything he was to say already written out. I was told to make bridging utterances that would lead on from one of his statements to another. Not being an employee, I refused to do any such thing. Although my resistance somewhat astonished him, we went ahead with a discussion on normal lines.

As so often during the war, we were talking about the future. I remember him saying that after the war I would be able to fly across to England, have a conversation with Wittgenstein, and fly back. To someone who was still wondering about how he was going to get to England in the cheapest possible cabin, this technological Utopianism was somewhat galling.

The strangest experience of all, however—and the biggest fraud —was 'The Army Wants to Know', which was part of the 'forces programme'. Ostensibly, members of the forces sent in questions, which we discussed on air. The 'we' was quite an interesting collection of people. I remember, at one time or another, the war historian C. E. W. Bean, the war correspondent 'Chester Wilmot', the pianist Lindley Evans, Frank Hutchens, Alan Stout, Julius Stone and myself. I was very much the junior—there, I suspect, as a result of Alan Stout's solicitations. We had as our chairman the very popular broadcaster Wilfrid Thomas. Although the questions were always presented as being from a particular soldier from a particular regiment, both these names and the questions were generally invented —how the ABC got away with this I do not know. We would mull them over and decide who was to answer them during a meal before the programme—although occasionally 'Wilfie' would throw in a joke, unprepared, question. Example: 'How does a giraffe get off the ground?' My answer: 'I thought it climbed up its own neck'. But things were not always as bad as that. Who, if anybody, listened to this once-a-week session? I do not know.

There were obvious censorship problems. When giving a solo broadcast, I was told to prepare my remarks in advance, submit them, and then not deviate in the slightest respect from my text. This was something I was not at all used to. My university lectures were always written out in case I was exceptionally ill or tired, but the lecture delivered was very different from what had been written out. I could not bear the thought of simply reading out what I had written. Broadcasting, however, I had to do so. The reason apparently was that some extremely ingenious spy had sent a copy of his talk to a foreign agent and then managed to convey a secret message by deviating from it.

In 'The Army Wants to Know' that could not happen; it was unscripted. With censorship at its tightest, however, there was always the risk that we should say something that was not supposed to be common knowledge. There were special problems after 'Chester Wilmot' joined us. He had just been expelled from New Guinea by General Blamey for criticising the supply side of Blamey's campaign; there was considerable risk that he would explode. So we had to be taped, with strict instructions to say nothing that would involve costly tape cutting and joining.

We were, by my standards, well paid, although a proportion of our earnings went to pay for the preliminary dinner. Fortunately, with severe price-fixing, the meals were relatively inexpensive. I had my first Chinese meal ever in one of Sydney's few Chinese restaurants, in the then minute Chinatown, with linoleum on cheaply made tables and service to match. I also dined in several better-known restaurants for the one and only time. All this acquainted me with peoples and places outside the Andersonian ambit. Did it corrupt me?

The broadcasts so far mentioned have, quite literally, vanished into thin air. One broadcast does survive, however, in the marble fixity of print, in a volume entitled *Prospects of Democracy*, edited by my old friend and rival W. H. C. Eddy. The whole volume illustrates just how concerned we were, for all the daily anxieties of the war, about the shape of the Australia to come, which, we believed, had to be very different from the Australia of 1939. In particular, there was a general, if by no means universal, recognition that Australia was in need of a larger population, which could be achieved only by immigration. The question in dispute was where the immigrants were to come from.

The *Prospects of Democracy* radio series, broadcast in 1943, had an exceptional pattern. On Monday morning an article on a particular topic would be published in the *Daily Telegraph*, at 8 p.m. a speaker would address the same topic, and at 9.30 p.m. the writer and the broadcaster, along with a third party, would discuss the issue. On this occasion Penton and I were respectively author and broadcaster, so the third speaker, George Ashton, had little chance of being heard. My talk had been entitled 'Majority rule—is that democracy?'. I had argued that it most certainly was not, that a democracy was to be defined in terms of the way political, cultural, racial, religious and social minorities were regarded and treated. That led to the question how we were to deal with migrant minorities from non-British countries. I read Penton as having said that we would have to learn how to assimilate such migrants; I argued, against the assimilation ideal, that what Australia particularly needed was much greater diversity—in short, what is now called multiculturalism. Reading John Docker's *Australian Cultural Elites*, where he writes about this long-forgotten discussion, I was quite surprised to find that I had raised such questions in 1943. If I now cite this discussion, it is to illustrate the degree to which what became central issues in post-war Australia were being debated even while the outcome of the war was still quite uncertain. In the light of subsequent experience, I should naturally modify what I had said, but not its main thrust.

It is likely that at some point in my argument I used the word 'liberal'—in the British, not the disconcertingly different American, sense. At this time the urban conservative party, known until its collapse in the 1943 elections as the United Australia Party, was considering whether to rename itself the 'Liberal Party'. (It has always been presumed in Australia that it would be fatal to go to the polls as the 'Conservative Party'.) Upset by my implication that the Soviet Union could not be regarded as a democratic society, a left-wing, crypto-communist paper in Sydney decided that to allege a conspiracy was the best reply. Sir Sydney Snow, a leading industrialist and prime mover in conservative politics, had a seaside house in Newport; I had been at the Summer School in Newport.

Obvious conclusion: we had conspired with the ABC to put on this series of lectures to lend support to the newly constituted Liberal Party. To anybody who knew me—and, I should imagine, to anyone who knew Snow, a man I had not so much as casually met—such an allegation would have been ridiculous. It was, however, a contribution to my education to see how easily the slightest coincidence could be made the basis for a conspiracy charge. No doubt, for those who read that newspaper the case against me was fully proved.

These civilian activities were related to my civilian-style war work. Once again there was an unusual degree of governmental foresight. Our reservation as university teachers had been based on the recognition that at the end of the war there would be a pent-up demand for university education. But it was also felt that preparation for that education should begin during the war. My old economics teacher, 'Bert' Madgwick, was Colonel-in-Charge.

The isolated soldiers, studying for the first time without a teacher, were obviously going to need help. So I wrote a pamphlet in 1942 with the self-explanatory title *Reading and Remembering* and two years later, as the discussion group method of studying came to be used extensively, *Talking Things Over*. These two pamphlets were so widely distributed not only during the war but, through the Melbourne University Press, for a quarter of a century later, that I came wearily to expect, when I was introduced to anyone, to get the response: 'Oh, are you the man who wrote *Reading and Remembering?*'. Unfortunately, such widespread circulation did little for my finances. At first distributed free, the pamphlets were later sold for sixpence, of which one halfpenny came my way. But if these works did nothing for my pocket or for my academic reputation, I felt pleased to discover how many people had found them useful.

There were other pamphlets of my authorship, designed for discussion groups, which were never published outside the Army Education Service. One of these, based on a civilian discussion course, was on propaganda. That had a rather odd history. The editors for the Army Education Service decided that it might adversely affect the morale of soldiers who were still at war, but, oddly enough, that it would be excellent during the prolonged period of demobilisation. They did the editing and sent me a copy, which I did not read, supposing that I already knew its contents. When John Mackie returned to take up a post in Alan Stout's department, he asked me for a copy of both *Reading and Remembering* and the propaganda pamphlet and with his customary diligence set out to apply to the second pamphlet the methods of structural analysis I had set out in the first pamphlet. He then came to tell me that at a certain point my methods did not work at all. The intractable material was in the chapter on newspapers. It turned out that the editor, a journalist, had so mutilated what I had written in order to play down my criticism of newspapers that it made no sense at all, containing even a straight-out contradiction. This was my first experience of the fact that although they have no hesitation in attacking academics, journalists are remarkably sensitive to criticism of their work.

I regularly wrote, too, a column for the *Current Affairs Bulletin* and attended schools for members of the Army Education Service, where my freedom to criticise senior officers came into full play. In general this work was worthwhile, although it was a considerable burden, but from the point of view of my wife this was a very dismal period. When I was at home, I was writing. Weekends and vacations meant nothing. When Doris was not alone with the children, she was sharing a house with a work machine. She did not suffer as other wives did who had husbands in a Japanese prison camp or on a fighting front and she had the advantage of understanding what I was writing and being able, when time permitted, to run a critical eye over it. But it will now be clear why, what with my overwork and her solitude, to say nothing of medical problems, I feel entitled to call these 'difficult years' by everyday standards.

There was one other form of wartime activity in which I was involved, of more dubious usefulness. As the war went on, and especially after the arrival of American troops, a degree of cynicism, unrest and black-marketing emerged. The American soldiers were received with gratitude, but they had possessions that were greatly sought after in a rationed Australia; more generally, where there is rationing there will be black, or at least grey, markets.

Where there is censorship, too, there will be cynicism. After all, we could read in our morning newspaper that 'the *Queen Mary* has just arrived in Cape Town' when it was visibly in Sydney Harbour.

The Darwin bombing was the worst instance. The government concealed the number of deaths by counting only those who were killed
on the land, excluding those who were killed in ships in the harbour
or nearby seas. In contrast, those who fled Darwin naturally tended
to exaggerate the death-rate. So rumours circulated and government pronouncements were received with increasing cynicism.

To help it face such problems, the government set up a body
entitled the 'Prime Minister's National Committee on Morale',
perhaps at the instigation of Alf Conlon, who became its chairman.
Its members were the anthropologists Ian Hogbin and Bill Stanner,
Julius Stone, Alan Stout, the historian R. M. Crawford and the physi-
ologist 'Pansy' Wright. Then there was a member of the judiciary,
Mr Justice Roper, the well-known journalist, S. H. ('Sid') Deamer
and Keith Barry of the ABC. There was also a Research Committee,
consisting of some of these people, myself and, I feel sure, others.

If I am precise about the membership of the main committee
but vague about the one to which I belonged, this is because in his
Government and the People 1945 Paul Hasluck lists the first but
not the second. His reference to the committee is far from compli-
mentary. Referring to the view that its suggestions for the remodel-
ling of the Department of Information had influenced the Minister,
Arthur Calwell, Hasluck bluntly comments that 'Official records do
not support the claims that have been made in public that this committee played a significant role in this or any other matter'. Hasluck
always refers to 'morale' in quotation marks, as if there were really
no such thing. But undeniably there were social problems that came
under this heading. They are clearly illustrated in Tucker's grim
Melbourne wartime paintings, in the Brisbane riots, in the variety of
jokes that circulated. There was the story, for example, of a train
from Brisbane to Sydney carrying American-impregnated nurses,
with the carriages marked 'Return when empty'. Such jokes often
masked deep resentment. While we certainly had real problems to
deal with, I have no evidence that our deliberations were anything
more than talk-fests.

It might well be asked what I was doing on such a committee.
Without losing interest in some of the central problems of philosophy, I had come to be particularly involved with the social sciences,
then largely neglected except in the case of anthropology and econ-

omics. Sensing my interest, Mills invited me to join a small group of economists who met weekly to discuss fundamental problems in economics. On the sociological front, I had read about the methods of social investigation represented in England by 'Mass Observation' and in the United States by polling. These revealed, I thought, how little was known about the way in which 'ordinary people' saw major public issues. I argued that we needed to make such investigations, and this view was later presented by Conlon to an unimpressed Prime Minister. A small office was set up to accept requests for help in such monitoring but, characteristically of the times, nobody came forward to use it. The fact remains that social scientists from around Australia began to talk together and the gaps in our knowledge of Australian society were brought into the open.

One advantage of my being a member of the committee was that it provided me with a permit to travel to Melbourne to attend a meeting, so I could resume disputes with the Melbourne philosophers. I still remember the anxious cries in the corridor: 'Mr Justice Roper has been double-booked'. The agitation this created, and the lack of concern about less highly placed travellers, brought home the fact that Australian egalitarianism had its limits. So did another occurrence that deeply disturbed me. On the return journey to Sydney, I found myself sharing a sit-up compartment with a sailor. It was cold and he offered to share with me his capacious great-coat, used as a rug. Throughout the night he talked fluently about his life as an ordinary seaman and the emergence on his ship of a Trotskyist group to which he belonged. Not until dawn did he ask me what I did. When I told him, he immediately withdrew into silence with a final 'You wouldn't want to talk with a bloke like me'.

With two other wartime organisations I had relations that I cannot recall in detail. (All my papers from this period I cast away before a trans-Tasman migration.) These two organisations were the Army Research Directorate, headed by Alf Conlon, which I could have joined as a Major and with which several of my colleagues were associated, and the Department of Post-war Reconstruction.

It is impossible to give a brief account of Alf Conlon's life and works. Various friends and associates have written about him in a volume entitled *Alfred Conlon 1908–63*, published by the

Benevolent Society of New South Wales, an organisation with which he was closely associated in his final years. But how much of what we are told in that volume is one to believe? Was he indeed responsible for the Australian manpower policy? Was the setting up of the Army Education Service his idea? Some of his admirers would have us believe this and more. One is troubled by disparities in detail. One contributor remembers him as always having a pipe in his mouth but never smoking it, another as perpetually smoking, yet a third as sometimes smoking, sometimes not, although there is general agreement that he would use the stem of his pipe to clean out his ear. It is not at all unlikely that he varied his smoking habits with different persons.

No doubt he was in some respects always the same person, squat and plain in appearance, never raising his voice, exuding a quiet authority that led one to turn to him for advice. Nevertheless he was one of the few people who could adjust his style so as to impress army men—with whom he could compete in expletives—academics and the directors of a benevolent institution. His long period of career uncertainty led to his being able to use with conviction the language of medicine, law and psychology. He also had an organisational tactic that irritated me. He wanted all discussions to pass through his hands. He would ask person A to talk to him about some issue and person B to do the same, but he did not want A and B to meet. He was to be the sole conduit. Obviously this meant that he was very often in conference. When I went to see him about some issue—goodness knows what—quite senior members of his staff would approach me plaintively: 'Will you tell Alf such-and-such? I can never get through to him.' To have worked in his unit would have been an interesting experience, but also intensely exasperating.

There is a story told about Conlon that, legendary or not, illustrates the skill ascribed to him. He had been a protégé of Adjutant-General Stantke—who, incidentally, claims the credit for setting up the Army Education Service. When Stantke fell from grace to be replaced by General Blamey, many in the army, resenting Conlon as an outsider, expected that this would be the end of him; when he entered the officers' mess there was a deadly silence. Yet in fact he was soon to be on similar terms with General Blamey. What had happened? He had gained access to Blamey, according to the story, and said to him: 'You have a difficult discussion ahead of you with the Prime Minister. Say A to him and he will come back with the objection B. You can reply with C, he will respond with D. You will reply with the proposal E which he will accept. That will give you all that you really wanted although you will please him by apparently making concessions.' The discussion ran exactly as Alf had predicted. Whatever the truth of this story, Alf lost nothing by Blamey's accession to power, although it is said that Curtin's death and his replacement as Prime Minister by Chifley did rather clip his wings.

It is generally agreed that 'Conlon's show' had a considerable effect on securing good relations between troops and the local inhabitants in New Guinea, no doubt because Conlon had at his disposal two sensible anthropologists in Stanner and Hogbin, although the role of such men as the lawyer John Kerr, the diplomat-to-be James Plimsoll, Harold Stewart and the poet James McAuley —who described the Directorate as having 'some of the elements of a Renaissance Court, with Alf as the Medici prince'—should not be underestimated.

In 'Alf's court' academics found themselves entangled in public affairs to an unprecedented degree. That was more obviously the case in the Department of Post-war Reconstruction, the wartime home of economists and political theorists. My own contact with the department was very limited, but I was interested in what it was doing. All of us who thought about the future of Australia were united on one point: that Australia should never again experience anything like the Great Depression. 'Nugget' Coombs has described in his *Trial Balance* the excitement with which he read Keynes's *General Theory* (1936) in which Keynes argued that unemployment was not inevitable. In his sensible way, Coombs tells us that he did not cease to read and re-read the classical economists. But Keynes, he thought, had shown for the first time that the economy had a structure in which a relatively small number of factors interacted upon one another. Unemployment, inflation and the like could be reduced by government action. This doctrine reached its peak in the

'Phillips curve', according to which inflation and unemployment varied inversely, so that if unemployment threatened it was only necessary to increase inflation and vice versa. Based on historical examples, it collapsed with the advent of a phenomenon it had ruled out as impossible, 'stagflation', where high rates of unemployment and inflation coincided. There can be no doubt that the plans developed by the Department of Post-war Reconstruction would have made of Australia a considerably more state socialist society than it subsequently became. But whereas civil servants and politicians were delighted by the success of centralised planning during the war and wanted it to continue in peace-time, the people at large rebelled against the regimentation it had involved. They voted against the nationalising of banking, they voted Labor out of power for many years to come. Still a change had come about as striking as the bulldozer. Federal power had greatly increased, and academics no longer kept themselves aloof from political power.

Partridge and Anderson argued in detail against centralised planning. Partridge did so both in an article in *Prospects of Democracy* and in a group discussion course on the temporarily popular Soviet Union—membership of the Communist Party had reached new heights—which led trade unions to threaten to withdraw financial support from the Workers' Educational Association. Anderson, as I earlier said, wrote his classical article, 'The Servile State'.

For some of us the position was more difficult. I agreed with Anderson and Partridge in their hostility to the Soviet Union. Civil liberties were to me as to them of pre-eminent importance. I stood by the principle that no government in a democratic country should make laws, the effect of which would be that if an authoritarian party came to power it would be easier for it to exercise control. Rationing had not worried us particularly; we had no car, so petrol rationing affected us only slightly, Doris made almost all our clothes, we grew most of our fruit and vegetables, we lived and ate very simply. Identity cards and censorship were a different matter. But, as I pointed out to Anderson, the state had made my academic life possible, with its libraries, its schooling, its university scholarships. Yet I did not feel particularly servile.

I could accept the view that markets were the best way of assuring that production and consumption matched, but not every social situation, as Partridge and Anderson would have agreed, ought to be described in the language of markets. I saw no reason for believing that private enterprise is always more efficient than the civil service, let alone less corrupted and more humane—I remembered the exploitation of my father. So I was not prepared to say that a society wholly based on private enterprise would automatically be less productive of servility than a mixed society. Some of the proposals being made for state intervention seemed to me good, others bad, depending on the kind of life they would encourage.

The wartime meetings of social scientists and humanistic scholars had one effect that no one had anticipated. The participants decided that they wanted to continue meeting. With the help of the Australian Council for Educational Research, two research councils were set up in 1943, one for the Social Sciences, one for the Humanities, both eventually becoming Academies. It says something for the width of my interests that I became a foundation member of both councils; it says more, however, for the fact that at that time there was not much competition for membership, whereas now there notably is.

It might have been expected that at the end of the war there would have been less to do. I was, indeed, no longer involved in work for the Army Education Service. But the government was right in its prognostications. Helped by government grants, students flooded into the universities, which were almost overnight twice the size of the pre-war university. I had committed myself to lecturing on logic and scientific method as a first-year course in the Faculty of Economics, and found myself lecturing in the evening to a class of several hundred students, using a microphone but still employing the question–answer style, very much in the manner of a secondary school, which was, I had decided, the best way of teaching logic.

The students were a very interesting collection, often achieving high positions in their later lives. It has been a solace to my vanity that so many of them in the years to come approached me to say how much they had gained from that course. But one felt that one had to control them, particularly by avoiding anything that their active minds could interpret as a *double entendre*. Brown-outs still continued and there was a truncated transport service. Sydney's British-made electricity system was fading away, but the British manufacturers of generators sought American dollars rather than Australian pounds. To come out of such exhausting lectures into a gloomy city was not cheering, and it now took an hour to get home by tram and train. Other nights I continued with my Adult Education lectures, fortunately held in the centre of the city rather than at the university. As for university philosophy, this, with an exhausted Anderson its centre, was very popular and additional staff impossible to obtain. Yet we continued with our conscientious marking. As well, I gave five seminars in the English Department on literary criticism, lectured on Descartes to the French Department, and even talked—only once—to the chemistry honours students, who, in opposition to what I had said, horrified their teachers by declaring that there were no hypotheses in chemistry, that one simply wrote down what one saw in the laboratory.

Partridge went off to Melbourne and persuaded me to take over the course on social philosophy offered to students taking the diploma in social work. I expected to be dealing with a group of hard-faced moralistic bureaucrats, but was quite wrong; they were not only intelligent, but immensely tolerant and ready to laugh about their experiences. Another prejudice blown out of the window. The course also had the advantage of paying me £100. At the same time the then Dean of Arts, the Greek scholar, Dale Trendall, mysteriously secured for me an unprecedented travel grant of £200. We were off!

11

All At Sea

THE DATE WAS 14 November 1947. 'Could that be the Passmores struggling up the passenger gangway? Surely they have not finally made it.' So I thought to myself as Diana 6, Helen 10, myself 33, Doris a shade older, made our snail-like way up the passenger gangway then down again to the two two-berth cabins that were to serve as our home for the next six weeks.

Certainly there had been occasions when it looked as if we should again be thwarted. A cable had reached us from the British philosopher Margaret Macdonald, then editor of the journal *Analysis*: 'Do not come; accommodation quite impossible'. But a little later, in one of those last-minute reprieves characteristic of the Westerns I had loved as a child, there was a cable from Alan Stout's daughter, Judith, who was studying and performing in London ballet. Would we like to take over her flat in Cornwall Gardens, Kensington? The rent would be £6 a week, half my pre-tax salary. Somehow, we decided, we could manage; and in fact we did, thanks to our economising habits, Doris's housekeeping skills, fixed prices, and the strength of the Australian pound as against the British currency.

When Doris and I travel abroad nowadays it is with a single suitcase between us; then it was with twenty-three cases, including extremely heavy cabin-trunks. Blankets, sheets, eiderdowns, towels, all had to be taken, along with the bulky overcoats. Doris had created summer as well as winter clothing, for we wanted to draw as little as possible on the rations we should be granted in London. Getting away from a house that had also to be made ready for tenants was not a simple matter. We allowed ourselves the luxury of

211

a final night in a now non-existent cheap hotel. There I sat up for most of the night marking examination papers for Alan Stout, helpful as always, to take back to the university. Travel is not meant to be easy.

Our departure was, in the manner of those times, a ceremony, a rite of passage. Friends and relatives crowded the wharves in the heart of the city. We were only a few yards from the site of the first Sydney hospital my most remote Australian ancestor had helped to construct. I was, I think, the first of his descendants to make his journey in the opposite direction. As departure time approached, coloured streamers were hurled from ship to shore, shore to ship, breaking only as a tug drew us away from the wharf, then falling desolately into the water, often enough to the accompaniment of tears. To many it would mean their final rupture with Sydney; others knew that, while they were leaving with the expectation of never returning, their ambitions might be disappointed and their return a confession of failure; others, like myself, expected to return but rather feared that they would be changed in ways they did not want to be changed, changed, as some of their colleagues had been, into pseudo-Englishmen. Would loves and friendships, some feared, be broken like the streamers?

For many of the passengers the voyage was six weeks of boredom. I loved it, and got out of the ship healthier than I had ever been before. One reason for my enjoyment was that, away from the anxieties of everyday life and not having to focus my eyes on anything smaller than a quoit, I turned out to be very good at deck games, as did Doris. By the exercise of low cunning, I consistently defeated young men who prided themselves on their athleticism. My sole, very modest, sports trophies are all labelled with the name of a ship. Perhaps the secret was the nursery food which, except for the eagerly anticipated Thursday Indian curries with their savoury supplements, constituted our diet. (We knew what we were in for when our first afternoon tea consisted of slices of buttered bread.) No doubt my release from the horrendous lecture programme of the preceding few years helped a great deal, along with my freedom from the telephone calls and mail that accompanied my editorship of the *Australasian Journal of Psychology and Philosophy* and a multitude of other responsibilities. I might well have felt bored after such a round of activity, however, were it not for our continuous and lively conversations on board the ship.

The passengers in 1948 were very different from the passengers one would now find on ships travelling from Sydney to London. Very few travellers at that time undertook the expensive seaplane passage to England—a ten-day trip, with hotel stops overnight. Every age was represented on our ship, with an age not too remote from ours predominant, and every kind of ambition. It should not be supposed that the more interesting people travelled first class. That was an area which we were not allowed to visit except by invitation. In contrast, first-class passengers were allowed to visit our region and some did so on the ground that the first-class area was lifeless. We, literally the lower classes, were indignant at such incursions, since we were cramped for space whereas they had an abundance of it.

They could reciprocate, however, by inviting us to have coffee, not in their grand dining-room but in a deck-café. Curiosity led us to accept such an invitation from Mary Somerville of the BBC. How that happened, I do not know, but it provided evidence that good conversation was not wholly limited to our class; their cakes, too, were a distinct improvement on our bread and butter.

For a person like myself, with a life-long passion for casual talking and people-watching, P & O *Stratheden* provided many opportunities. It was fascinating to watch the way in which like-minded passengers congealed into social groups, and to observe the processes of social manipulation. A striking example of this was the behaviour of a man in his early-middle years who was on his way to England to defend his doctoral thesis in an oral examination. He first made himself conspicuous by his solicitous attention to elderly lady passengers, adjusting their deck chairs, bringing them rugs, making sure that the beef tea distributed on the deck every morning at 11 a.m. found its way to them. His tender loving care won the admiration of the many unattached young women on board. In just a few days the elderly ladies found themselves deserted and the young women were no longer unattached.

Other passengers were eccentric rather than calculating. There was the man who even in equatorial regions strode up and down the boat deck in a greatcoat, resolved that it was not women and children who would be the first to leave the sinking ship. He was untouched in his solitary peregrinations. An eccentric woman, however, found herself confined. Shipboard respectability did not allow her to free herself of clothes and perambulate naked through the passageways, especially on the captain's deck.

Even ignoring such manipulations, such eccentricities, the passengers were a miscellaneous collection. There was a medley of missionaries, a young ballet dancer who saw in me something of a father-figure, a publisher, a circle of academics, along with many passengers going to see friends and relatives for the first time in many years, more than a little worried about the changes the war would have made. The anxiety was palpable, the more so the closer we got to British shores.

Of the many passengers three or four had a special impact on me, as distinct from being remembered only as pleasant company. One of them, Gwyn James, was the Melbourne University Press publisher who had published civilian versions of my *Reading and Remembering* and *Talking Things Over* but whom I had known personally only through a somewhat acerbic correspondence. He once wrote me a letter in which he set out formally ten or so responses to complaints of mine and concluded with a sentence beginning 'If you consult your contract'. I triumphantly replied to each of his responses in turn, concluding with 'I have never had a contract'. This is on a par for my correspondence with publishers. A later letter was triumphantly displayed by an English publisher as an example of invective. I have heard it described as 'the best thing you ever wrote'.

At sea, however, Gwyn James was most notable as a counter-blast to the American historian, Craven, a history professor from the University of Chicago who had been one of the then extremely rare visitors to Sydney University. If the right ear was burnt by James's virulent attacks on the United States, the left was frozen by Craven's chilling contempt for the British, whom he condemned as whiners, pretending to be badly off only in order to wrench money out of the United States. I should add that he later visited us in our London flat, after having eaten two successive meals in an attempt to assuage his hunger, and solemnly informed me that 'the

English were not getting enough to eat'. But he then had a new theme: 'the ordinary Englishman is completely stupid'. His evidence —'I went up to a bus queue to ask where the bus went to. Nobody knew'. It did not occur to him that Londoners catch their bus by numbers and generally have no idea where it terminates.

On the ship I had asked him, in the idiotic way we Australians do, how he liked Sydney. He had liked it, he said, except for one thing: he could not get warm, not once. His wife told me that he insisted that his Chicago flat be kept at eighty-five degrees Fahrenheit. He was unhappy on the ship until we approached the equator; he lay in the sun when we were withdrawing from it. None of these remarks are of great significance, but his behaviour helped to prepare me for some of the weirder sides of American life.

The two missionaries I talked to—among the thirty or so on board—affected me in a different way. One of them was returning from home leave to the school for which he was responsible in what was then called the United Provinces, now Uttar Pradesh. He obviously loved his Indian students but had long ago given up the idea of converting them to Christianity; it was enough to educate them. The other was a young medical missionary. I had some slight acquaintance with her in Manly, where she lived a very protected life; her father used to meet her at the Manly wharf each day to walk her home. Every Hindu temple, she told me, was a place where unspeakable orgies occurred. Since they were unspeakable, she naturally could not tell me what they were. Unless they could be converted to evangelical Christianity, she did tell me, the Hindus would be eternally damned. Although in the past I had met no missionaries except Jesuits in training for New Guinea, I had nonetheless happily generalised about them—as do anti-Semites who have never met a Jew. Hereafter my wife had to live with a husband who if she ventured an 'always' would automatically respond with some such expression as 'well, quite often'. Empirical generalisations, I concluded, were likely to be false; adherence to them could readily lead to fanaticism.

For all such socially interesting encounters, spending six weeks in a match-box cabin certainly had its disadvantages. In stormy weather climbing up the ladder to the upper berth and disposing one's body on it without hitting the ceiling required gymnastic skills that did not come easily to me. The cabin window had to be closed except in the calmest weather, so the atmosphere could be somewhat stifling. Fortunately the Indian Ocean was preternaturally calm. And all was saved by our Goanese cabin steward, Almeida, who made our voyage quite luxurious, by my not very demanding standards. Just to ask for a bath was to have a deep, hot, salt-water bath willingly prepared in the admittedly austere public bathroom. What more could any man want? Except perhaps to return to one's cabin after lunch to find one's sandshoes cleaned, all traces removed of the formidable sweating produced by tropical deck-tennis. And this with no sign of either grovelling or contempt. We could talk freely, the first time I had any substantial contact with someone from the Indian subcontinent. He obviously loved his family, and his absence from them for two years at a time was a hardship into which only extreme poverty could have driven him. His hostility to his Portuguese governors was apparent; he saw them as exploiting the Goanese to the profit of the army.

If we got on well with our Goanese cabin and table stewards, our relationships with the pursers at the information desk were very different. They were a type of Englishman we had never met before. I diagnosed them as Public School products who combined incompetence with arrogance, obviously regarding our concerns as unworthy of their attention. When they did deign to answer our questions it was almost always with gross misinformation. We met another such Englishman later in the voyage. He purported to be from the British Embassy in Cairo. Boarding the ship at Port Said, he spent much of his time explaining, rather implausibly, why he was not in first class. Directing our attention to snow-clad mountains, he condescended to explain that they were Moroccan. When I pointed out that they were on our right-hand side, not our left, that in fact we were looking at the Spanish Sierra Nevada, he was not at all disconcerted. I began to worry whether the Englishmen whose company I had enjoyed in Australia were untypical, suddenly realising that most of them were either in fact Scots, not English, or came from Northern England. An alarming thought: were Wodehouse's characters not entirely fictional?

Only once did our lowly state create a problem for us. The ship's captain was a brother-in-law of Alec McDonald, then Professor of the History of the Ancient World in the University of Sydney. Alec had given the captain the names of academics on board, and we suddenly received an invitation to have drinks in his cabin. In its idiomatic sense, we had 'nothing to wear'. However, in the traditional Australian style, our deck neighbours came to the rescue with this or that. But problems remained. The invitation told us that our cabin steward would lead us to the captain's cabin. For once Almeida rebelled. To his knowledge, no one from our nether regions had ever been invited to the captain's cabin. He had no idea where it was and, in any case, he could certainly not afford the time to take us to the giddy heights where it would most certainly be. So, asking the way to the captain's cabin as we rose floor by floor, generally being misinformed, we finally made our own way there. I do not think the captain was any happier with the occasion than Doris and I were; he was a naturally taciturn, self-contained Scot. The revelation, for us, was the swift and silent service of the Chinese steward, something far beyond our previous experience.

In a way, that experience was to be characteristic of our future life. We are made awkward by ceremonial occasions. I did not buy a dinner jacket until I was forty-two years old and it is many a long year since I last wore one. There was a period when responsibilities forced me to take a prominent place in social life, but I did so at considerable psychological and physical cost.

So far I have written as if the *Stratheden* were simply a floating hotel. It was that, but after all, we were on it to travel, not simply to chatter or to play deck-games. At first the ship took us on a route that was still, in outline, comfortably familiar. Melbourne was not previously unvisited, Adelaide and Perth were. But everywhere we were greeted by fellow philosophers who entertained us in a familiar language, with familiar food, in a familiar social style. Particular architectural styles, particular flowers or shrubs, minor differences in life-styles or vocabulary might strike our attention, but basically we were still at home. We crossed the equator with the traditional rough-and-ready ceremonies. Nowadays the equator is silently crossed with no pagan invocation of Neptune, no ducking in a baptism-like manner, no issuing of documents to serve as a warranty that one has changed hemispheres.

It was with our arrival in Ceylon that we knew ourselves to be in foreign parts. True enough Ceylon was still a British colony; when we picked up a local newspaper, written in English, it was to find the whole front page devoted to the knighting of the cricketer Don Bradman. Nevertheless the Australia we had left was still a 'White Australia'. There had been nothing to prepare us for the brightness of the saris in the streets, the music and chanting from a Hindu temple we passed, the courtyard of the mosque where we were greeted in a friendly way, the hawkers in the streets, the noisy vivacity of the street markets.

The Eastern style of marketing was felt by the Australians to be harassment; many of them fled back to the ship. Our fair-headed children attracted particular attention in the market we entered. A variety of food was being thrust upon the children, and it seemed rude to refuse it. But we had been told on the ship under no circumstances to eat the peeled fruit that was the normal gift. We certainly did not want to have to entrust our children's care to that Somerset Maugham character—the ship's doctor. He may, for all I know, have been an admirable doctor. But we could not get used to the smell of whisky he breathed out when walking past our breakfast table each morning.

Fortunately, our missionary friend, Weekes, was with us and he addressed the more troublesome vendors with a word that caused them to flee. Many years later, I used the same word to produce the same effect on pestering gypsies in Rome. Don't ask me what it means. A group of passengers soon developed around Weekes. Fifteen of us wanted bananas. Ruth Weekes, used to such markets, took over. There followed a process of counting and recounting, prices and counter-prices, all enunciated at such a loud level and high pitch that Diana was left trembling. But we finally found our way back to the ship, clutching bananas and ready to wash them in Condy's crystals before removing their skins.

Colombo was important as our first experience of an Asian city. It left on our minds an impression of Asia as friendly and picturesque. That impression was enhanced when on a later journey we were able to go to Kandy and the tea plantations that surrounded it. As has so often happened to us in visits to other parts of the world, we saw the apparently friendly co-existence of diversified peoples but not the fearsome underlying animosities.

It was our next stop, Bombay, that created for many thousands of Australians an image of Asia that remained with them. Our two days in Bombay, with its deformed beggars lining the streets, its dirt, its crowds, so disturbed many of the passengers that they thought it quite wrong of the ship to let us go on shore. Even before we did so Doris was horrified to note that it took thirty-five coolies to join the gangways to the ship; their emaciation was obvious.

Nonetheless, we found Bombay, on a grand tour of it, fascinating in its diversity. And one personal contact with its inhabitants displayed their kindliness. To tour, we had shared a taxi with other passengers, but we asked that we be dropped in the centre of the city to make our own way back to the ship. I think we wanted to make some small purchases but we also wanted to see the city at ground level. We got lost. I approached a cheerful-looking postman to ask the way. He insisted on taking us back to our ship, although it was well out of his round; we chattered away as we walked. I have never forgotten him, although so much else in Bombay has the opacity of a dream.

Yet I have never again set foot in India, for all that I have admired its arts, have had good personal relations with many Indians, wrote an article for the first number of the *Indian Journal of Philosophy*, was delighted that the first translation of my *A Hundred Years of Philosophy* went into Hindi, and know full well that Southern India is very different from Bombay. This may be in part because a friend of mine had his health seriously affected for life as a result of a visit there and my own interior is what Victorians used to call 'delicate'. But there can be no doubt that images of Bombay streets played a part in my not even going ashore when my ship berthed on a later occasion in that city. For many years they even put me off visiting Asian countries. In later life, I have made many visits, especially to Japan, but it was a long time before I started doing so. I suspect that a visit to Bombay created stereotypes in many Australians beside myself.

We did not leave India quite behind when we left for Aden, except in a purely geographical sense. An elegantly dressed group of Parsees was now, if invisibly, on our ship. They had not toiled up the gangways. A rear doorway in the hold had been opened up so that they could enter from a private motor boat. They got off, under similar circumstances, in Aden. All this reminded us that the horrendous poverty we had seen in Bombay was not inconsistent with the co-presence of ostentatious wealth, which showed no signs of 'trickling down'. This was more damnable to Australians in 1948 than it would be to Australians in 1996, who are becoming accustomed to a similar situation.

Two other groups of passengers from India were distinctly visible. We had discovered a peaceful lounge, which was ideal for reading or quiet conversation. It was now occupied by a group of women who were obviously the wives of minor officials, leaving an India that was being torn apart in the final steps towards independence. Their arrogance was manifested not only in their treatment of the stewards but in their loud, high-pitched voices, saying nothing of any consequence. So we were forced to flee from our peaceful hide-out, no doubt to their gratification. Our fear of what might confront us in England was accentuated, especially as we had already encountered similar women in Roseville, in this case sent there from Singapore, who in the same high-pitched voices treated our Italian greengrocer, to all of us a member of the family, as if he were not a human being but something of a much lower order.

In contrast the group of Indian students who had joined us in Bombay combined, in a way previously unknown to me, a lively personality it was a joy to communicate with, considerable intellectual capacity, a volubility that exceeded even my own, with an equally developed capacity to be exasperating. I taught them to play deck tennis. One habit I could not get them out of. They would call 'out' when the quoit was anything up to a foot in, and 'in' when it was a foot out, whenever it suited their purpose. It was obvious that they would not be the easiest of people to govern. I politely refused an invitation to contribute to the left-wing journal one of them edited. But so long as one could think of our relationship as theatre it was one of the more enjoyable features of our journey.

Aden was to be our next point of call. It was, in the outcome, to be a direct experience of Middle-Eastern instability. Our radio communications were cut off on our slow voyage across the Arabian Sea, but when we did arrive we found frigates drawn up beside one of the wharves and were told that we had to stay on board. The explanation we were given was that there were riotous encounters between Jews and Arabs, which the navy had to mediate. More likely it was one of a long series of violent disputes between the British and Arabian nationalists in search of independence.

There is no better place than a ship for studying the origins, the growth, the dissolution, of rumours. The rumour in this case was that the Suez Canal was not open to ships and that we could get to London only by taking the long journey around the Cape of Good Hope. That rumour was particularly worrying at our dinner table. The P. & O. practice was to place a member of staff at each table in the dining room, in our case an engineer. The engineer, a Scottish pessimist, had been telling us for some time past that one of our engines was defective—hence the slowing in speed—and that, at best, we should arrive in London a day late. It was scarcely consoling to hear it rumoured that we might have to go around Africa.

The rumour turned out to be a furphy. Was there a malicious passenger who enjoyed generating them? We set out to round Arabia. Now we could see why England had appropriated Aden as a naval base and clung on to it with such tenacity. For it dominated the Red Sea, through which ships, on the shortest route, would have to pass to reach India.

'The Red Sea'—red from algae. Now we were beginning to make our way through an area that had everywhere an historical resonance, whether from biblical times or from ancient literature, as with Daedalus Lighthouse. Historical, literary, mythical memories were aroused in our minds. There is a stretch of the Suez canal that is very narrow. We made our way along it like ships in a desert. On the Egyptian side of us lay what were metaphorically called camel-trains, along with tilled fields and disconcertingly Australian shrubs and trees. To bring us back to reality we felt the need of eating the Turkish delight sold on deck by a hawker who had joined us in Suez and would leave us at Port Said. On the starboard side there was a sealed road, from which a series of signposted roads led into the interior. From the ship one could read the signposts but it was scarcely possible not to see them as pointing to the past. Could these biblical towns, Jericho for example, still exist, as places where human beings lived out their lives, buying and selling?

Of Port Said as we saw it on this voyage I remember only two things—one is that when we bought a small 'Egyptian' purse from a hawker it turned out to be labelled 'made in Birmingham'. The second was that England still had garrisons and naval ships in Egypt, visible at such places as Alexandria. I began to reflect on what we had seen since we arrived at Colombo. As I now describe those thoughts they contain dates that I did not then so precisely know, but, in general terms, my description of what we had seen remains —we were witnessing the decline of that British Empire to which we still thought of ourselves as belonging. It had been pleasant to disembark in Bombay with no formalities except the display of our passport (Craven's American passport wrought no such miracles, so that he was left fuming on the ship), to be going from one pink area on the map to another, to find signposts in English and to be able to have conversation with, let us say, our Indian postman.

At the same time we knew that we were at the end of an epoch. Ceylon was to be granted independence just two months after we visited it. India had officially gained its independence in the very year of our arrival there. Aden, a British colony since 1839, was not to achieve independence for another forty years, as part of South Yemen, but was subject to many riots. Just a year earlier British troops had withdrawn from Egypt except from the Suez Canal area, where they were to stay for another nine years. We were sailing through the sudden collapse of the British Empire and expected that to be a matter of general concern when we arrived in England. But war-exhausted England was not particularly interested; daily bread was its main concern.

Our voyage across the Mediterranean was to me a frustration. We could see, because of the mud it brought with it, the river Nile making its way into the Mediterranean but nothing of the wonders it had passed through. The Greece, the Italy, the France I longed to visit formed, at best, a remote shadow on the starboard horizon.

Not until we approached the Straits of Hercules did we encounter scenery more closely, in the form of the Sierra Nevada and Gibraltar. Meanwhile our summer clothes had been packed away, our winter clothes replacing them. Gradually the decks were enclosed, games became impossible. The ship, from our point of view, was gradually dying.

Then it was across the Bay of Biscay to Tilbury, where our voyage was to conclude. Had we disembarked in Southampton, as was more usual, and travelled by train to Waterloo Station rather than from Tilbury to Liverpool Street our initial impression of England would have been very different. But there we were in the gloomy surroundings of Tilbury, very much the worse for war but at no time a resplendent entry to London.

It was now 17 December, cold and damp, although not horrendously so. We arrived at 5.30 a.m. in darkness. At first light I was on deck, where I met my first Englishman on his own territory, a 'wharfie'. He spoke, and I found, to my surprise, that I had great difficulty in understanding him, although I had so often been told that Australian speech was cockney. But I finally made him out: 'A lot of Goanese on this ship. Not that I mind the Goanese. It's them bloody Froggies I can't stand.' I recoiled in astonishment. That, in general terms, was an experience I was to have again and again in the London of 1948. I was not living in the twentieth century but in the London of Dickens.

Next came our first ever Customs examination. The journey from Port Said to London had a dark shadow hanging over it. A lengthy document had been handed out to us, signed H. M. Customs. I preferred to think of this as the name of a particular person rather than as an abbreviation for an institution, as a more specific object of my wrath. The form had obviously been designed for English tourists returning from a weekend in Paris. We were to mention every item in our possession that had not been bought in England. That meant, in our instance, everything. The general designation 'wearing apparel' was forbidden. Did this mean that we were to write down how many pairs of socks we had, exactly what underwear, in all of our twenty-three cases? It was no use asking our fellow-travellers; this was for all of us our first such experience. The information desk displayed its customary zero helpfulness. 'Surely you know how to fill in a form, sir. Just supply the information you are asked to provide.'

In the end I hopefully wrote 'clothing' instead of 'wearing apparel', but naturally faced the customs desk with more than a little trepidation. Then but a single question: 'Any tobacco goods or alcohol, sir?' 'No'. Next, to my astonishment, his hand raised to his face to conceal what he was saying: 'I'm just going on board for a double whisky myself'. This was a strange introduction to England. No wonder I was feeling all at sea, if no longer literally, at least metaphorically.

Next came the boat-train to Liverpool Street—exceptionally ill-suited to the reception of hectic, child-surrounded bearers of heavy luggage. From the windows we looked out at some of the dreariest scenes in London, accentuated when the train was held up for an hour so that we could better appreciate the architectural glories of Kentish Town. One could recognise the effects of the Blitz but that did not seem to be the sole explanation of its gloom. I knew the London of a century ago quite well from Dickens but it did not occur to me that London in 1948 would still be so grim. Almost without exception British films had not been set in the poorer regions of the city. That is why such plays as Osborne's *Look Back in Anger* were to cause such a stir. Secrets were being given away.

Liverpool Street Station was another nightmare. We could understand nothing of what was announced over the loudspeakers. Our luggage was heavy, our children exhausted. Then I saw a taxi. 'Can you take us to Cornwall Gardens?' 'That depends on how much you are prepared to pay. It will cost you a pound.' I had no option but to accept.

The name 'Cornwall Gardens' had misled our naive Australian minds. We expected a row of houses, each with its garden back and front. But when we turned out of Gloucester Road into Cornwall Gardens our eyes lit on long rows of identical houses, opening directly on the street and confronting their opposite neighbours across a mini-park, fenced but with gates at intervals. Each house had two points of entry. One, also gated, led down to a basement. For the first time I fully understood T. S. Eliot's invocation of 'the damp souls of housemaids sprouting despondently at area gates'. Steps led down to an 'area' in front of the basement door. There were no housemaids to be seen; the erstwhile servant quarters, we discovered, were now all tenanted. Even if the housemaids had su. vived, it was not easy to imagine them sprouting in weather so cold and damp, although easy enough to imagine them being despondent.

For our part, we were called upon to ascend a few stone steps to the columned portico that sheltered the front door of our Victorian neo-classical house. There was an elegantly shaped name-plate—brown in colour, with three names on it in rococo gilt. But who was this mysterious 'Passuedes' whose name stood where ours should have been? We never did find out. Fortunately Judith Stout was there to hand over the keys and reassure us that the flat was really ours. It turned out that the name-plate was by no means an accurate description of the inhabitants of number 73. The owner-ship of that building was so complex that I never really mastered it. Presumably the ultimate owner was a member of the aristocracy, as in most of central London. He would sell a ninety-nine-year lease. The lessee would in turn let out particular flats to sub-tenants, who would then lease them to such short-term tenants as ourselves. But that is not the whole story. We found that we were sharing our flat with three basement-living men. No flat, it seemed, had but a single tenant. There were at least twelve persons whose names should have appeared on the name-plate.

Our flat was on the ground floor, so a stream of visitors would ring our bell asking us where they could find Mr X or Mrs Y. If a tenant tried to improve the situation by affixing a visiting card to the name-plate, our landlady's landlady, who often walked by the house, would immediately tear it off. I thought at the time this was an attempt to keep up appearances at whatever cost to other people. It may rather have been a matter of by-laws, with possible legal problems for a woman who already, we were told, had more than enough of them. But whatever the cause, this action increased our sense of being 'all at sea', of not understanding what was going on.

Our own flat had been the public section of a wealthy town-house, of the sort familiar to us from fiction. It consisted of what had been the reception room, the drawing room and the dining room, all grandly furnished in a High Victorian style. Considered only from this point of view, we have never before or since lived in such grandeur. Our extraordinarily large number of visitors, many of them Australians living in very humble conditions, entered our flat with astonished envy.

If, however, our visitors ventured beyond the reception room, they would find a double bed, constituting our bedroom, occupying the centre of the former drawing room. My study was a large table, nicely placed alongside the large window, so that I could look out on the 'gardens' as I wrote—once being asked through an open window whether this was the Polish embassy. The former dining room had to perform a similar variety of functions. There was a rather uncomfortable bed-sofa that, with quite a few complaints, the children had somehow to share as their bed. A new kitchen-ette, which Doris found surprisingly satisfactory, was enclosed by curtains. Taking a bath involved a visit to the basement. The bathroom we had to share with the three sub-tenants, one an un-employed actor, who now and then acted as a steward on a cross-channel ferry to profit by the opportunities for smuggling, another a playwright who adopted the same method of keeping alive, the third an Alexandrian Egyptian who was busy studying transport. I remembered what the 'embassy' man had said on the ship: 'It would be ridiculous to have a private bathroom on a six weeks trip like this; you could not possibly want more than six baths on such a voyage', and we changed our habits accordingly. The only real problem was that the actor had so many unguents that it was hard to find space for our soap. But generally speaking our relationships with our co-tenants were not the source of any serious problems. The Alexandrian had an ex-Air Force radio, which he occasionally shorted, with the result that the fuses went and our flat would be suddenly in darkness. But he would always emerge on the scene apologetically, if not very helpfully. I became something of an expert on fuse-changing.

To my astonishment, our landlady told us on arrival that our gas bill, which was bound to be considerable, would in fact, without their knowing it, be paid for by our co-tenants. To keep their gas going, they had to put coins into gas-meters—as was common enough at the time—which we then extracted to pay the bill. These gas-meters had been rigged; we would find that the amount we extracted was enough to pay the total bill. Financially, this was an unexpected windfall, but I found it rather shocking. That attitude put me in a difficult position. Foreign coins and buttons often found their way into the meters. Financially challenged—or in the franker language of the time 'poor'—as we were, I could not resist asking that the buttons and foreign coins be replaced by coins of the realm. This is one of the only two cases in which I can remember cheating anybody. (The second instance was a misunderstanding. Since it involved cheating an Aden taxi-driver, it might deserve a place in the *Guinness Book of Records*.) Our financial problems had been exacerbated by the discovery that, although money reached us from Australia only once a month, rent had to be paid in advance on every 'quarter day'—an expression that I imagined to have died out in the Middle Ages.

The other tenants of No. 73 were a miscellaneous lot. There was the woman whom I thought I heard talking amorously to a lover as she climbed the steps, but the loved one turned out to be a dog. There was a theatre manager who engaged in frightful battles with his mistress, which sometimes terminated in the hurling of underwear through a window into the light-well.

But it was the Stonors, inhabitants of a second-storey flat, who meant most to us. He had known wealth as the son of a Liverpudlian cotton merchant who was, however, badly hurt by the Great Depression. This was an interregnum, before he became wealthy again as a result of joining with his brother to form a Radio Rentals Company. Like most married couples, the Stonors were an oddly matched pair. She, a war widow, was a kindly and able woman— later a Brighton magistrate—but bore all the marks of a conventional Southern upbringing. He was exceptionally vivacious, by no means Southern English in his attitudes. They shared their flat with two young women, one a nurse, one a doctor. Their combination was a very useful one for introducing us to English ways. I had come to realise that what I had thought of as our English tenants when I was a boy came either from the Midlands, as did Uncle Harry, or from Scotland and that this was true even of the academics from the United Kingdom I had most often talked with: Stout, Powell, Gasking. There was now a new social world to be dealt with.

I have for some years past felt the need for an abbreviated way of referring to 'the home counties middle-class English'. When this group refers to 'the English' they usually mean themselves. They have even managed to persuade the world that their dialect is standard English. In fact they constitute a relatively small group, but are—or perhaps one could more safely say 'were'—extremely influential. I shall call them 'the English' in quotation marks. They are often surprisingly ignorant of the rest of England, as the Liverpudlian Stonor was clearly not.

The Stonors, just because they were so different, helped to educate us. One night I complained to them when they were entertaining us that I simply did not know what to make of such statements as 'You really must have dinner with us some day. At the moment we are rather tied up.' Rather cruelly Stonor replied 'It's really quite easy. When you are leaving tonight my wife will say this, this, this and this'. When the time came, she had no alternative but to say precisely what he had predicted in precisely that order. He was teaching us that these remarks were simply a ritual that had to be gone through even if the hostess was silently thinking: 'One thing is certain. I'll never invite them again'. The lesson helped us. But it took a long time for me to have any confidence in my interpretation of the expression 'Really?' in its many variations between the very rare 'That's interesting, tell me more' and the very common 'How boring; what conceivable interest could I have in that?', or 'How dare you speak to me: who do you think you are?'

The Stonors also helped to relieve the gloom that was settling on us, the spiritual equivalent of the London fogs that helped to create it. We all agreed that the Christmas party they invited us to, just a week after our arrival, was the most enjoyable we had ever attended, with its mixture of ages and sexes. It was a traditional party with traditional games. Helen was to win the musical chairs, I proved to have some skill in charades. But the liveliness and the spirit of welcome that pervaded it were the important things.

We had arrived with only one letter of introduction. Neither of us can recall who provided it, but the recipients had been told when and where we would arrive. A ring at the door brought with it a gift of bread and potatoes, immensely valuable as an accompaniment to the Australian tinned food that was our sole resort until we could get ration tickets. Professor Jones-Parry, like many others, had been allocated to the Civil Service during the war, and remained there, eventually to become Sir Ernest.

The atmosphere in their household was sedate although, as being Welsh, not given to the leading vices of the British upper classes. There was no question of their sharing their flat; they rented it in its entirety. But they had been prepared to live in Cornwall Gardens during a period when the buzz-bombs seemed to have an enthusiasm for finding their target in Kensington. They often cared for our children while we went to theatre performances the children would have found boring.

Under instructions from our children we went first to nearby Kensington Gardens to see the statue of Peter Pan. Even during the winter months when we had to cope with temperatures below freezing point, including a week of ice and snow so severe that everyone feared that the ferocious winter of the previous year might be repeated, we still found that park a refuge. Near by were the great South Kensington museums. The streets around us were peculiarly fascinating to Doris and myself, so many of the houses being marked with plaques to designate former famous inhabitants. 'So this is where John Stuart Mill's maid burnt the manuscript of the first volume of Carlyle's *History of the French Revolution*!' Or detail would fascinate, as when we actually saw in a window a bird in a gilded cage. The children loved the pantomimes, the decorations, the sight of the great Christmas tree in Trafalgar Square, a gift from the Norwegian government. Christmas reality at last coincided with the Christmas of the books they had read.

What was depressing was the Dickensian atmosphere that still prevailed, even in Kensington. And even more sombrely the atmosphere of Hitchcock. Each evening, as in a Hitchcock film that had terrified us, the lamplighter came by to light the gas-lamps that so inadequately lit our square; every now and then the coal cart arrived, a manhole cover was removed and coal poured into the cellar. A small boy covered in coal-dust was always involved in this procedure. The coal-fires produced the ruddy smog that reduced visibility to little more than zero. At its worst, buses had to be preceded by a man carrying a torch. The very short days sometimes revealed a round white object we took to be the sun, although it gave no warmth whatsoever. On one occasion, at a free film in the Imperial Institute, the fog inside the room made the film scarcely visible. When it snowed, the snow lay dirty in the street. Doris innocently put a bowl of junket to set by an open window; it was soon covered in black spots.

More than that, I felt socially lost. Always a talker, whether with friends, casual acquaintances, shop assistants or perfect strangers, I now found myself cut off from the greater part of humanity. I had been baffled when Alan Stout had recoiled as if bitten when he was addressed one day by the lift-driver in Grace Brothers. Now I had to learn not to talk to strangers, and accept my inability to have any sort of conversation with 'the working class'. When friends would write from Australia to ask me 'how ordinary workers saw the political situation', I could only reply that my sole information on this point came from newspapers; no working-class man I met would commit himself to an opinion, when this would involve doing so to a 'colonial gentleman' like myself.

A few examples. I asked the milkman what the weather was like. 'Well, Mrs Cartwright, four doors down, did say it was a nice day.' The three long queues at a pantomime each had an attendant. I asked one of them whether a particular line was for the cheapest seats. 'I can't say, sir, *this* is my queue.' A librarian at the Warburg Institute had generously devoted time to showing me around the somewhat extraordinarily arranged library, in which if you went to take a particular book from the shelves you would find it surrounded by other books Warburg thought one ought to read, however remote they would have been from one another in a traditional library classification. I forgot to ask the librarian at what time the library opened and put that question to an attendant at the door. 'I can't say sir, and it's none of my business. But I have seen the gentlemen come in about nine o'clock.'

In all this I felt not only a complete refusal to take responsibility but a degree of contempt. The first characteristic came out in a tendency to say 'I believe' before any positive statement. When I asked from what platform a train left, the response 'Platform 5, I believe' sent me off to find a printed timetable, until I realised that the 'I believe' did not convey even a smidgin of doubt. (Oddly enough, the philosopher G. E. Moore had never noticed this usage. In a series of lectures directed at workers, he told them that saying 'I believe' rather than 'I know' conveyed a degree of doubt. When his audience denied this, he simply urged them to think again. It is astonishing that 'ordinary language philosophy' should be developed in a country where 'ordinary language' is so diversified.)

Was this simply a case of animosity towards Australians? Not at all. Even now such animosity is largely confined to the 'English', or to journalists obsessed by Murdoch's misdoings. In 1948 Australians were relatively popular. It was still remembered that Australian pilots had taken part in the Battle of Britain, to say nothing of other battles where our infantry were by no means of negligible significance, with many of them killed. Australian food parcels were naturally welcomed although few realised that Australia had introduced rationing so that food and clothes could be sent to England. The complaints I heard were simply that Australia had not increased its production so that more could be sent to England; nobody seemed to know that Australia had experienced a savage drought, from which recovery was necessarily slow. Neither did they generally know that Australia was deliberately buying from Great Britain, when it could get supplies more cheaply and rapidly from the United States.

I had no special difficulty except with a salesman at Harrod's who insisted that I was not an Australian but a South African. 'I know a South African when I hear one,' he insisted. We did more than once wonder why the French called the English a nation of shopkeepers.

Attitudes to children were also a source of problems. But here, as so often, one has to distinguish private from public attitudes. No one could have been kinder to our children than were the friends we had already made and would make in the future. But the public attitude was a different thing. We had been accustomed to a situation

where children's concessions were the rule; it made quite a difference to our budget that this was now not so. When we were leaving,
the landlady told us that she would have charged us thirty shillings
a week less had she not expected the children to be destructive. We
did not get a refund. But what struck us more forcibly were such
phenomena as the sign outside a large Kensington store: 'Prams and
dogs are not admitted. Kennels are provided in the basement'—not
somewhere to park the prams.

We had a key to the central park of Cornwall Gardens,
although our children's going there was regarded with obvious suspicion by those, the vast majority, who did not know them. But one
day they committed what we were to discover was the crime of
crimes. They had become friendly with a young girl, the daughter
of a journalist, and took her into the park to play. They were
questioned, and it emerged that the journalist's daughter lived in a
basement. The dictum followed: 'No one who lives in a basement
can enter the garden'. Our children were bewildered to the point of
tears and never entered the garden again.

With Tuesday 6 January school began. We naturally looked for
a state school, of the sort we, and our daughters, had been to in
Australia. The very sight of the nearest such school—The Bousfield
—depressed us. Our depression was deepened by an encounter with
the headmaster. He again took us back to Dickens in his pomposity.
We were assured that it was not inconceivable that our girls should
go on to secondary school or even—hold your breath—the university. Headmasters in the Manly primary school I had attended or the
Chatswood primary school Doris attended would have taken this
for granted. The headmaster had never before met an Australian,
but was glad to be able to 'cement imperial bonds'. As he went on
he was doing more and more to loosen them.

Private schools were beyond our means. Some sent their
children to dame schools 'to avoid state schools', but they were
educationally useless—Dickens again. So off to The Bousfield it had
to be. Helen and Diana had never been to a co-educational school.
There was a good deal of roughness and class disorder. Helen was
pestered by beaux, who would telephone her on the slightest excuse.
Diana would sit gloomily over her fatty lunch, in solitude, not

allowed to leave the dining hall until she ate it all up, but obstinately refusing to do so. (Later we discovered that she had a defect in her jaw that made chewing this sort of food very difficult, but she would in any case have rebelled against it.) There is general agreement that the food in 1948 was worse than it had been at any time during the war.

There were odd cultural interchanges. Our daughters taught their fellow students skipping games that still flourished in Australia, although British experts described them as obsolete; and vice versa.

The teaching cannot have been so bad as we feared. Helen won a scholarship to Godolphin and Latymer. But that was after only a few weeks at The Bousfield, so Australia could take most of the credit. (She could not take it up, as she had to agree to stay at the school until 16 years of age, but we got her into Fulham Secondary Central for our last term there. That left her contented but Diana isolated.) Having to send the children to The Bousfield was one of the things that made us gloomy, longing for nothing more, after the first six weeks, than to secure a berth back to Australia.

Yet there were already consolations—especially theatre-going. Provided that one did not mind sitting at the back of the very cheapest seats, London theatres were incredibly cheap. One could get into Covent Garden for only half a crown and it cost us very little more to see a wonderful *Valkyrie* with some of the greatest singers of the time, such as Kirsten Flagstad. Cheaper still were the ballet and opera at Sadler's Wells, where we could take our children for a shilling each. On a very low income, a person could educate himself or herself culturally. So much, too, in the form of galleries and museums, was free. The 'user pays' doctrine had not yet arrived.

One theatrical piece particularly interested us, in a sociological sense. That was a revue, 'Penny Plain and Tuppence Coloured', which had been enthusiastically reviewed as a sharp satire. In fact we found it self-congratulatory, any laughter at British ways always turning out to be the laughter of approving recognition, not of satire. That led me to reflect on how many of the famous satirical writers were of Irish, not English, origin, from Swift to Shaw.

Restaurants, too, were surprisingly cheap. With fixed prices, the maximum price for a meal was supposed to be five shillings. It is true that when, on a special occasion, we decided to have lunch at the White House, various extras succeeded in lifting the price to seven shillings and sixpence. On the other side, when we took the girls to dinner in a Lyons Corner House we sat in terror throughout the meal, not believing that two and sixpence each could buy us waiters in dress-suits and an orchestra in the corner. But it did. The quality of the meals was a different matter. Margaret Macdonald once took me to a meal in a large hotel. It consisted of Brown Windsor soup, a chicken bone with reconstituted potatoes, and a plate of jelly.

12

Semi-detachment

W HY WAS I taking my study leave in London rather than making the customary pilgrimage to Oxford or Cambridge? No doubt London was an ideal centre for my informal education, with its galleries, its museums, its theatres. No doubt, too, as the transport centre of England, it let us explore England, even Scotland, whereas both Cambridge and Oxford are ill-adapted for such journeys. But I was not in England on vacation; I was there to work, and work I certainly did.

There was a special reason for working in London. I had become interested in a group of moral philosophers who had tried to base moral conduct on reason. I intended to write a book about them. On the traditional account, their founding father was a Cambridge philosopher, Ralph Cudworth. I knew from J. H. Muirhead's *The Platonic Tradition in British Philosophy* that there were unpublished Cudworth manuscripts in what was then called the British Museum, now the British Library. It seemed only proper to read them before I wrote what was meant to be the first chapter of my book on the British Rationalists.

Since Muirhead had listed the manuscripts and briefly indicated their contents, I expected to have no great problems in making my way through them. A quick survey, however, soon revealed that my task was much more complicated than I had supposed. At first sight, the majority of the manuscripts were in a handwriting so execrable as to be totally unreadable. At second sight, however, I recognised what I had learnt to call the 'secretary hand'. This was gradually replaced in the course of the seventeenth century by the 'italic' hand, which is still the hand we all write with varying degrees of legibility. Muirhead, I soon discovered, had based his description of the secretary-hand manuscripts on an italic summary. That was not all. What some librarian had bound together as the first three chapters of an incomplete work were, I found, in fact chapters 1, 2, 3, of quite different books. The entire set of manuscripts had to be re-ordered. When I did so, a picture of Cudworth appeared that was very different from the traditional picture.

That is why what was meant to be a chapter became my first book. In the unlikely event that any of my present readers are interested in my struggles with the manuscripts, the appendices to that book will gratify their curiosity. The broader biographical interest of the struggles lies in the fact that I came to realise that, had I written in Australia, I should have misinformed my readers on a wide variety of points, including where to find Cudworth's anthologised poems. I discovered that not even the vast resources of the British Museum satisfied my needs. I needed a network of libraries—the elegant library of the London Society of Antiquaries, the Dr Williams Library, the Warburg Library, the library of the Bedford College—and to read Cudworth's correspondence and relevant unpublished manuscripts by John Locke I had to make a trip to the Bodleian Library, Oxford.

In all these cases I was treated with a courtesy and helpfulness that went far beyond duty. The one exception was the British Museum. The attendants under the great dome of the main library reminded me of the pursers on the *Stratheden*. In the manuscript room the librarians were obviously engaged in their own research and so simple a question as whether a particular signature was by a librarian they refused to consider. Also I had supposed the librarians to be reliable. But their ordering of the manuscripts threw some doubts on this. The British Museum was, to be sure, a magnificent collection, a privilege to work in, but it confirmed my view that the larger an organisation, the more indifferent it is to the needs of those who make use of it, if they are at all unusual. There are diseconomies as well as economies of scale.

That, however, is a side issue. The crucial point is that I realised that if I returned to Australia I should have to abandon my more sweeping scholarly ambitions. The seventeenth century was to my mind the century of genius and I had hoped in the long run to write about it as such. Yet it became more and more obvious that I could not write such a book in Australia. After all my diligence, I was rebuked by a reviewer for not having worked through the State Papers, where I could have found material that would have let me demonstrate what I had only conjectured about the relationship between Cudworth and the Third Earl of Shaftesbury. But time had not permitted such explorations. Perhaps it was all for the best that I did not go ahead with this work; but that is not how I saw the situation in 1948. It was a test match, as I then thought, between Australia and Scholarship.

Cudworth occupied a great deal of my time; during the last few weeks, almost all my time. But in the various branches of the University of London I encountered minds of the highest order. My timetable was a full one. In the morning I took my daughters to their 9.30 a.m. school, at first in the dark, dank, weather of a London winter. That involved walking against a stream of pale-faced, black-suited, bowler-hatted commuters. They were obviously affected adversely by the horrors of the war and the largely unexpected hardships that followed it. Everywhere, too, destroyed or seriously damaged buildings were vivid reminders of a by no means remote past. Yet well before the war, confronted by a similar situation, T. S. Eliot had appropriated Dante's 'I had not thought death had undone so many'. I felt that I was walking against columns of silent ghosts.

Next it was a dash by way of the Gloucester Road underground station to Holborn, which became the centre of my academic life. From there I made my way to the British Museum. Then it was a wilder dash to the London School of Economics, especially, but not only, for Karl Popper's lectures and seminars. From there it was an even wilder dash to University College for A. J. Ayer's seminar. Or perhaps to what was then the Women's College, Bedford, for Margaret McDonald or the political philosopher Harry Acton. Or perhaps through a particularly devastated route to a private discussion group led by A. C. Mace, then the leading exponent of traditional philosophical psychology. There might, in the evening, be a meeting of the Aristotelian Society or the Institute of Philosophy, both of which I addressed. (I still have nightmarish memories of being unable to find the Aristotelian Society on the night I was to address it, lost in a Bloomsbury fog.) There might even be a foray through the devastated East End to Queen Mary College, to talk about Plato. On Sundays there was often a meeting of a small discussion group hosted by Margaret McDonald. There I learnt more about Wittgenstein—he had just resigned from Cambridge and retreated to Wales. It was, too, a wonderfully diversified group of personalities. The quick-witted Margaret McDonald, living refutation of the view that close philosophical reasoning was not for women, the very Cambridge John Wisdom, conjoining psychoanalysis with Wittgenstein's new-style philosophy, O. K. Bouwsma, the best type of mid-Westerner, totally devoid of pretentiousness, steadily refusing East-Coast offers, and then me, the wild colonial boy.

Of all the philosophers I have so far mentioned in this chapter, Karl Popper is the only one with whom I had any contact before I left Australia, and then only by letters. In a series of articles on logical positivism, I had criticised the then prevailing picture of Popper's thought, which supposed him to have substituted a falsifiability theory of meaning for the logical positivist verifiability theory, whereas he was in fact interested in finding a way of determining the conditions under which a proposition could count as being scientific. Popper was then lecturing in Christchurch, New Zealand, where the *Australasian Journal* circulated. He wrote to thank me and thus began a highly argumentative friendship that lasted for a lifetime.

Popper was not at that time particularly well-known. His *Die Logik der Forschung* had appeared in 1934 but was not translated into English, then in a greatly enlarged form, until 1959. He first came to public notice when *The Open Society and its Enemies* appeared in 1945. In that same year I urged that he be invited to be a Senior Lecturer in Sydney, a position that I otherwise expected to fill. This may seem to have been a strikingly self-sacrificing act and, given my financial situation, I suppose that in a way it was. But I was desperately anxious to have someone appointed who would bring fresh ideas into the department in a way that was not merely antagonistic. The Returned Soldiers' League violently objected on the ground that this life-long enemy of Nazism was an 'enemy alien'. (There was a tendency, in quarters like the Returned Soldiers' League, to believe that anyone who was anti-Nazi before an approved date was almost certain to be a communist.) This matter was settled, however, when the London School of Economics appointed him to a Readership.

There Popper had already established a band of disciples, like Andersonians, convinced of its own superiority, but never fully accepted by the British philosophical world as a whole. (There are legends about a conflict between Popper and Wittgenstein that involved the brandishing of a poker.) In Europe he eventually exerted a very considerable influence. At a world conference of philosophy in Düsseldorf in 1978, our meeting place was surrounded by Marxist students with placards bearing, in German, the inscription 'Down with imperialistic Popperianism'. That was a testimony to his growing influence.

A number of things distinguished Popper from the most influential British philosophers of that time. His background was scientific, but he also had a close personal connection with music in Vienna, especially with Schoenberg. He had been deeply involved, too, with Viennese social democracy. At a time when English philosophy was preoccupied with 'ordinary language', these interests were distinctly unfashionable. But they suited me fine.

It is also true that he upset English philosophers by his discussion methods. He was very much the old-style Germanic philosopher, perpetually dominating. At his seminars, where doctoral students read papers, they were not allowed to get through more than a paragraph or so before Popper would break in, often to say precisely what the student had written in the next paragraph. I felt sorry for the students and conveyed my feelings to his colleague, J. O. Wisdom (not to be confused with John Wisdom; that not only one, but two, philosophers should be called 'Wisdom' is hard to believe). He, to my astonishment, conveyed my feelings to Popper, who characteristically assumed that I was complaining that I did not have enough opportunities to talk. But even in conversation it was impossible to intervene in order to say 'that is not what I meant at all'. One can easily understand why such a conversational style did not recommend him to the Oxford philosophers and why pokers might have been brandished at Cambridge when two Austrians confronted one another. Nevertheless, our friendship persisted, even if, like many another, he could not understand my choice of topics to write about.

Popper was by no means the only source of fascination at the London School of Economics. The building might be all but impossible to find one's way around, the food appalling, the library surprisingly inefficient, the accommodation for graduate students minimal, but the Senior Common Room abounded in interesting people, whose lectures I could attend. Politically, the School was at a turning point. Under the influence of Laski it had graduated hundreds of students as socialists. But now with such teachers as Friedrich Hayek, who had published his *The Road to Serfdom* (1944), the movement was in the opposite direction, accentuated by Popper's *The Open Society and its Enemies*. There was a parallel here with what happened in Sydney with Anderson's *The Servile State* (1943).

There was much beyond that. I could talk with Terence Hutcheson, whose *The Significance and Basic Postulates of Economic Theory* was of central interest to me; listen to and talk with the maverick visitor Rex Knight and with Edward Shils, of whom I was to see a great deal more in later years. There were seminars, too, which brought together such figures as Robbins, Knight, Hayek, Meade and Paish. It was an overwhelming experience for a relatively young Australian, made easier to take by the courtesy that was extended to me.

There was one instance, however, that reminded me of the darker, less comprehensible, side of 'English' life. In the course of one of his lectures the sociologist Morris Ginsberg mentioned that there had been no further studies of the extent of social mobility in England since his investigations in the early 1920s. I mentioned this fact to the secretary of the British Institute of Philosophy, who had just conveyed to me an invitation to lecture to the Institute as if such an invitation was roughly equivalent to being awarded the Nobel

Prize. His response staggered me. 'It's all very well for Ginsberg. He is a Jew, and a Polish Jew at that. But it's not good form to talk about that kind of thing, not good form at all.'

We were astonished by the general lack of attention to the economy and to social relationships. Harry Acton, one of the few philosophers we met who had a grammar-school background, once told me there were no longer any class distinctions in England. In Australia we had been deeply concerned about England's post-war economic conditions. Economic news had always been on the front pages of our newspapers—a consequence of our rather simple economy, where the price of wool mattered to everybody. In England, in contrast, one had to root through the back pages of the newspapers to get any economic news and most philosophers had no idea of what was happening on the economic front.

To move now to University College. A. J. ('Freddie') Ayer's seminars were of a unique character, so much so that when I idly picked up a novel from the shelves of our local library—a novel principally concerned with his womanising rather than his philosophising—I had only to read the first paragraph to say to myself 'Ayer's seminar, 1948'. Ayer, I am plausibly told, hated the novel.

Of Franco–Jewish origin, Ayer had a series of mannerisms that I cannot adequately describe—the way in which he fiddled with this or that on the desk in front of him, the fluctuations in his distinctive voice. He was what I think of as being one of the eccentric Etonians, the scholars, as distinct from the 'English' Etonians, who live up to the stereotypes. His enthusiasm for soccer, generally thought of as a working-class game, and his constant appearances on television distinguished him, in the public eye, from most British philosophers. Ayer had become famous, or in some quarters notorious, for his *Language, Truth and Logic* (1936), the leading British exposition of logical positivism, with its rejection both of metaphysics and ethics. He was not short of self-confidence. Years later we were walking past Foyle's bookshop, then the leading London bookshop, to find one window entirely devoted to three books, Ryle's *The Concept of Mind*, Ayer's book and my *A Hundred Years of Philosophy*. 'There', he said, 'are three permanent classics'. About 'permanent' one can have one's doubts. But Ayer's success was fully justified as the author of a book that combined great clarity with the defence of revolutionary theses.

Back to the seminar. It was not merely Ayer's personality that made it remarkable. It was conducted in what was taken to be the manner of the logical positivist Rudolph Carnap. (Later in life I heard Carnap conduct a seminar. It was quite informal, not at all like his books, which the members of Ayer's seminar were imitating.) I was very much odd man out, attacking the notion of sense-data, it then being a holy doctrine that these were what we immediately perceived, with no possibility of error. Nevertheless, I got on reasonably well with members of the seminar. We often lunched together in a nearby 'Express Dairy'. Almost every member of that group was later to become a professor, although what I took to be the brightest of them was destroyed by alcoholism.

Of those I met in Ayer's seminar the most important for my future life was Richard Peters. He was not at all interested in Ayer's philosophy. I suggested that he should attend Popper's seminars, which he did. In our general attitude to life, Peters and myself lay at opposite extremes. The artistic life of England meant nothing to him; he preferred to live in the country, at first in Surrey, later in Thaxted, Essex. It was very pleasant to spend a weekend with him but I should not have cared to live in such an environment, especially given the animosity of the villagers to 'foreigners', counting Londoners under that head. Then, too, he was a Quaker, the first I had ever met, and a staunchly patriotic Englishman, thinking it improper for a 'colonial' to offer even the mildest criticism of English ways. I have never confined my friendships to people who agreed with me; otherwise I should have lived a very lonely life.

I have sometimes been conjoined with Peters and Israel Scheffler of Harvard as the founding fathers of analytical philosophy of education. But when, in later years, I led a series of seminars in the London Institute of Education, Peters began by saying that it was a tribute to his belief in free speech that he had invited me to address his students. His philosophy of education made reason central; I am often now supposed to have made critical thinking central, but I have always conjoined that emphasis with the encouragement of imagination, both being needed for creative thinking. This is made plain in my *The Philosophy of Teaching*.

I forget where I met the American, Morris Lazerowitz. The first encounter with him that I remember was in relation to an opera company, appearing in London as the Cambridge Opera Company. When I remarked that I had been unable to get tickets to their performances, he told me that he had connections with the company and would have got tickets for us had he not discovered that English philosophers were not interested in such things.

It was quite an occasion when Lazerowitz rang one morning to say that we could go up to Cambridge that afternoon to talk with G. E. Moore. Moore was one of the heroes of that time—with the Bloomsbury group for the last chapter of *Principia Ethica*, and with philosophers in general, if by no means all of them, as having, with Russell, destroyed the Idealist monolith, F. H. Bradley.

Moore was then seventy-three years old, confined to his bed by a blood-pressure-derived illness. His wife informed me that it was a condition of my visit that we did not talk philosophy. But that was all Moore wanted to do; gossip was alien to him, as was 'polite conversation'. I defended, he attacked, my Heraclitean views until his wife drove me out of his bedroom. She is often depicted as a gorgon; but she certainly added years to Moore's lifespan.

His was a curious case. Most of his articles and his later book on ethics are very difficult reading, so anxious was he to carry carefulness to its extreme point. They did not impress me, but the man himself did. He left me with an impression of total honesty and lack of pretentiousness. I was reminded of what Samuel Johnson said about Burke: 'you could not stand five minutes beneath a shed with that man when it rained but you must be convinced that you had been standing with the greatest man you had ever seen'—or at least one of the greatest men, in what has been in this respect my very fortunate life.

My visit to Moore was not, however, of great importance in my future life. What happened on 9 February most certainly was. Gilbert Ryle rang from Oxford to ask Ayer, a former pupil, to invite me for dinner to one of the best-known London clubs, the Travellers. He would meet us there. As editor of *Mind*, Ryle would have received the *Australasian Journal of Psychology and Philosophy* and he might have read, at least, my 'Logical Positivism' articles. Just before we arrived in England, I had received my first *Mind* citations in an article by Rush Rhees, who had been a pupil both of Anderson, when he taught in Wales, and of Wittgenstein. This might have been enough to attract Ryle's attention to me. (Rhees, incidentally, was lucky to get away with citations; Ryle had a deep animosity to footnotes.)

Of that night I remember almost nothing, except that the strange staircase in the club had taken its present shape so that the elderly Talleyrand could ascend and descend it. But I must not have been hopelessly stupid, overwhelmed though I certainly was by the combination of Ryle, Ayer and club-land formalities.

For Ryle soon got in touch with me and invited all four of us to stay in his country house at Bucklebury, Berkshire, where he lived with his twin sister Mary. She was not only intelligent and kindly but courageous. Wanting to adopt a child, she found that her choice was limited by her being both single and slightly crippled. She agreed to accept an 8-year-old Liverpool girl whose past history had been horrendous. No doubt one reason for our being invited to Bucklebury was that our girls could provide some company for her. At times they found what she said and did puzzling but they got on well enough together. She later became a nurse, married, and helped Mary in her declining years.

Our days with the Ryles were somewhat Spartan. It was breakfast at 8.15, then tidying up our rooms, sparing Mary as much as possible. Ryle and I would then retreat to his study, there to discuss, day by day, a chapter in his *The Concept of Mind*, which was near to completion. Let not any desperate graduate student seize upon this revelation to undertake a thesis on 'Passmore's influence on *The Concept of Mind*'. For although when I criticised this or that— particularly, as I remember, his reliance on 'dispositions'—he would always assure me that in the final version my discontents would be allayed, as in fact they never were. (Years later, when he stayed with us in New Zealand, we sat up until midnight discussing his paper on sensations. Doris was present on this occasion and thought, as I did, that on several occasions he gave way. She was upset when the next morning he put his paper in an envelope and sent it off unchanged.) He did, however, ask me how to write a blurb for *The Concept of Mind* and I made one up by way of an example. He seized upon it and used it, just as it stood. That may confuse critics who suppose the blurb to be his, rather than my, description of his intentions. It was he who was responsible for my being asked to write *A Hundred Years of Philosophy*, although he kept silent whenever I cursed whoever had done so. Ryle never confessed and the publisher did not give the secret away for many years.

In Bucklebury, after philosophical mornings we would sit down to a very simple but well-prepared lunch, take a short rest, then go for long walks often through muddy fields—we had no previous experience of such mud—back to another simple meal. Finally, after the children were all in bed, an onslaught on *The Times* crossword puzzle. Mary had a genius for anagrams.

This simplicity was by no means foisted on Gilbert by Mary. At Magdalen the tradition was that the Fellows took it in turn to draw up the menu for the following week. One could tell it was Ryle's week when rice pudding was conspicuous.

Ryle took us to his rooms at Magdalen so that my first sight of Oxford was of one of its most beautiful colleges. I was never formally attached to it as a visitor as I later was to Corpus Christi and later still to All Souls. But even in those years Ryle and I gave a joint seminar at Magdalen on philosophical reasoning. I quite often dined there and loved to walk in its gardens, which included a deer park. Perhaps my memories of Magdalen are sweetened by memories of venison and raspberries in 1948, when the food in London was so awful.

My relationship with Ryle was in many ways an odd one. His favourite novelist was Jane Austen, by no means Dostoevsky or Joyce; he showed no signs of having any interest in painting or music. Yet he meant more to me than anyone else I met in England. His death in 1976 left a permanent gap in my life; Oxford was never to be the same for me again. On Ryle's side, Ayer once said that Ryle had only two friends, Harry Weldon—of whom more later—and myself. I cannot accept this view; it gave vent, I think, to a degree of jealousy on Ayer's part. Ryle had been his tutor and Ayer might well have expected him to be a close friend. But temperamentally they were miles apart. There was no flamboyance about Ryle; it was the essence of Ayer. The solid respectability of our family was much more to Ryle's taste than Ayer's womanising.

Ryle's background was very different from mine—his father was a doctor, his grandfather a bishop. He liked the fact that the bishop wrote books with such titles as *Knots Untied*, which was exactly what he thought of himself as doing. Friendships, however, are often based on shared animosities. As well as sharing a naturalistic view of things, with its animosity to any form of 'new age' goings on, we both hated any form of pompous pretentiousness. Unlike most of the 'English' he genuinely liked Australians, because he found the ones he met free from this vice. That liking was widely reciprocated. The only background we had in common was that we were both brought up in seaside resorts, he in Brighton, I in Manly. That, I earlier suggested, is something of a prophylactic against pomposity. The severity of his criticism had led him, in earlier years, to bear the nickname 'Butcher'. I do not think that anyone ever described me in these terms, but perhaps they did. His military career, leading him to the rank of Major, I certainly did not match. He kept very quiet about it and thought that others should do likewise, especially when, as I discovered from others less discreet, the career included the breaking of ciphers and spy flights over Germany.

At this time, Gilbert Ryle was scarcely known outside Oxford. Ayer and Popper were somewhat better known. But of all the philosophers I met the best known to the general public was C. E. M. Joad. Perhaps I can best indicate the quality of Joad's books by saying that if I received an undergraduate essay that seemed too good for a student to have written but was not of so high a quality that I could safely denounce him or her for plagiarism, I would turn to relevant passages in Joad's writings and there I would find the essay. His writings were voluminous but he was best known publicly as a member of the 'Brains Trust', a distinctly up-market version of our 'The Army wants to know'. His favourite phrase 'it all depends on what you mean by . . .' had become a national joke. I cannot be sure where I met him but it was most likely at a meeting of the Aristotelian Society. He invited me to visit him in his house at Hampstead; he also had a country house.

I was warned by others who had accepted such an invitation that this was unlikely to be a standard 'English' visit and they were right. The door was opened for me by a graceless housekeeper who indicated with a thumb the room to which I was to make my way. From near by I heard Bach-like sounds from a harpsichord. I had been warned that Joad's general practice was to make his guests wait until he completed whatever piece he was playing. I was favoured, however, since he ceased playing and came through to the sitting room. At some point in our conversation I remarked that the academics I had met were almost invariably childless. The 'English' have many strange views about Australians and one that Joad shared was that they are easy to shock. So he, a bachelor, responded with: 'I have children all over England.' I refused to be shocked. A little later, forgetting Joad's association with the *New Statesman*, I remarked that it was getting worse and worse, so far as that was possible. That really did shock Joad.

Nevertheless, he insisted that I accompany him to the first-year lecture he was about to give at Birkbeck where, though generally known as 'Professor Joad', he in fact held a Readership. We travelled on the Underground. Just a day earlier Joad had been found guilty of travelling without a ticket. We were obviously under inspection— Joad's face was well-known to Hampstead intellectuals—by passengers trying to make out whether this time we had a ticket. I did not care to ask him whether it was the cost of supporting so many children that made such economies and his inveterate publishing necessary.

The lecture was in many ways brilliant, considered as an introduction to philosophy. No doubt, it was unorthodox in style. Joad rolled on the desk, supporting himself on his elbow. It was a constant discussion, swinging between Joad and his class, notable for its vivacity. Yet his later-year students and his assistants thought very poorly of him. If nowadays I was asked whether someone was a good university teacher, my first response would be: 'Do you mean for first-year classes or for honours classes?' Of course, some are good for both, but by no means all.

Spring had now arrived, a time for weekend visits to Kew Gardens or the nearby Surrey countryside. Much that we saw was lovely, in a soft spring light. But to find ourselves walking along paths with 'Trespassers will be prosecuted' on either side of us was somewhat disconcerting, particularly to our 10-year-old Helen, who confused 'prosecuted' with 'executed'.

A visit to London's Epping Forest brought out the difference between our attitude and that of the ordinary Londoner. There were considerable crowds on the outskirts of the forest but only deer further in. Puzzled by the interior emptiness, we looked up a guide book. There we discovered a warning. On our first visits to the forest, it told us, we would not feel confident enough to venture into the interior but it was perfectly safe if we took such-and-such a church tower as our guide. How we laughed!

We also went on our first holiday, staying in a guest-house recommended by Peters, located in the village of Winscombe, Somerset. We were completely at home there, able to chat without restraint with road-workers and without 'No Trespassers' signs to disturb our walks over the Mendip Hills. There were buses to such lovely towns as Wells and Bath, such historic sites as Glastonbury. As a Manly boy, I insisted on visiting Weston-super-Mare, where I discovered businessmen from Birmingham perambulating the shore in dark suits with gold watch-chains across their breasts.

The Mendip Hills fascinated us. Here centuries of history lay before our eyes, from the Iberians to the Romans attracted there by its lead-mines. There were huge barrow cemeteries. Every now and then we encountered strange bursts of water. I have never been anywhere so eerie. At the end of this walk we met by chance the headmaster of the Quaker school where Peters had been educated. He took us to his school, which calmed the emotions the Mendips had created.

A later visit, on the recommendation of Mrs Jones-Parry, was to the Welsh tourist resort of Llangollen. We were to stay with her aunt, who would let us have rooms; we were to prepare our own meals. We loved Wales, although it could be disconcerting to enter a shop where the customers were talking English but switched to Welsh as soon as we arrived. When we began to talk, however, they would switch back. We were obviously not 'English'. The food, after London, was wonderful in its freshness, and when we got back from our walks there were somehow hot meals on the table, in spite of our original contract. Fresh eggs for breakfast after the dreadful dried eggs of London were a particular delight, and the lamb more than lived up to its reputation. Walking into the mountains, we were suddenly hit by cold rain. A farmer winding his car up the dirt road saw us and insisted on driving us back to Llangollen. With petrol rationing what it then was, that was a real sacrifice. Once more we felt at home.

Then it was back to my intellectual life, although that came to be linked with a good deal of travelling. Ryle had handed me Weldon's *States and Morals* for review in *Mind*. I wrote a lengthy review, which was immediately published. Weldon invited me to spend the weekend in his rooms—a two-bedroom suite in Magdalen College—so that we could discuss my review. We never in fact did so but I had an experience of the way life in such places could be lived—although admittedly Weldon had sybaritic tastes. As I awoke in his guest bedroom, his 'scout' produced an orange drink and told me that my bath was running. Returning from my bath I found that he had fliped my socks so that I could more easily put them on. Fortunately Wodehouse had prepared me for this Jeeves-like behaviour. But when I was to leave I did not know Wodehouse well enough to be quite sure whether I should, or should not, pack my case. Compromising, I put my clothes into my case without closing it down. This was before breakfast. Returning from breakfast—the typical Oxford breakfast, silver-served in deadly silence—I met the scout on the staircase: 'I noticed, sir, that you had thrown a few things into a suitcase; I ventured to pack it for you.' And packed it certainly was, each item in tissue paper. I might have wondered where the wealth came from to make all this possible. But on the wall of the Senior Common Room I had seen the gun that the steward (have I got the vocabulary right?) once used to persuade the college's tenants to pay their rent.

Weldon took me to a seminar where Isaiah Berlin and the historian Alan Bullock were among those present; it was my first acquaintance with the philosophy of history. Berlin I was later to encounter in many different places, most recently by chance at Pesaro, where we were both attending the Rossini festival. Our backgrounds were as different as could be, but we had the firmest of foundations for an academic friendship: we admired one another's work.

Another visit to Oxford involved meeting George Paul again; he was now a fellow of University College, a college he obviously loved. It cast quite a new light on him to watch him take a hand-kerchief out of his pocket to rub a small patch of dust off the woodwork. But his position in Oxford was rather a sad one. From his room he showed me crowds of students pouring into Peter Strawson's lectures; he attracted no such crowds. He was, too, very much a Cambridge man and in my experience very few former Cambridge men were totally happy in Oxford. I once made a similar remark to a distinguished interpreter of Mycenaean texts. He became silent. 'You're thinking of all the exceptions?' 'No. I'm thinking I can't think of any exceptions.'

Paul took me to visit J. L. Austin. Knowing nothing about his formidable Oxford reputation, I argued with him as I would with anyone else. The subject was a proposed course in British epistem-ology. I suggested that it should begin with Robert Boyle rather than with John Locke. When we left Austin, Paul was angry with me. 'You can't talk to Austin like that.' Austin obviously did not mind; in later years, we shared his house and I had the use of his room at Corpus Christi while he was in California. His Oxford colleagues could not believe the stories that came back about his open friendli-ness. He was an interesting example of a man who, through the sharpness of his mind and the unsparing nature of his criticisms, had built a ring of fire around himself. Our Sydney graduates liked to have him as their supervisor for the Oxford Bachelor of Philos-ophy. Acid though his criticism could be, they greatly preferred such criticism to the indifference some other supervisors displayed. But after all Sydney had broken them in.

I said that my work was often combined with travel. So Tony Flew, famed as a vigorous controversialist, invited me to talk at the new Keele University, Newcastle-under-Lyme. What I most vividly remember from that occasion was the train journey through the industrial towns, the 'five towns' of the novelist Arnold Bennett. That sight, coupled with a later visit to a mill at Leeds, incredible in its dust and noise, showed me an England very remote from the England of the 'English'. These were the days in which smoke-stacks were taken to be a clear sign of prosperity and no one had heard of environmentalism.

Ryle took me with him to Swansea, where I was able to talk with Rush Rhees. For the first time, I understood why the State I was living in was called New South Wales. For the coastline of New South Wales was very like the coastline of South Wales. Human beings had increased the degree of that resemblance. The coastline hills were in both cases the homes of coal-mines. The steel-mills at Port Talbot, Wales, were geographically matched by the steel-mills at Wollongong, New South Wales.

Then it was all the family to Edinburgh on the Royal Scotsman, so familiar to us from fiction and in this case bearing the sub-name 'Commonwealth of Australia'. The intellectual attraction of Edinburgh lay in the person of Norman Kemp Smith. He had recently published a book on Hume that greatly disquieted me, since it contained a great deal that we had separately discovered and that I had intended to include in a book. I finally got around the problem by writing a book called *Hume's Intentions*, which had a quite unorthodox structure. Those who heard me lecture on Hume were always surprised to discover how different my lectures were from my book. They were the more conventional book I would have written had it not been for Kemp Smith's book. It was Kemp Smith, incidentally, who advised the Cambridge University Press to publish my book.

Kemp Smith belonged to the same generation as G. F. Stout and displayed the same kindness and generosity. His chauffeur-driven car took us to some of the most interesting places in the border country. He demanded a grandfather's rights; we were not to protest at whatever he offered our children.

We felt very much at home in Edinburgh. I liked the fact that the porter who carried our luggage to the train happily argued about politics with me. I feel fairly confident, however, that he would not have done this had we been 'English'. On an expedition to the

Forth Bridge, we found ourselves on a punt conveying both every-day Scots and a set of 'English' on their way in expensive cars to the north for hunting and shooting. I suspect that the 'English' were quite unaware of the intense hostility their presence created, but to us it was palpable.

Returning south, I abandoned my wife and family at Durham for the leading British philosophy conference—the joint conference of *Mind* and the Aristotelian Society. It was like the Australian conference in being relatively small. There was no question of submitting a paper; to be invited to deliver a paper or to chair a session was a considerable honour. The chairman was by no means confined to organising the discussion. I remember an occasion when the Welsh-born Oxford professor H. H. Price delivered from the chair a devastating analysis of the papers we had just heard. In general, the papers and the consequent discussion, which by no means ceased when the session ended, were of high quality.

There were other virtues of this meeting. It provided an opportunity to talk with philosophers one would not otherwise meet. The physicist–philosopher David Baum affected me in much the same way as Moore had done—as being a very remarkable personality, not merely clever. Outside the meeting, there was Durham Cathedral, of great significance in the history of architecture. As Popper and I wandered through it, he jokingly argued that future archaeologists would be bound to conclude, all written evidence notwithstanding, that microphones were invented before this cathedral was built, since otherwise the preacher could not be heard.

Yet Durham itself greatly depressed me. It was a concrete illustration of class division. What I shall call 'Upper Durham', geographically as well as socially 'upper', contained the great memorials of past power and the modern symbols of wealth, splendid houses. I had visited coal-towns in Australia, but had never seen anything like the dirt and poverty of 'Lower Durham'.

Another bifurcation also troubled me. I noticed that the Oxbridge philosophers never talked to the provincial and Scottish philosophers. At a later conference, with my customary tact, I asked for an explanation of this strange phenomenon. The answer: 'They all talk so slowly; we can't endure that'.

A later expedition in London led me along Mile End Road to Queen Mary College, originally called East End College. Amid all the devastation one building stood unharmed. I soon smelt what it was—a fish-shop. Fish-shops were one of the features of London life to which we found it hardest to reconcile ourselves. Hygiene was widely dismissed as 'American'. The fish were laid out open to the dirt and fumes of the street, with flies perpetually resting on them. A pre-war lecturer at Queen Mary told me that when he walked along the bombed road he thought to himself: 'Well at least that fish-shop, which made me cross the road to avoid the smell, will have gone.' But there it was, the sole survivor. Were the smells so potent that the bombs deviated? Or did the Germans deliberately not hit it, as a form of negative chemical warfare?

The next expedition was on a much larger scale and of central importance in my life. The first post-war World Conference of Philosophy was to be held that August in Amsterdam. Resolved to attend, I submitted a paper with the title 'Can the social sciences be value-free?' or more precisely a summary of it. The summary had to be written as early as February. It was accepted. In retrospect I find it surprising that I thought of myself as being able to afford to go, but apparently I was working on the principle that no such opportunity would come my way again. A bottom-class cabin in a boat to The Hague was relatively cheap, too, as was a room in the Bijenkorf (Bee-hive) hotel, which contained the smallest bedroom I have ever inhabited in a lifetime of small rooms. I could not open my suitcase without putting it on the bed. One other member of the Ayer seminar was there but rapidly left; I stoically bore it. Still, I did not go to the bathroom to find someone sleeping in the bath, as later happened in a similar Amsterdam hotel.

The meetings, held in the 'Free University', not far from the notorious red-light district, extended over nine days. The general setting came as something of a surprise. The opening ceremonies, as later the plenary addresses, were held in a great hall decorated with Persian carpets on the walls, a form of decoration I had never previously encountered. It was also a novelty for the president's opening address to be interrupted at intervals by a string quartet, on the pattern: speech—first movement—speech—second movement—

speech—third movement. But if that was disconcerting, it was also charming.

In contrast, the presidential address, eloquent and deeply felt, was highly disturbing. The Dutch philosopher, H. J. Pos, vividly reminded us of what had happened in the past. The congress was to have been held in 1941 at Groningen with its president Leo Polak, a philosopher of whom Pos spoke with admiration and deep affection, who ended his days in a Nazi concentration camp. I knew on what a scale such things happened but there was something especially disturbing in this very personal account.

I had already been reminded of the war as our train from the Hague passed through what had once been Rotterdam. There was nothing visible except a great expanse of grass. In London we had just been vividly reminded that a Third World War could not be ruled out, looking overhead at the planes carrying food to blockaded Berlin to satisfy ourselves that they did not bear Russian insignia. We were unexpectedly invited to have lunch with Stephen Roberts, an expert on foreign affairs, but when we telephoned him to fix a date he had fled incontinently to Australia.

If a Third World War was to break out, it was sufficiently obvious that it would be instigated by the Soviet Union, assisted by the Eastern European countries it now controlled. It was an indication of this control that so many of the papers at the conference, particularly by distinguished Polish philosophers, could not be read by their authors; they were not allowed to be present.

A controversy arose out of the international situation. I was now, along with Boyce Gibson from Melbourne, a member of the Federation of Philosophical Societies, which has the supreme governing rights over international conferences. A proposal was put forward at its meeting that philosophers should not be allowed to attend such conferences unless they were prepared to sign a declaration that they held fast to the general principles of democracy.

This motion was warmly supported by a somewhat uncanny alliance between Sidney Hook and a representative of the Vatican, a man whose sinister appearance lived up to the worst Protestant nightmares. I opposed the motion on the ground that we should do all we could to facilitate the presence of philosophers from Eastern

Europe, to keep them in contact with the democratic philosophical world. Hook was furious with me but I won the day.

In later years we did have present some very distinguished, certainly not communist, Polish philosophers. And that was also true of the Paris-based *Institut International de Philosophie* to which I was elected a few years later. No doubt the Soviet Union and East German philosophers whom we later invited to talk would sometimes develop strange illnesses just before they were to come to our meetings and would be replaced by official hacks. But that was not always so, and in any case it was sometimes illuminating to discover what the latest official line was. One could quite often derive amusement and instruction from their attempts to construct defences against their critics. As for the Poles, figures like Kotarbinski, the most gentlemanly of philosophers, Ajdukiewicz and Ingarden were distinct acquisitions. Allowed to do research but not to teach in their own countries, they were finally permitted to travel, perhaps because the published proceedings of the earlier conference they had not been allowed to attend included a long list of Polish philosophers killed by the Nazis. But the ways of Poland, as distinct from the Soviet Union, were not always easy to comprehend.

Contacts with Continental philosophers I should not otherwise have met were one of the joys of the Amsterdam conference. There was, for example, the Jesuit historian of logic, I. M. Bochenski. His appearance and manner were reminiscent of a Rabelaisian monk; one could not imagine him as a 'Grand Inquisitor'. He invited a small group to dinner at a Chinese restaurant. 'There is only one phrase,' Bochenski told us, 'that you have to learn in every language: "I like good food."' Unfortunately, his advice was no use to Doris and myself. What we had to learn in every language was: 'How can we get something cheaper?' That is the cost of our travelling so much: never to have eaten in any but the simplest restaurants. But that does not mean that we have always eaten poorly; I would set a Bologna cafeteria against any restaurant anywhere. And our economy is just as well. Bochenski's grand meal left me physically devastated.

Amsterdam, then, meant much more to me than the obvious success of my paper. Unfortunately in the excitement of the moment

I lost it but it was gratifying to discover that the summarised version had been reprinted in Feigl and Brodbeck's *Readings in the Philosophy of Science*, the first of my articles to be thus anthologised.

Giving such a paper at an international gathering was no easy matter in the days before English became an international language. The official languages were supposed to be English and French. Although nervous about talking French, I was reasonably confident that I would be able to understand comments on my paper. But I discovered that, although the Italians and Spanish spoke French with enviable fluency, they made not the slightest attempt to pronounce it in the French manner. It was easier to understand the philosopher who broke the rules by talking German, even though my knowledge of German was distinctly less developed than my knowledge of French. The worst case was a Spanish monsignor. He spoke at length; I responded in English; he looked satisfied. After this interchange, a French philosopher came up to me, asking how I managed to reply to the monsignor, since neither he nor his French colleagues could understand a single sentence of what the monsignor had said. I explained: 'I was confident that the monsignor knew no English. I replied by saying things that I thought would be of general interest to my audience in relation to my paper. He looked happy because I had replied at some length.'

So far as English philosophers were concerned the great event was a lecture by Bertrand Russell. I have written a good deal about Russell and spent many recent years as General Editor of his *Collected Papers*. The question has often been raised, not unnaturally, whether I ever met him. Our sole contact was when I cornered him, in a manner that now seems somewhat disreputable, in the foyer to the auditorium. We were at once surrounded by photographers; all that I can recall of our encounter is my astonishment at his so turning his head that photographers could capture his best profile. Moore is often grouped with Russell but as personalities they were at opposite extremes.

Of other English philosophers, the one I saw most of in Amsterdam was Stephen Toulmin, a King's College Cambridge man, later to make his name as an historian of science, and his lively wife Alison, born into wealth. In their relatively youthful company, I encountered an episode that I have always remembered as an extreme example of being 'English'. We had, all three, gone for a walk. At first it led us through the Amsterdam red-light district. There was nothing peculiarly 'English' in Alison taking both arms as we walked past the large windows which, uniquely, displayed prostitutes engaged in a peaceful domestic task, such as knitting. What domestic task they performed after a man entered and the blinds came down I am in no position to say. Her 'Englishness' came out, rather, when our walk took us to the 'Old Church'. It had been badly damaged but was now in the hands of a television crew, with leads tangled all over the floor. It was plain that no entrance was permitted. But being specifically told so by one of the workers did not satisfy Alison, who responded with: 'Not even although we are English?' The reply was mild but delivered in a tone that scarcely concealed a sense of absurdity: 'Not even although you are English.' I wondered what response I should have got had I tried out: 'Not even although we are Australians?' under similar circumstances in England.

Something happened in Amsterdam that was far more important for my future life than anything I have so far mentioned. I fell in love. At first I thought of it as just a temporary affair that would not last. But instead it turned out to be a lifetime passion. I fell in love only, I then thought, with Amsterdam but it turned out to be a love for Europe, which we have now explored from Lisbon to Istanbul, from Moscow to Sicily. A love, fortunately, that is not besotted. Bombs in Barcelona, riots in Milan and France, attempted cheatings and robberies in Italy, visiting Auschwitz and witnessing the sickening prostrations in the nearby cathedral, hearing the old German prejudices from a German hotel-keeper, being bugged in Bulgaria, being told over a loud-speaker on the border that it was no longer possible to enter Yugoslavia, being in Madrid when a military coup was attempted—this was all living history, Europe an enlarged schoolroom, but scarcely likely to inflame one's affections. Not to mention the discomforts of what were almost always cheap hotels and cheap meals. Yet I have never hesitated to take every opportunity to visit Europe.

What did I love in the Amsterdam of 1948? I had time for only a very brief encounter with its great galleries, doing what everybody does by taking a brief look at the Rembrandts. In fact, although I made several intervening visits to Amsterdam, only in 1995 did I discover some of its most striking riches. Europe is like that. But what particularly fascinated me was Amsterdam's architecture, in its masterly combination of unity and diversity. One of the things I had most hated in Sydney were the streetscapes. England had given me some better examples, even in those years of bomb-damage and grime, but they often fell into monotony. There were exceptions, like High Street in Oxford, but even then the traffic was disrupting, not to be compared with Amsterdam canals. A long bus trip to the North of Holland revealed many other triumphs of town architecture, the towns all displaying some form of architectural harmony.

As my life has gone on my passion for architecture, painting and sculpture has greatly intensified. So, too, has my delight in visible history, as displayed, let us say, in the Schleswig museum, where history over more than a thousand years linked with literature—in this case with *Beowulf*. Half a century of travelling through Europe has increased my affection for it; there is always something to be discovered and, often, woven into my writings. That does not stop me from also being fascinated by Japan, which I have visited nine times.

A curious fact about my travels is that I am often taken to be a local inhabitant. In Amsterdam, I was sitting at a high counter drinking coffee alongside two men who were engaged in a vigorous argument. There was a sudden silence and it was obvious that they expected a judgement from me. In Norway an elderly woman became very angry with me when I did not answer her question. This sort of thing is not confined to Northern European countries. In Athens a Sydney classicist once came to our hotel and triumphantly announced that, after many trips to Greece, he had at last been addressed in Greek, to which I could reply that this had happened to me on my very first day in Greece. I do not understand this phenomenon but I think it somehow helps on our travels.

Returning to London from Amsterdam was in some ways, but not in all respects, returning to what was now a familiar way of life. During my absence Diana had been taken ill, which was terribly distressing to Doris, who felt deserted. But what were by now old friends rallied around; Mrs Jones-Parry sent for a doctor, others brought in previously unknown neighbours with a nursing background. Diana turned out to have nothing worse than a case of food poisoning.

Our English friends' concern made us feel much more at home. On the other side I now had to cut myself off from the intellectual friends I had made. For my work on Cudworth just had to be finished before we left, with much checking to be done, since my capacity for misquoting cannot easily be paralleled, although Doris is good enough to say that I generally improve the original. I managed to get for her a reader's ticket to the manuscript room. She could read the secretary hand. Sunny days no longer meant a stroll in the parks. They meant sitting by the windows in the manuscript room, getting the maximum light to read the fading ink. I could no longer go to the seminars. There I behaved in a stupid manner, which I later repeated in Oxford. I thought it would be self-important to announce that I should be no longer attending, whereas in fact my not doing so would very likely have been taken to be rude. Thus I may have fortified the stereotype of Australian rudeness, which is so often, as in my case, awkwardness.

In my last months in London I was offered my first professorship. This was in Pietermaritzburg, Natal, at that time one of the most pleasant areas of South Africa. The approach was made by Malherbe, a philosopher Vice-Chancellor of considerable ability and with a most attractive personality. I was to be paid a salary just about double what I was being paid in Sydney. I was also to get a car and Doris was told that servants would be readily available. Since I was then determined never to own a car and Doris hated the idea of servants, these were not very effective inducements. I said 'No', thus beginning a long history of saying 'No'.

My love for Europe was accentuated by two visits to France. The first visit occurred under circumstances that are still mysterious. Four of us, the Borries and ourselves, were having lunch in Bush House, quite close to the London School of Economics, a restaurant I had never before eaten in. Someone—his name turned out to be Nelson—who was quite unknown to me came up to our table and addressed me: 'They would like to see you in Australia

House'. I knew nobody there in person except attendants. What could be going on? I certainly did not expect what happened next: 'Could you represent Australia at a Unesco Conference in Paris?' I began to calculate: 'Well, not at the end of the month when I have to talk to the Aristotelian Society.' The reply was startling: 'I don't mean at the end of the month; I mean tomorrow.' There were obviously practical problems: 'I do not have a visa.' This was an easy one: 'We can get you a diplomatic visa, if you leave your passport with us.' Another problem: 'How am I going to get there in time?' 'You'll be flying.' I had never been to France, had never flown, had never represented anyone anywhere. The children were flabbergasted.

I found myself then, very nervously, in the Paris airport. The flight from London had been unexpectedly agreeable. If slow, it was also low, and on the clear autumnal day one could clearly see the contrasts between the broad English and the narrow French farmlands, reflecting the difference between England and France in the rules of inheritance—a history lesson from the air. But what was I to do next in this unfamiliar airport chaos? There was no sign of anyone there to meet me. Then an announcement in French came over the air with my name at the end of it. I had been listening to the announcement but only casually. Thinking back over it, however, I decided that I was to go to a particular entrance where a car and driver were awaiting me. So along I went.

The meeting, I was there told, was to be held in the Abbaye de Royaumont, some sixty kilometres from Paris, founded in the twelfth century and partly in ruins as a result of the French Revolution. We were out there, it emerged, so that we would concentrate on our proceedings rather than being tempted by Parisian fleshpots or, at least, by its historical monuments. It was to be *Folies Politiques* rather than *Folies Bergères*.

My only companion in the car was a very distinguished member of the French Academy, the historian Georges Lefèbvre, a famous, if controversial, historian of the French Revolution. He spoke not a word of English. So I had two options, deadly silence for the next sixty minutes or speaking French for the first time outside a classroom to a member of the French Academy, that great protector of the French language. I chose the latter alternative and often interpreted for him on other occasions. How he must have suffered!

Our meetings had, however, an official interpreter, Polish in origin. She had been a translator at the 1946 Paris Peace Conference, where Australia had been represented by one of the more controversial figures in Australian politics, H. V. Evatt, then Attorney-General and Minister for External Affairs. Some have spoken of Evatt's performance on that occasion as robust or vigorous but she saw it rather differently: 'I did not like translating for your Dr Evatt; he was so rude.' I had to persuade myself to be exceptionally polite, to rid her of any tendency to generalise unfavourably about Australians. One other experience with the translator was a warning. A French speaker had remarked, in French: 'You all know what my feelings are towards the English'. In her translation 'towards' appeared as 'against'. Fortunately, some of us could immediately protest. But if, say, the original language had been Polish and the Pole knew no English, none of us could have done so. The Italian phrase 'traditore, traduttore' ('translator, traitor') came very vividly to life.

My memories of the meeting are of a marginal character. Of those who were present, apart from Lefèbvre, I remember by name only our chairman, the American sociologist Otto Kleinberg, and T. H. Marshall, whom I already knew as head of the Social Science Department at the London School of Economics. I know that we talked about tensions and I know that I insisted, in Heraclitean style, that tensions were sometimes a good thing so that we had to consider when they were and when they were not.

Finally came a day off, Sunday in Paris. We were driven into Paris, lined with autumnal trees, by Kleinberg, whose wife was staying in Paris at the Hotel Lutetia. That name reminded me that I was in a city of Roman origin. But this was modern Paris and Kleinberg had a very modern car, with a roof that could be made to open or close by pressing a button. I had never before been surrounded by so large a gawking crowd. It became obvious that if Paris once worshipped Rome, it now worshipped The Car. Then there was an extended lunch at the Closerie des Lilas, once a favourite centre for literary Paris. One of my colleagues, a Canadian sociologist, was determined to see the Mona Lisa. When we arrived at the Louvre it was just about to close, with Sunday crowds pouring down the staircases. But he had the qualities that have made Canada great. We got there for the required two-minute look. I was overwhelmed by the great gallery where the Mona Lisa was to be found, and was determined that my wife and family should see the glories I was so superficially examining.

At the end of the conference we were paid a small sum of money. It was, of course, in francs, and francs could not be taken out of France. We left in less grandeur than we arrived, dumped where the bus left for Le Bourget, in an area by no means richly endowed with shops. But I managed to get hold of a large book on Cézanne, and Breton dolls for my daughters. The French Customs officials were delighted. 'Breton dolls, how wonderful. And for your daughters, how charming.' My reception on the English side was, shall I say, much less exuberant.

Back in Cornwall Gardens two important things had happened. Our landlady in Roseville had written to say she had decided to sell our house and was making us the first offer. But she would not sell it at the fixed prices the government had established. We were called upon to pay £1200 'key money', as it was called, an illegal payment, which would not be met by any mortgage lenders, even if we could find such a lender. We could only reply that we had no way of paying the money. After our return she continually pestered us to leave, saying that we could easily find accommodation elsewhere. This was in fact next to impossible, as a result of the fact that no houses had been built during the war years. The only accommodation available was in places far remote from the university. That pestering was an important factor in our finally leaving Sydney for Dunedin.

Secondly, a Senior Lectureship was advertised by the University of Southampton. Should I apply? During the period in which I was all at sea, I would not have been at all attracted by such an advertisement. But my attitudes had changed since I had visited the Continent. The feelings generated by Amsterdam had been deepened by my experience of Paris. Could I, returning to Australia, bear to set such distances, still by ship, between myself and Europe?

Southampton was in easy reach of Europe and reasonably close to the theatres and museums of London, with open country near by.

But there was one very serious problem. We were not willing to entrust our children to English state schools, after what we had seen of them, and the salary attached to the position was too low to allow us to send them to any half-decent private school. I began to understand why so few of the academics we met had children. At the same time, the pressure increased both from Karl Popper and from John Findlay—although neither of them had been completely happy in New Zealand—to apply for the Dunedin Chair. They thought of it, I suppose, as a step on my way to better things, as it had been for both of them.

For the rest, life continued much as before. I lectured in various places, most notably to the Cambridge and the Oxford philosophical societies. Determined that my family should see the Cambridge colleges, I accepted an invitation to stay with the moral philosopher A. C. Ewing; my wife and family found cheap, but pleasant, accommodation in a bed and breakfast guest house. The Moral Science Club placed its central emphasis on discussion; the speaker spoke only for fifteen minutes. I have no idea what I talked about and remember no feedback.

The Oxford senior philosophical society was rather different, much larger and permitting the lecturer considerably more time. There were members of the group who remember the occasion better than I do. Jack Smart, eventually to be my successor as professor of philosophy in the Institute of Advanced Studies, tells me that induction was my principal theme; David Pears, now an Oxford professor, tells me that the discussion was difficult going. At that time philosophy at Oxford was much more varied than it now is, with many remnants of its neo-Hegelian past. I apparently did not know what to make of such questions as: 'Are you denying that the universe is through-and-through rational?' I suspect that I fell back on Joad's: 'It all depends on what you mean.'

As for Cudworth, Australians came to my aid when it seemed impossible to do all I had to do, especially in the way of checking the large number of secondary sources. They were two former members of our Roseville tennis group, Max Hartwell and John La

Nauze, both of them, fortunately, much better at being accurate than I am. It was a nice feeling to have this co-operation; in a way it prepared me for returning to Australia.

Meanwhile, however, we were to leave our flat on 15 December, and whatever the pressures might be, I was determined that my family should see the Paris that had so fascinated me on my very short visit there. A colleague in the French Department, Derek Scales, as I previously said, was researching there and was willing to make our arrangements. So we set out on the cheapest but longest route, crossing a channel that lived up to its reputation for unfriendliness, were met by Scales and taken to a hotel, which then bore the delightful name of 'Hotel de L'Univers et du Portugal'. It was situated in the Rue Croix des Petits Champs, very conveniently for our purposes, with a good cheap restaurant near by. Close at hand, too, was the café Ragueneau, founded in 1603, once a principal resort of Molière. That still survives with a proud and informative proprietor, serving delicious pastries.

This is not a travelogue; I shall take for granted the extraordinary buildings with their historical echoes that we managed to examine on the first of what were to be many visits to Paris. Doris's first impressions of Paris were a great deal less favourable than mine had been. Finding that her warm brown stocking had twisted about her leg, she went into a woman's lavatory to adjust it. There she found, as is customary in France, a woman seated at a table with a plate on it to receive coins in payment for the use of toilets. There was also a policeman. Doris moved around a corner out of sight of the policeman to do her adjusting, and was about to leave when the woman demanded payment. We had just arrived and Doris had no small coins. But in any case, as the policeman protested, she had not used the facilities. Nevertheless, Doris had to come to me for coins and take them back to the woman.

Doris was by now close to tears, and the event cast a deep shadow over her experience of Paris. Time and time again when I meet people who have been unhappy in Paris, this is the kind of story they tell about French officials—including such lowly examples as toilet-minders. I remembered my contact with the English wharf-labourer: 'I can't stand them Froggies.' Doris was now inclined to sympathise with him.

I had the advantage of remembering the Customs officials who had been delighted by my purchase of dolls. As a French attitude, this was even more notable now that we had our daughters with us. The contrast with public, as distinct from private, London was striking. The hotel had what was a novelty for our girls—revolving doors—and the proprietor encouraged the girls to play with them. In a large department store, the girls were given balloons. But on an upper floor with a high roof, Diana's balloon escaped to the roof. Chairs were placed on tables, the department collaborated, the balloon was rescued. There was, I admit, a downside to this story. Overnight in their bedroom the balloons gradually gave up their contents; the resulting smell of garlic was all-pervasive.

During our tour of the glorious Sainte-Chapelle, the guide brought the girls to the front of the group. That, I fear, was not much use for them, innocent of French as they were, but it was fine for us. There were splendid puppet shows, especially in the Jardin du Luxembourg, where I insisted on their eating in the Closerie des Lilas, although I was not well enough to do so and, stupidly, shivered in the park while they ate—stupidly because I could easily have sat in the restaurant, explaining the situation, without eating, but was too shy to do so.

Then it was back to London, bidding farewells, sadly. Mary Ryle was determined that the children should have an English Christmas before we sailed on 23 December, even though that meant abandoning her usual familial party. Doris was exhausted by a combination of packing, cleaning and Paris; the Bucklebury household and Mary Ryle's ministrations were a wonderful solace, followed by two days in what was for us a luxury hotel, the Cumberland, where our daughters were fascinated by the large fluffy towels.

I shall not follow us home on the *Mooltan*. We were on what was essentially a migrant ship, modified to hold 1000 passengers including 123 children, on it only as a result of confusions by the shipping company. The cabin we occupied had an upper berth, recently added, which constantly jumped in syncopated harmony with the ship's engines; the carpenters could do nothing about it, although they built a wooden pillar. Any delusions of grandeur were rudely shaken out of me, night after night. Otherwise, the ship was a masterpiece of organisation by the Department of Immigration, who found ways of keeping the children busy the whole way back to Australia, so that one could forget that they existed. But it was obvious that a percentage of this collection of migrants would soon be back in England. They could not cope with change. In fact, I decided that the ship should have sailed back to England after a week to unload the grumbling migrants—cheaper in the long run. This was my first contact with the 'New', if still 'White', Australia.

The little boy from Manly died on this voyage. My position, I came to realise, had completely altered. Whereas my former referees had been purely Australian, I could now call upon the recommendations of Ryle, Popper and Ayer. There was no 'cultural cringe' in this recognition. It was a simple fact that these names counted for much more than did Anderson, Alan Stout and Boyce Gibson, who would support me only if no member of his department was applying. Meanwhile however, I was returning to Sydney, to a teaching programme so arduous that I had no hope of writing further books.

It would have helped had I been promoted to a readership, which limited teaching hours to give more time for research. But Anderson, who was persistently severe in his attitudes to promotion, refused to put my name forward. Along with our housing problems, that led me, at last, to apply for the philosophy chair in the University of Otago. There was a considerable suspicion about Australian applicants, but the Vice-Chancellor told me that the many British philosophers he had consulted were unanimous in warmly supporting me. That concretely brought home to me my changed position.

I spent five productive years in New Zealand, so much so that I often encounter the belief that I am a New Zealander by origin. A staff of five for a hundred students was very different from a staff of five for over two thousand students. But, as a result of the illnesses of some of my senior colleagues, I accumulated many administrative responsibilities, acting, although not officially, as a deputy Vice-Chancellor. Excessive administration turned out to be as troublesome as excessive teaching. When the opportunity arose of returning to Australia to a research post in the newly founded

Australian National University, as a colleague of my old friend Partridge, with no fears about accommodation, I did not hesitate to accept, although it meant leaving Dunedin, to which we had all become very attached. Less importantly, it meant abandoning a Professorship for a Readership. My father's death, too, led me to feel that I ought to be closer to my mother. So after a very fruitful year at Corpus Christi, Oxford, with Carnegie help, I was back in Australia. Canberra has been my principal place of residence ever since.

Then why not describe myself as being fully Australian? That ought to be apparent from the story I have told. Whenever I have had the opportunity to get to Europe I have done so, although never for more than a year at a time. Neither have I ever refused an opportunity to visit Japan. Much that I have written depends on my having taken these opportunities. I have spent a considerable amount of time, too, in North America, always fruitfully, but never with the awed affection I feel for Europe.

Should I therefore describe myself as a citizen of the world rather than as a semi-detached Australian?

I am deeply concerned about many of the changes that have taken place in Australia during the last fifteen years, undermining the reasons I used to give for remaining in Australia rather than moving to the United States. But I still want to insist that I am an Australian. If I criticise, it is because I care. That is why I prefer 'semi-detached Australian' to 'citizen of the world'.

'Citizen of the world' would, however, be reasonably accurate in so far as it would bring out both my capacity to feel at home in a wide variety of countries and on the other side the degree to which my work is familiar to international students and teachers, which constantly surprises me. I did not expect to be danced around by young Korean teachers on the footpath outside the 1988 Brighton conference or, in 1995, to find myself singled out from the members of a smaller conference for a photograph and interview in the leading Finnish newspaper, with an emphasis on what I had meant to Finnish students. I still get many requests for permission to translate my books and essays. The fact that there is an entry on me in both the Cambridge and the Chambers biographical dictionaries but not in the comparable volume edited by the Australian Barry Jones might suggest that my own country neglects me. But that is not so; it has bestowed honours upon me. Inclusion in biographical volumes is a very chancy business; I was astonished to find my name in the British biographical dictionaries, indeed even embarrassed.

A final comment. In the manner characteristic of our times, there is now a tendency to denigrate my principal teacher, John Anderson, and my own account of him might selectively be used as a weapon in that denigration. So let me again insist that I could not have wished for a more mind-opening teacher. The *Europa International Who's Who* is neither particularly oriented towards Australians nor towards philosophers. Yet it has included such pupils of Anderson as Mackie, Armstrong, Kamenka, Stove and myself. Few Australian teachers could say as much. We all went our own way but were nevertheless permanently marked by Anderson's influence, as were very many others whose lives were lived outside the academic world, even, sometimes, knowing him only at second hand, in the manner of Robert Hughes or Germaine Greer.

Index